The
Grape Escapes 2

Temecula Wineries
& Tasting Rooms

By Bob & Cindy Rhodes

www.TheGrapeEscapes.com

First Published by Dog Ear Publishing
4010 W. 86th Street, Ste H
Indianapolis, IN 46268
www.DogEarPublishing.Net

ISBN 978-1-59858-573-5

Library of Congress Control Number: Applied For

This book is printed on acid-fee paper.
Printed in the United States of America.

Disclaimer: The information contained in this guidebook was correct at the time of publication, but is subject to change. Telephone numbers and website information are provided to assist the reader in obtaining more current information. The recommendations and opinions expressed herein are solely the authors' own. *No fees or any type of compensation or benefits have been paid by any of the wineries, tasting rooms, or merchants to be included or mentioned in this guidebook.*

On the Cover: Old Town Arch on Front Street, Temecula, Photo by Cindy Rhodes; Antique Grape Press at Keyways Vineyard and Winery, Photo by Cindy Rhodes; Grape Cluster Photo provided by Foote Print Winery.

Additional copies of this guidebook can be ordered online at
www.TheGrapeEscapes.com

"Great wine is about nuance, surprise, subtlety, expression, qualities that keep you coming back for another taste."

~ Kermit Lynch
Adventures on the Wine Route

"Saying thank you is more important than good manners."
~ Albert Painter

ACKNOWLEDGEMENTS

Although only our two names appear on the cover of this guidebook, it was not developed without the cooperation, information, guidance, and assistance provided by numerous individuals.

First and foremost, our thanks go out to the winery owners, winemakers and PR staff who patiently answered what must, at times, have seemed like an unending series of questions.

In addition, we would like to extend a special thank you to the owners and managers of the wineries and tasting rooms and the other merchants who have generously agreed to be part of our *Grape Escapes Discounts and Promotions Program*. Your support is greatly appreciated.

We also wish to thank Carolyn Fittipaldi at the **Temecula Valley Convention and Visitors Bureau** for her assistance in helping us discover all that Temecula has to offer.

Extra special thanks to Le Roy Guilford (*ShopTemeculaWines.com*) for sharing his time and expertise, as well as assisting us in obtaining wines from winemakers who do not have tasting rooms. Thanks also to Lisa Osslund for introducing us to **Orfila Vineyards & Winery.**

For their proof-reading assistance, we wish to thank our friends, Renee and John Jones.

And let us not forget our neighbors, Cheryl, Cherie, Nancy, Jim, John, Renee, Glenn, Sharon and Chris who unhesitatingly responded to our call for wine-tasting and performed their assignment above and beyond the call of duty.

Have fun. Be inquisitive.
Ask questions and *enjoy* your wine tasting adventure!

TABLE OF CONTENTS

Title   **Page**

THE WINERIES AND TASTING ROOMS

Temecula's Hidden Gems - Wineries without
  Tasting Rooms or not open to the public

The information contained in this guidebook was current at the time of publication, but is subject to change. Telephone numbers and website addresses are provided to assist the reader in obtaining up-to-date information.

The recommendations and opinions expressed herein are solely the authors' own. *No fees or any type of compensation or benefits have been paid by any of the wineries, tasting rooms, or merchants in order to be included or mentioned in this guidebook.*

Additional copies of this guidebook can be ordered online at
www.TheGrapeEscapes.com

WHO SHOULD BUY THIS BOOK?

Why everyone, of course. And not just one or two copies. You should purchase lots of copies for family, close friends … not-so-close friends.

Okay, we admit we're teasing. We also admit that it is possible to have a perfectly good wine tasting adventure in Temecula Wine Country without the aid of a guidebook. If, however, your aim is to find the best of what Temecula Wine Country has to offer, then *The Grape Escapes* is for you.

***The Grape Escapes* is thoroughly researched!**
Many travel writers never actually *visit* the wineries they describe, much less taste the wines. Some writers simply conduct research online and by phone. For us, this approach is just not good enough. We sampled 250+ wines from over 40 wineries in the Temecula area with the sole purpose of helping our readers find just what they are looking for – whether it is great reds, great whites, wine tours, the best picnic areas, the best tasting room shopping, or the best of a particular varietal.

***The Grape Escapes* will save you time!**
There are numerous publications that tell you *where* the Temecula wineries and tasting rooms are located, but only *The Grape Escapes* helps you find the tasting rooms that offer the best wine tasting *experience*. Our guidebook provides specific, descriptive information on the facilities, services and outstanding features of all of Temecula's wineries and tasting rooms. We also attempt to answer all of your other "Where do I go to find…?" winery questions.

***The Grape Escapes* will save you money!**
In the Temecula area, tasting fees generally run from $6 to $10 per person. In some cases, however, the tasting fees at a few of the exclusive tasting rooms can run as high as $30 per person. As a result, the cost during a day or weekend of sampling can really add up. Many of the wineries participating in our ***Grape Escapes Discounts / Promotions Program*** provide

Two-for-One or **Complimentary Tasting** if you present a copy of this guidebook. In addition, some of our favorite and recommended wineries have generously agreed to provide *significant discounts* (one winery offers up to **30% off**) on wine purchases.

Simply put, if you are going wine tasting in Temecula, *you cannot afford to be without this guidebook.*

USING THIS GUIDE

The primary purpose of this guide is to help you make the most of your time in Wine Country. It is also designed to help you break out of your routine and to approach wine tasting in perhaps a slightly different way.

To begin, we have three Rules of Wine Tasting:

Rule #1: Wine tasting should be fun!
Rule #2: You should learn something new.
Rule #3: See Rule #1.

Okay, so we only really have two Rules of Wine Tasting. If we were going to have a third rule, it would be that you "gotta have a plan." Now wait. We heard the mental groan. You're asking, "Do we really have to have a plan?" Well, no. You don't *have* to have a plan, but a plan is a key part of the first two rules of wine tasting. In Temecula Wine Country there are well over 400 different wines on the winery tasting menus, so a plan is certainly helpful in making the most of your limited time and helping you find great wines to taste.

One of our goals is also to help folks expand their wine tasting experiences to include "undiscovered" Wine Country. We hope, through the information contained in this book, to take you to wineries and tasting rooms that you might not otherwise discover on your own.

How to Use This Book ...

This guidebook is comprised of three major sections. Not to worry. You do not need to read all the chapters before beginning your *Grape Escapes* adventure. Each of the chapters can be used alone or combined with others to create a unique, personalized and enjoyable wine tasting excursion.

The first Section of this book, "**The Wineries and Tasting Rooms**," describes each of the wineries we visited, their hours, the wine varietals they serve and our favorite or "recommended" wines at each tasting room. Why list our favorite wines? It is not unusual to find tasting rooms with over 20 wines on their menu. Since you will probably not be able to taste all of the wines on their menu during a single visit, our recommended wines provide you a good place to start.

The second Section, "**Create Your Own Wine Tasting Adventure**," describes the tasting rooms and what they offer, such as tours, picnic areas, art, shopping, entertainment and restaurants. We hope this information will help you make your wine tasting adventure fun and exciting. Not everyone approaches wine tasting in the same way. If you love meeting winemakers, check out our chapter entitled *We're Off to See the Wizards*. If you see winemaking as competitive sport and want to go in search of **medal-winning wines**, we help you here as well. We have identified the wineries where we feel you will have the best opportunity to actually *taste* award-winning wines.

The third Section of this guidebook, "**The Wines**," focuses strictly on the wines. Here is where we give the results from our sampling of the 250+ wines. If, like Bob, you are a nut for Zinfandels, we suggest wineries and tasting rooms for you to visit, such as **Thornton** and **Stuart Cellars**. If your taste runs to white wines, no worries. We have these covered as well. We fell in love with the wonderful Riesling and Viognier produced in the Temecula Valley. Our guidebook tells you exactly where to find these varietals and other wines that scored well in our evaluations.

We suggest you carefully review the **Table of Contents**. The tongue-in-cheek chapter titles are usually self-explanatory. You can read about each of the wineries / tasting rooms and create your own wine tasting adventure or you can choose wineries based upon our recommended stops for particular varietals. If you are looking for a specific activity, such as winery tours, picnics, gift shopping or meeting the winemakers, we have chapters on these topics as well. No matter which way you choose to explore Temecula Wine Country, we are confident you will have a *great time*.

Grape Escape Discounts and Promotions

Watch for the ✪ – it is **your key to saving money** during your wine tasting adventure! Our **Grape Escapes Discounts Section** lists the names, addresses, phone numbers, hours of participating wineries and merchants, and describes their money-saving offers. Each time one of the participating wineries or merchants is mentioned in this guidebook, you will see the ✪ symbol followed by a description of their promotion.

Special Information

Temecula area wineries and tasting rooms have a lot more to offer than just good wine. We have included special entries such as "☞ **Authors' Tips**" and "⇨ **By the Way**" notations that provide advice, guidance, and interesting tidbits of information about Temecula, wine, wineries / tasting rooms, winemakers, merchants and other wine-related matters.

Winery and Tasting Room Listings

When we suggest a winery or tasting room, we usually list the address, phone number, and operating hours so you do not have to flip back and forth to other Sections.

DESTINATION: TEMECULA
(The Center of It All)

We lived in Southern California for 15 years and visited the Temecula area often, so we thought we knew a lot about the region. *Wrong!* Performing research for this guidebook opened our eyes to all the exciting activities this thriving region has to offer – not just the Wine Country, but the entire Temecula area. We spent two weeks in Temecula and discovered that the area has evolved into a wonderful *year-round destination* with an abundance of entertainment and recreational opportunities.

Chances are if you are reading this Section, you are planning to visit the Temecula Wine Country. Congratulations! We promise that you will not be disappointed. Temecula is an easy commute from San Diego and Orange County and about 90 minutes from Los Angeles, Palm Springs, and Southern California's world famous beaches. Not only does Temecula have wide open spaces, rolling hills, vineyards, equestrian trails, and mountain views, it also offers visitors premier restaurants, casinos, resorts, spas, unique recreational activities, and internationally recognized entertainment venues. Temecula is truly "The Center of It All" and the perfect *base* from which to explore everything that Southern California has to offer.

Hollywood, Disneyland, Knotts Berry Farm, Universal Studios, Legoland, Wild Animal Park, Santa Rosa Plateau Ecological Reserve, Mount Palomar Observatory, Sea World, Balboa Park Museums, and the **San Diego Zoo** are all an easy drive from Temecula. Although there are hundreds more cultural, educational, and entertainment opportunities a short distance away, Temecula itself has plenty of activities to keep you busy for days at a time. There is **Wine Country**, of course, but that is just one of the many attractions in the area.

One of the most frequently visited and widely recognized local landmarks is **Old Town Temecula**. Just 150 years ago, the Butterfield Overland Stage used to wind its way through the Temecula Hills on the way from Yuma to San Francisco. Old Town is a reminder of that earlier time. You get a sense of the Old West by strolling along the wooden boardwalk of Old Town Temecula and visiting its art galleries, quaint shops, restaurants and taverns that now inhabit the rustic buildings. Be sure to take time to enjoy a performance at **The Old Town Community Theater** – a contemporary 357-seat theater that features music and stage productions throughout the year. In addition, Old Town Temecula hosts numerous festivals and special events you won't want to miss.

On the following pages we have listed a few of the area's major recreational / cultural venues and recurring festivals / events. *For more information about the Temecula area, check out the internet links and resources listed at the back of this guidebook.*

Note: The information contained in this guidebook was current at the time of publication, but is subject to change. Telephone numbers and website addresses are provided to assist the reader in obtaining up-to-date information.

The recommendations and opinions expressed herein are solely the authors' own. *No fees or any type of compensation or benefits have been paid by any of the wineries, tasting rooms, or merchants in order to be included or mentioned in this guidebook.*

RECREATIONAL ACTIVITIES

Hot Air Ballooning – If you have never flown in a hot air balloon, now is your chance. There is simply nothing like flying over Wine Country's rolling hills, horse ranches, and vineyards in the early morning stillness. It is a magical and surprisingly peaceful experience. Since you are sailing with the wind, you feel no breeze at all once aloft. If this is your first flight, you will be wondering why you waited so long to try it. You will be planning your next trip before you touch down. We recommend **A Grape Escape Balloon Adventure.** Give them a call at (800) 965-2122 to schedule your flight or check out their website: *www.hotairtours.com.*

✪ *Grape Escapes Discount!* - Present a copy of this book and receive **10% off** the regular rate for a hot air balloon ride.

Note: While **A Grape Escape Balloon Adventure** and **The Grape Escapes** guidebooks share similar names, they are two separate and distinct business organizations and not affiliated in any way.

Beaches – Dozens of Orange County and San Diego beaches are only an hour away.

Bicycling – Bring your bike! Temecula has miles of cycling trails and many more bike trail routes planned. Check out the City of Temecula website: *www.CityofTemecula.org*

Casinos – Vegas style gambling and excitement await you at the **Pechanga Resort and Casino** located outside Temecula. The Pechanga Casino, with its 522 luxury rooms, is the largest casino in Southern California. Other major casinos that are nearby include: **Pala Casino and Resort** (Pala, CA) and **Harrah's Rincon Casino** (Valley Center, CA near San Diego).

⇨ **By The Way** – According to the Temecula Valley Chamber of Commerce Business Resource Guide, Temecula has been ranked as "the best city in Riverside County to live in."

Camping – Temecula is a great camping destination. The following are just a few of the area's camping spots.

> **Lake Skinner Campground** – 37701 Warren Road in Winchester, CA. For more information, call (800) 234-7275 or visit their website: *www.riversidecountyparks.org*
>
> **Pechanga RV Resort** – 45000 Pechanga Parkway in Temecula. For more information, call 1-877-977-8386 or visit their website: *www.pechangarv.com*
>
> **Vail Lake Resort** – 38000 Hwy 79 South in Temecula. For more information, call (866) 824-5525 or visit their website: *www.vaillakeresort.com*

Dining – There are hundreds of restaurants to choose from in Temecula and in Wine Country ranging from casual, family-friendly to first class. Whether you are looking for steak, seafood, chicken, vegetarian, Italian, Chinese, Mexican, BBQ, or a juicy burger – you will not go hungry in Temecula. We promise.

If fine dining is what you are looking for, one of our favorite restaurants is **Frankie's Steak and Seafood.** Located at 41789 Nicole Lane #1 in the Creekside Shopping Center in Temecula, this fantastic restaurant has an outstanding wine list, great service, and superb cuisine. We recommend the Rib Eye paired with a glass of **Villa Vessia Cabernet Sauvignon.** The locals frequent this premier restaurant, so you may want to make a reservation. The Dress Code is California Casual. Visit their website for more information: *www.frankies-restaurant.com* or call (951) 676-8040.

Golfing – There are a number of golf courses in Temecula or within a half-hour drive. The following courses are open to the public:

> **Cross Creek Golf Course** – 43860 Glen Meadows Road, Temecula ◆ Phone: (951) 506-3402
>
> **Redhawk Golf Course** – 45100 Redhawk Parkway, Temecula ◆ Phone: (951) 302-3850
>
> **Temeku Hills Golf** – 41687 Temeku Drive, Temecula ◆ Phone: (951) 694-9998
>
> **Temecula Creek Inn** – 44501 Rainbow Canyon Road, Temecula ◆ Phone: (951) 694-1000

Not a golfer yet? Not to worry, you can take lessons while on your holiday. Contact:

Temecula Valley Golf School – (951) 699-2283 or (800) 996-2283
International Golf Management – (310) 595-0726

Museums – Looking for a great way to spend a morning or an afternoon? The **Temecula Valley Museum** is open Tuesday through Saturday 10 AM to 5 PM. Tel: (951) 694-6450. **Temecula Children's Museum** is open Tuesday through Sunday. Tel: (951) 308-6370.

Parks – The City of Temecula has 36 sport and nature parks. If you are looking for a relaxing morning or an afternoon in the sun, one of their parks will certainly be just what the doctor ordered. For more information, visit their website: www.*CityofTemecula.org*

Shopping – There are tons of shopping opportunities in Temecula, from antiques to collectibles to stylish shops, boutiques and malls.

Spas – How about a massage? The friendly and professional staff at **South Coast Winery, Resort & Spa** have just the ticket. Call (866) 994-6379, extension 7284 or email them at *spa@wineresort.com*

Water Parks - In this land of year-round sunshine, if you can't make it to the beaches, visit one of the local water parks: **Splash Canyon Water Park** in Temecula, the **Wave Water Park** in Vista, **Knotts Soak City** in Chula Vista, or **The Wave House** in San Diego.

FESTIVALS AND EVENTS

Below are only a few of the major events and festivals that Temecula hosts each year. The dates listed for the following events are subject to change. For additional information and links to the event / festival coordinators, visit these websites: *www.temeculacvb.com, www.temeculawines.org, www.temeculacalifornia.com* and *www.localwineevents.com*

Winter Barrel Tasting – Over 20 Temecula wineries offer samples of their soon-to- be-released wines along with specially prepared food. This event is usually held in **January**.

Regional Wine Tasting – Wineries from Mexico to Canada pour hundreds of their best wines and talk with guests about the individual characteristics of each wine region / appellation. This event is usually held in **March**. Website: *www.temeculawines.org.*

Old Town Bluegrass Festival – This two-day event features the best of bluegrass entertainment at multiple sites in Old Town Temecula. This event is usually held in **March**. Website: *temeculacalifornia.com*

Temecula Spring and Fall Rod Runs – This pair of annual events feature pre-1974 classic cars and hot rods, concerts, food, and charity auctions. The Rod Runs are held in **March and October** each year. Website: *www.rodruntemecula.com*

Thornton Winery Champagne Jazz Series – Internationally celebrated contemporary jazz artists perform live in a unique outdoor setting at this beautiful winery. Programs in this concert series are usually held from **April through October**. Website: *www.thorntonwine.com*

Grape Day – This conference venue features seminars on the latest advances in winemaking and vineyard management. This event is usually held in **April**. Website: *www.temeculawines.org*

Temecula Music Fest – This multi-day festival features different styles of music, food vendors, and art. Each day a different style or music theme is presented. This event is usually held each year in **May**. Website: *www.temeculamusicfest.com.*

Western Days – Celebrate Temecula's Wild West roots with mock gunfights, bank robberies, rope tricks, Native American dancers, cowboy poetry, a chili cook-off, and Western music and exhibits. This event is usually held in **May**. Website: *www.temeculacalifornia.com*

Temecula Valley Balloon and Wine Festival – Dozens of hot air balloons fill the air in Temecula each year during this unique festival. In addition to the Balloon Glow and Laser show and balloon rides, the world-famous festival offers top-name entertainment, wine and beer tasting, arts and crafts vendors, a kids' fair and delicious food. The Wine Garden features different premium wines from numerous Temecula Valley and other Southern California wineries. This event is usually held in **June**. Website: *www.tvbwf.com*

Plein Air and Street Painting Festival – Artists and others wanting to "express themselves" draw and paint giant murals on Old Town streets and listen to great music. This event is usually held in **June**. Website: *www.temeculacalifornia.com*

International Jazz Festival – The festival features free and ticketed concerts by internationally recognized performers at several locations throughout Old Town Temecula. Activities also include music and rhythm workshops and clinics with the performers. Proceeds benefit multiple music-based charities and foundations. This event is usually held in **July**. Website: *www.musiciansworkshop.org*

Vine 2 Wine (Vineyard Tasting and Sunset Barbecue) – Tour a vineyard, talk with Temecula's winemakers, sample their wines, and enjoy a sunset BBQ. This event is usually held in **August**. Website: *www.temeculawines.org*

International Film & Music Festival – In this five-day festival, filmmakers and musicians from across America and around the globe participate in and enjoy numerous independent film screenings, live concerts, workshops, and artisan exhibits. This event is usually held in **September**. Website: *www.tviff.com*

Grape Stomps – These fun and exciting events are held at multiple wineries during the Fall season, generally **September**. Website: *www.temeculawines.org*

Old Town Quilt Show – Over 150 members of the Temecula / Murrieta Valley Quilters Guild host a one-day outdoor quilt show in Old Town. Dozens of colorful, intricate hand-made quilts are displayed. The Guild makes quilts for the military wounded, babies, and HUGS for Children (a nonprofit organization that assists foster families). This event is held in **October**. Website: *www.temeculacalifornia.com*

Erle Stanley Gardner Mystery Weekend – Mystery buffs, crime-solving fans and writers of all ages flock to Old Town to "solve" cases and to participate in mystery writing competitions and publishing workshops. This event is usually held in **November**. Website: *www.temeculacalifornia.com*

Harvest Wine Celebration – Over 20 wineries join together to let you sip new, unreleased wines and barrel samples and enjoy specially selected wine-pairing foods. This event is usually held in **November**. Website: *www.temeculawines.org*

Dickens of a Christmas – Experience an old-fashioned Holiday Season in Old Town with bell ringing choirs, carolers, sleigh rides, Christmas music, Santa Claus (with his elves), and festive displays. Dickens characters and a variety of holiday musicians entertain every weekend from **mid-November through mid-December**. Website: *www.temeculacalifornia.com*

TYPES OF WINE YOU WILL FIND IN THE TEMECULA AREA

Twenty years ago, Temecula was considered to be "White Wine Alley." A lot has changed since then. One of the worst things to happen to Temecula Wine Country was the severe outbreak of Pierces Disease in the late 1990s. This devastating disease, which is caused by a bacterium carried by an insect called the Glassy Winged Sharp Shooter, causes the infected grapevines to starve and die.

As a result of the infestation, millions of dollars worth of vines had to be destroyed. Many vineyard and winery owners suffered severe financial setbacks. After removing the diseased plants, a significant number of vineyard owners decided to experiment by planting different varietals that are less susceptible to Pierces Disease. Temecula Wine Country now has a lot more variety on its tasting room menus. The newly planted varietals are thriving and the wines being produced are better than ever.

You will, of course, find the traditional favorites – Chardonnay, Cabernet, Syrah, Merlot, Sauvignon Blanc, Zinfandel, Port and a variety of blends in abundance. If, however, you are looking for Riesling, Sangiovese, Nebbiolo, Gewürztraminer, Cortese, Sherry, Grenache, Tempranillo, Cab Franc, Barbera, or other less common varietals, you need to know which tasting rooms offer these wines. That is where we come in. We tell you the tasting rooms that are likely to be pouring these and other less common wines.

If your wine tasting experience is limited to the more traditional varietals, Temecula is a great place to expand your horizons. Instead of Chardonnay, try Viognier. Instead of Cabernet Sauvignon, try Cab Franc, Syrah or Barbera. We think you will be glad you did.

☞ **Authors' Tip:** *If you are a white wine lover, you must sample the Temecula Wine Region's Viognier and Riesling. These varietals grow extremely well in the Temecula Valley and the area's winemakers are producing some outstanding wines using these varietals.*

GETTING STARTED ON YOUR WINE TASTING ADVENTURE

A fun-filled *Grape Escapes* adventure requires very little equipment. All you need is a winery guide map, a cooler, a trip plan, and maybe a picnic basket. Why the cooler? Temperatures inside your car can reach 120 degrees or more in the summer and heat can destroy wine. The cooler will help protect your wine purchases from the heat.

During your wine tasting adventure, be sure to follow the:

ABCs of Wine Tasting

A – A Trip Plan. The most important part of a successful wine tasting excursion is the **trip plan**. This is where our guidebook comes in. You can develop your own trip plan after reading the write-ups on each of the wineries, by selecting wineries based upon our favorite picks for each varietal, or by selecting wineries that feature specific activities that appeal to you.

B – Begin with Breakfast or a hearty lunch if you are starting your tasting adventure in the afternoon. Do not even think about beginning your wine tasting trip on an empty stomach.

☞ **Authors' Tip:** *Leave the cologne and heavy perfume in the bottle while in Wine Country, or those hints of rose petal, honeysuckle, cedar, and sandalwood (or was that cat's pee?) may not be coming from your wine glass. (And, yes, "cat's pee" does occasionally show up as a wine descriptor – but, it is not one we use.)*

C – Control your Consumption. Know which wines you wish to focus on – whether they are reds, whites or specific varietals. It is tempting to try to sample everything on the menu, but don't. Simply put: tastings do add up.

Let's say you visit seven tasting rooms. Let's also assume each winery pours you seven one-ounce servings. That is 49 ounces – or **two full bottles of wine**. Even if you pour out half of everything you are served, you will still have consumed an **entire bottle of wine**.

☞ **Authors' Tip:** *Since many wineries have 20 or more wines on their tasting menu, it is not practical to try and taste them all. To provide you with a starting point, we have listed our recommended wines at each of the wineries. You might also want to ask your tasting room host to serve you the wines that he or she thinks are the best. This is a good way to reduce the number of wines you sample without worrying that you might miss an undiscovered gem.*

D – Designate a Non-Drinking Driver. It is best to agree on who will be the Designated Driver before you embark on your *Grape Escapes* adventure. This will ensure that you have a safe and enjoyable tasting experience.

⇨ **By The Way – "D" is also for "Dump Bucket." Use it frequently when sampling; that's what it is there for.**

☞ **Authors' Tip:** *Now a word about spitting. If you are going to be visiting a lot of wineries, spitting is a must. Some people feel it is OK to spit directly into the dump bucket. We do not. We like to take a few sixteen ounce plactic cups with us - the ones with the large mouth. This way we can discretely dispose of wine without swallowing or publicly spitting it out. At the end of our visit, we simply discard the contents of our cups into one of the winery's dump buckets. Your spit cup will need rinsing as the tasting day wears on. We recommend keeping a bottle of water in yor car for that purpose. Do not be surprised if the Tasting Room host offers to rinse it for you.*

"It takes 5,000 nuts to put a car together, but only
one to scatter them all over the road." ~ Darryl Somers

"PARDON ME. HAVE YOU SEEN MY DRIVER?"

(Transportation Services)

Admit it. You've always wanted to ask someone that question. Go ahead; clear your throat and say it out loud in your best upper-crust voice. *"Pardon me. Have you seen my Driver?"*

We are huge supporters of using designated or professional drivers in Wine Country. If no one in your group is willing to serve as the Designated Driver, we suggest you contact one of our recommended Temecula wine tour and transportation providers listed below.

How did we develop our list of recommended transportation service providers? Actually, we didn't. We polled a large number of the top wineries in the area and asked who they believed did a great job for their customers. Our three recommended companies are the ones that came out at the top of the list.

We also wish to mention that the Temecula Valley Winegrowers Association has begun an innovative program to help reduce the occurrence of visitors who are intoxicated when they arrive in Temecula Wine Country. The **Responsible Partner Program** asks transportation providers who operate tours in Wine Country to comply with a code of conduct and promote good behavior. These tour companies are asked to discourage the consumption of hard liquor and beer by their clients and to ensure that visitors to Temecula Wine Country are aware of and adhere to wine tasting etiquette and courtesies. If you would like to know more about the Responsible Partner Program, please visit: *www.temeculawines.org/ limo_partners.asp*

WINE COUNTRY TOUR AND TRANSPORTATION PROVIDERS

The Grapeline® – Temecula
Website: *www.gogrape.com*
Telephone: (951) 693-5755 or 1-888-894-6379
Email: *temecula@gogrape.com*

The tour company most frequently recommended to us by Temecula wineries was **The Grapeline®**, owned and operated by John and Kim Kelliher. In addition to being nice people, the Kellihers are very active in and dedicated to the Temecula wine community. They, and their excellent staff, know all about the wineries, the owners, and winemakers. As a result, they are able to fashion a personalized, high-quality and delightful wine tasting experience for their customers.

The Grapeline® offers two public tours designed to fit their customers' needs. The **Vineyard Picnic Tour** includes a picnic lunch at a winery and four wine tasting stops. (Note: Food and tasting fees <u>are</u> included in the price of this tour.) Weekday rates begin at $88 per person. Weekend rates are slightly higher. One of the advantages of this tour is that many of the wineries have a separate tasting area for Grapeline® passengers – not so important on weekdays, but a very nice feature on weekends when you (and perhaps 100 or more guests) are "jockeying" for a spot at the tasting bar. Also, on this particular tour, you will receive an exclusive *Value Passport* that provides discounts on wine and merchandise purchases at the wineries. Reservations are required for the tour.

The other public tour is **The Grapeline ® Wine Country Shuttle** which offers a unique all-day transportation system that tours wine country. You can catch this **hop-on / hop-off shuttle** from most area hotels during the hours of 10:30 AM to 4:30 PM. Weekday rates start at $42 per person. Weekend rates begin at around $52 per person. (Tasting fees and food are <u>not</u> included in the prices.) The Grapeline® Wine Country Shuttle stops at some of the top winery restaurants in the area. So, no need to worry about going hungry.

John and Kim also offer **private tours**, aptly named the **De Portola Charter**, the **Cabernet Tour**, the **Road Less Traveled Charter,** and the **Chardonnay Luncheon Charter**. These tours typically include a behind-the-scenes winemaking tour at the first winery stop or a private tasting with one of the more colorful winemakers or owners.

☞ **Authors' Tip:** *For private groups using The Grapeline®, we recommend the Road Less Traveled and De Portola Charters. Rates begin at $88 per person on weekdays and start at $98 per person on weekends.*

One of the features we like about The Grapeline's® operation is that they have an outstanding group of drivers / hosts who, in addition to performing the driving duties, are there to ensure that you have the best and safest possible time in Wine Country.

We spent some time with "Wes," one of the excellent Grapeline® driver / hosts. Wes hosts tours in Wine Country several days each week and understands the area intimately. He is able to match the likes and needs of his guests with the wineries. We asked if he would be willing to share some of his passengers' favorite stops. According to Wes, his passengers especially enjoy the following wineries and tasting rooms: **Bella Vista**, **Wilson Creek**, **Oak Mountain**, **Wiens**, **Stuart**, **Leonesse** and **South Coast**.

Sterling Rose Limousines
Website *www.sterlingroselimo.com*
Telephone: (951) 699-9151 or 1-800-649-6463
Fax Number: (951) 699-2502
Email: *sales@sterlingroselimo.com*

Sterling Rose Limousines is fanatical about providing the highest standards in luxury transportation. Their slogan is "Excellence in Elegance," and they have a large and varied fleet of late model vehicles that can accommodate groups ranging in size from two people in one of their smaller sedans to as many as 28 persons in their limo coaches.

When Sterling Rose says they are a family-owned business, they really mean it. It is owned by Heidi and Steven Levin. Steven's sister, Wendy, is the Operations Manager and her husband, Rudy, is the General Sales Manager.

Steven's uncle started in the transportation business back in 1952. Soon thereafter, as a youngster, Steven found himself already in the business by cleaning the cars and performing oil changes. Bottom line is that Steven has cars (and possibly a little 10W30) in his blood – along with a desire to provide the best possible transportation services to his customers.

About now you are probably saying, "*Well*, they can't possibly be THAT good." Wrong. But, don't take our word for it. Sterling Rose Limousines has been named **"Operator of the Year"** by Limousine and Chauffeured Transportation Magazine (LCT) out of **9,000 nationwide transportation companies**.

Sterling Rose offers a variety of wine tour packages that are included with your tickets. Most tours include stops at four or five wineries. You can check out their website to see the list of wineries from which you and your group may select. While you are there, check out their "Testimonials" link. Sterling Rose has a long list of satisfied customers.

Charter rates are reasonable. A sedan may be hired for $50 per hour (weekdays) with a minimum of only two hours. You can hire one of their larger shuttles for as little as $100 per hour. Their larger vehicles generally have a three or five hour minimum rental period. Weekend rates are 10% to 20% higher than the ones quoted here.

Sterling Rose offers a **10% discount** off its published rates to all **Active Duty Military** personnel. Oh, and one more thing. If your company might be interested in exploring the possibility of a corporate event or retreat to Temecula Wine Country, give Steve or a member of his staff a call. They will be delighted to assist you.

West Coast Chauffeur & Transportation
Telephone: (951) 926-1902
Website: *www.wctrans.com*
Email: *kat@wctrans.com*

West Coast Chauffeur & Transportation has a fleet of limos, coaches and stretch SUVs designed to provide stylish luxury transportation for one to 20 people. Your good times start immediately upon entering one of their vehicles. West Coast's limos are designed to impress and entertain with fiber optics throughout, onboard TVs (one as large as 40"), and Surround Sound speakers.

But West Coast did not make our list just because of their vehicles. According to Les Linkogle, Owner of *Briar Rose Winery*, West Coast excels at taking superb care of their customers. Trust us. If Les recommends someone or something, pay close attention.

If you are not exactly sure what you want to do and where you want to go in Temecula Wine Country, not to worry. West Coast specializes in helping you customize a Wine Country package that will satisfy even the most discriminating. They offer tasting packages for $30 per person. This price includes your tastings at four wineries. Check out their website to see which wineries are included in this offer. They can also provide a gourmet sandwich lunch for an additional $11 per person.

Sedan rates at West Coast Chauffeur & Transportation begin at $200 for four hours of wine tasting. This rate rises to $440 for their stretch SUV. *There is also a 20% service charge*, not included in the prices quoted above.

✪ *Grape Escapes Special Benefit* - Present a copy of this book and receive a **complimentary bottle of champagne for your party** when West Coast serves as your transportation provider in Temecula Wine Country.

☞**Authors' Tip:** *The Temecula area has a free community newspaper called Neighbors that contains the latest news on Temecula Wine Country. You can also find updated information on entertainment and, occasionally, discount coupons offered by the tasting rooms in this newspaper.*

"Whoever said money can't buy happiness simply
didn't know where to go shopping." ~ Bo Derek

FAVORITE (Non-Winery) PLACES TO BUY TEMECULA WINES

SHOPTEMECULAWINES.COM

Proprietor:	Le Roy Guilford
Telephone:	1-888-460-WINE (9463)
Website:	*www.shoptemeculawines.com*
Hours:	Online 24 hours
Email:	*customerservice@temeculawinesonline.com*
Address:	LP Guilford Companies, Inc.
	c/o 2466 Cavalcade Court
	Perris, CA 92571

Wines:	All Temecula Wines

Yes, Virginia, there is a Santa Claus and he has moved to Temecula. He now goes by the name of "Le Roy Guilford." He carries <u>all</u> of the Temecula Valley wines and is a wealth of knowledge on the area's wineries, tasting rooms and wines. His *ShopTemeculaWines.com* website is ultra user-friendly and many of the wines he sells are offered at a *discount*. That's why we think of him as Santa Claus.

If you have been a good little boy or girl who is over the age of 21, but are not able to slip away to Temecula for a few relaxing days of wine tasting, then Le Roy (and your friendly UPS delivery guy) will bring Temecula wines to your door. You can even pretend they came down the chimney.

☞ **Authors' Tip:** *In addition to being the owner and cellar master-extraordinaire of www.ShopTemeculaWines. com, Le Roy Guilford is the host of Wine Country Talk Radio broadcast from Anaheim, CA on most Saturdays at 1 PM at KLAA, 830 on your AM dial. Via his website and radio show, Le Roy writes and talks about Temecula wine with a passion and authority shared by few others. Le Roy sums it up his passion this way, "It's All About the Wines."*

TEMECULA HOUSE OF WINE
(Wine Shop, Tasting Bar and Garden)

Proprietor:	Carlos Palma
Telephone:	(951) 699-0929
Website:	*www.palomarinntemecula.com*
Hours:	10 AM to 8 PM weekdays
	10 AM – 10 PM on weekends
Address:	28522 Old Town Front Street
	Temecula, CA 92590
Wines:	All Temecula Wines

If you visit Temecula, but are not able to make it to Wine Country – that is simply a darn shame. Some things are just wrong and that's one of them. Having said that, we are not here to judge you. Instead, we're going to try to help.

The **Temecula House of Wine,** located at the historic **Palomar Inn** in **Old Town,** opened in March of 2006. Owner Carlos Palma is a fan of Temecula wines. In fact, they are the only wines he carries. His goal is to bring Wine Country to his customers and patrons that cannot make it out to Wine Country.

If, after tasting at Carlos' place, you decide you do have time to make it to Wine Country after all, Carlos also arranges private tours.

⇨ **By The Way – Not content just to expand his wine tasting operation, Carlos' plans call for increasing the number of rooms in his hotel from 10 to 27.**

At the time we spoke with Carlos, he indicated that by the Summer of 2008, he will have completed both a tasting bar and a tasting garden that will feature five to six Temecula wines each week. There will also be food, cheese and music on the weekends.

Carlos also carries most of the private label wines of some of Temecula's top winemakers who do not have tasting rooms. Some of his most popular selling wines are by **Leonesse Cellars, Boorman Vineyards**, and **Santa Maria Cellars**.

✪ *Grape Escapes Discount!* - Present a copy of this book at the *Temecula House of Wine* (28522 Front Street) in Old Town Temecula and receive a **10% discount** on all wines purchased on the day of your visit. If you purchase a case or more of wine during your visit, you will receive an additional **5%** (total 15%) **discount**. Tel: 951-699-0929 ◆ Hours: 10 AM to 8 PM weekdays and 10 AM to 10 PM on weekends ◆ Website: *www.palomarinntemecula.com*

LONGS DRUG STORE

Longs Drug Store is located on Rancho California Road. It is on the left-hand side just before you reach Wine Country, and is probably the best "worst kept secret" in Temecula. If you want to buy great wines from all over California at discount prices, Longs is the place to go. Don't believe us? Well, if you stick around long enough, you are apt to meet the many of the staff members from the various wineries in Temecula. Most shop at Longs because the wines are priced 10% to 20% less than at the wineries.

Angel Castaneda, liquor and wine manager at Longs, personally tastes and selects all of the 500+ labels in stock. He stocks top California wines and a good selection of international wines as well. Angel knows wine. His is one of the best California wine selections we have seen anywhere.

Longs Drugs
30640 Rancho California Road
Temecula, CA 92591
Tel: (951) 695-1710

TEMECULA SUPERMARKETS

Two other Temecula area stores have great wine selections and attractive prices, **Stater Brothers** and **Barons**. We think Barons Market is the best place to begin your wine tasting adventure. This is simply a wonderful store. Stock up on their great selection of olives, breads and cheeses. While you are there, you can check out their wine selection of well-priced Temecula wines.

Barons - The Marketplace
31939 Rancho California Road
Temecula, CA 92592
(951) 693-1111

Stater Brothers Markets
Two Locations:

31813 US Highway 79 S	27475 Jefferson Avenue
Temecula, CA 92592	Temecula, CA 92590
Tel: (951) 303-1244	Tel: (951) 676-2548

☞ **Authors' Tip:** *This may be the best advice we give you in the entire book. Before you even think about going to Temecula Wine Country, you have to stop off at Barons - The Marketplace. Why? Glad you asked. This is a magnificent market. They have meats, some amazing cheeses, dozens of types of olives, more peppers than we can name, fresh-baked bread, crackers, fresh fruit, desserts... everything you need to have the most perfect picnic of your life. This is truly a great store.*

While you are there, check out the wine section as well. They have an excellent selection of local wines. Chances are the prices here will be at least 10% lower than those in the tasting rooms.

Don't have a cooler? Not to worry, Barons will fix you up with an inexpensive "cold bag."

GRAPE ESCAPES DISCOUNTS AND PROMOTIONS

OK, here is the fun part. Not only are we going to *help you find* some great wines, wineries, and tasting rooms, but we are actually going to *save you money* in the process.

For example, the friendly folks at **Callaway Vineyard and Winery** will provide you a **20% discount** on all wines purchased on the day of your visit, PLUS they also offer **Two-for-One tasting**. All you have to do is show them your copy of this book.

As they say on those late night TV advertisements, *but wait – there's more!* In addition to Callaway, many of the wineries listed below provide **two-for-one tastings**, and / or provide significant discounts on wine and tasting room merchandise when you present your copy of *The Grape Escapes 2*.

GRAPE ESCAPES PARTICIPATING WINERIES

Boorman Vineyards Estate Winery
21630 Ave de Arboles, Murrieta, CA 92562 ◆ Tel: 951-600-9333 ◆ Hours: By Appointment Only ◆ Website: *www.boormanvineyards.com* – Present a copy of this book and receive a **free "back-stage" tour** of the winery with the winemaker. *Advance appointment is required.*

Callaway Vineyard & Winery
32720 Rancho California Road, Temecula, CA 92591 ◆ Tel: 951-676-4001 ◆ Hours: Daily 10-5 ◆ Website: *www.callawaywinery.com* – Present a copy of this book and receive a **20% discount** on all wines and tasting room merchandise purchased on the day of your visit. Also, present a copy of this book and receive **Two-for-One tasting!!!**

Foote Print Winery
36650 Glen Oaks Road, Temecula, CA 92592 ◆ Tel: 951-265-9951 ◆ Hours: Fri 12-5, Sat-Sun 10-5, Mon-Thurs by Appt ◆ Website: *www.footeprintwinery.com* – Present a copy of this book and receive a **Two-for-One tasting!!!**

Frangipani Estate Winery
39750 De Portola Road, Temecula, CA 92592 ◆ Tel: 951-699-8845 ◆ Hours: Daily 10-5 ◆ Website: *www.frangipaniwinery.com*– Present a copy of this book and receive a **30% discount** on all wines purchased on the day of your visit.

Keyways Vineyard & Winery
37338 De Portola Road, Temecula, CA 92592 ♦ Tel: 1-877-539-9297 ♦ Hours: Daily 10-6, Winter 10-5 ♦ Website: *www.keywayswine.com* – Present a copy of this book and receive **Two-for-One tasting** from their "standard" tasting menu. Sorry, but offer is valid on weekdays only.

La Cereza Vineyard & Winery
34567 Rancho California Road, Temecula, CA 92591 ♦ Tel: 951-699-6961 ♦ Hours: Daily 10-5 ♦ Website: *www.lacerezawinery.com* – Present a copy of this book and receive a **10% discount** on all wines and tasting room merchandise purchased on the day of your visit. Sorry, but offer is not valid on weekends.

Longshadow Ranch Vineyard & Winery
39847 Calle Contento, Temecula, CA 92591 ♦ Tel: 951-587-6221 ♦ Hours: Mon-Fri 12-5, Sat 10-4 (Sat Bonfire 5-9 PM April through October), Sun 10-5 ♦ Website: *www.longshadowranchwinery.com* – Present a copy of this book and receive a **10% discount** on all wines purchased on the day of your visit.

Maurice Car'rie Winery
34225 Rancho California Road, Temecula, CA 92591 ♦ Tel: 951-676-1711 ♦ Hours: Daily 10-5 ♦ Website: *www.mauricecarriewinery.com* – Present a copy of this book and receive a **10% discount** on all wines and tasting room merchandise purchased on the day of your visit. Sorry, but offer is not valid on weekends.

Mount Palomar Winery
33820 Rancho California Road, Temecula, CA 92591 ♦ Tel: 951-676-5047 ♦ Summer Hours: Mon-Thurs 10-6, Fri-Sun 10-7; Winter Hours: Closed Mon & Tues; Wed-Thur 10-5, Fri-Sun 10-6 ♦ Website: *www.mountpalomar. com* – Present a copy of this book and receive a **Two-for-One tasting!!!**

Oak Mountain Winery / Temecula Hills Winery
36522 Via Verde, Temecula, CA 92592 ♦ Tel: 951-699-9102 ♦ Hours: Daily 11-5 ♦ Website: *www.oakmountainwinery. com* – Present a copy of this book and receive a **10% discount** on all wines purchased on the day of your visit. Also, present a copy of this book and receive **Two-for-One tasting** for up to four guests. Offer does not include the souvenir logo glass.

Orfila Vineyards & Winery
13455 San Pasqual Road, Escondido, CA 92025 ◆ Tel: 760-738-6500 ◆ Hours: Daily 10-6 ◆ Website: *www.orfila. com* – Present a copy of this book and receive **free tasting** for up to four people in your party. In addition, you will also receive a **15% discount** on all wines purchased (except the Ambassador Reserve Merlot), plus a **10% discount** on all tasting room merchandise purchased on the day of your visit. Present a copy of this book and receive an additional **5% discount** (total of 20%) on a case or more of wine. Also, present a copy of this book and receive a **free "backstage" tour** of the winery. Appointment required.

Palumbo Family Vineyards & Winery
40150 Barksdale Circle, Temecula, CA 92591 ◆ Tel: 951-676-7900 ◆ Hours: Fri 12-5, Sat-Sun 10-5, Mon-Thurs By Appointment ◆ Website: *www.palumbofamilyvineyards.com* – Present a copy of this book and receive a **complimentary tasting for two people** in your party.

Ponte Family Estate Winery
35053 Rancho California Road, Temecula, CA 92591 ◆ Tel: 951-694-8855 ◆ Hours: Daily 10-5 ◆ Website: *www. pontewinery.com* – Present a copy of this book and receive a **Two-for-One tasting!!!** Offer valid Monday Through Thursday, excluding holidays.

Robert Renzoni Vineyards
37350 De Portola Road, Temecula, CA 92592 ◆ Tel: 951-302-8466 ◆ Hours: Daily 11-6 ◆ Website: *www.robertrenzonivineyards.com* – Present a copy of this book and receive a **10% discount** on all wines and tasting room merchandise purchased on the day of your visit. Also, present a copy of this book and receive an additional **10% discount** (total of 20%) on a case or more of wine.

Tesoro Winery
28475 Old Town Front Street, Temecula, CA 92590 ◆ Tel: 951-308-0000 ◆ Hours: Daily 10-5 ◆ Website: *www.tesorowines.com* – Present a copy of this book and receive a **Two-for-One tasting** for up to four people in your party!!! Present a copy of this book and receive a **10% discount** on all wines and tasting room merchandise purchased on the day of your visit.

Wiens Family Cellars

35055 Via Del Ponte, Temecula, CA   92592 ◆ Tel: 951-694-9892 ◆ Hours: Daily 10-5 ◆ Website: *www.wienscellars.com* – Present a copy of this book and receive **Two-for-One wine tasting**, plus a **10% discount** on all wines purchased on the day of your visit. Also, present a copy of this book and receive a **free "back stage" tour** of the winery with the winemaker. *Advance appointment is required.* Phone (951) 694-9892 to schedule.

Wilson Creek Winery & Vineyards

35960 Rancho California Road, Temecula, CA 92591 ◆ Tel: 951-699-9463 ◆ Hours: Daily 10-5 ◆ Website: *www. wilsoncreekwinery.com* – Present a copy of this book and receive **Two-for-One tasting** for up to four guests (a $20 value). PLUS, present a copy of this book and receive a **10% discount** on all wines purchased on the day of your visit. Offers good Monday – Friday only, except on holidays.

And, if this is not reason enough to visit Wilson Creek – (one of our favorite wineries), present a copy of *The Grape Escapes 2* and receive a **free glass of Almond Champagne** for up to four guests (one glass per entrée) with your purchase of an entrée at the **Creekside Grille** located at Wilson Creek Winery. This is a $28 value and is valid Monday – Friday only, except on holidays.

TOUR COMPANIES AND MERCHANTS

A Grape Escape Balloon Adventure – **40335 Winchester Road, Suite E, Temecula, CA 92591 ◆ 1-800-965-2122 ◆ Reservations Required. ◆ Website:** *www.hotairtours.com*   Present a copy of this book and receive **10% off** the regular rate for a hot air balloon ride.

Note: While **A Grape Escape Balloon Adventure** and *The Grape Escapes* share similar names, they are two separate and distinct business organizations and not associated in any way other than participation in the GE2 discount program.

Temecula House of Wine (Wine Shop, Tasting Bar and Garden) **28522 Old Town Front Street, Temecula, CA 92590 ◆ Tel: 951-699-0929 ◆ Hours: 10 AM to 8 PM weekdays and 10 AM – 10 PM on weekends ◆ Website:** *www.palomarinntemecula.com* – Present a copy of this book and receive a **10% discount** on all wines purchased on the day of your visit. If you purchase a case or more of wine during your visit, you will receive an additional **5%** (total 15%) **discount**.

West Coast Chauffeur & Transportation
◆ Tel: 951-926-1902 ◆ Website: *www.wctrans.com* – Present a copy of this book and receive a **complimentary bottle of champagne** for your party when West Coast serves as your transportation provider in Temecula Wine Country.

⇨ **By The Way** – One ton of grapes can be used to produce about 700 bottles of wine.

☞ **Authors' Tip:** *Some wines only get better with age. If you discover a red wine that you like, consider purchasing at least three bottles. You can "lay down" two of the bottles and enjoy them in a year or two, or longer, depending upon the type of wine.*

THE WINERIES AND TASTING ROOMS...

"Wine makes daily living easier,
less hurried, with fewer tensions
and more tolerance."
~ Benjamin Franklin

TASTING ROOM PRICE CODES

Average Wine Prices:
We have included price codes in the write-ups on each winery. The only thing better than finding a great wine is finding one that is "bargain-priced." The following codes denote the *average price* of the wines on the winery's normal tasting menu.

$ - The average price of wines listed on the tasting menu was $17 or less.
$$ - The average price of wines listed on the tasting menu was $18 - $25.
$$$ - The average price of wines listed on the tasting menu was $26 - $35.
$$$$ - The average price of wines listed on the tasting menu was $36 or higher.

☞ **Authors' Tip:** *A word about price. Are the higher priced wines better? Sometimes, but not always. Certainly, the higher priced wineries have some outstanding wines, but so do less expensive wineries, such as South Coast, Falkner and Mount Palomar. These wineries offer great wines with average retail prices of around $20 per bottle or less.*

⇨ **By The Way** – **A barrel of wine holds about 1200 glasses of wine.**

☞ **Authors'Tip:** *Because winery owners and staff are friendly people, it is hard not to want to buy at least one bottle from each winery you visit. However, we recommend you only purchase a wine if you truly like it.*

Temecula Wine Country

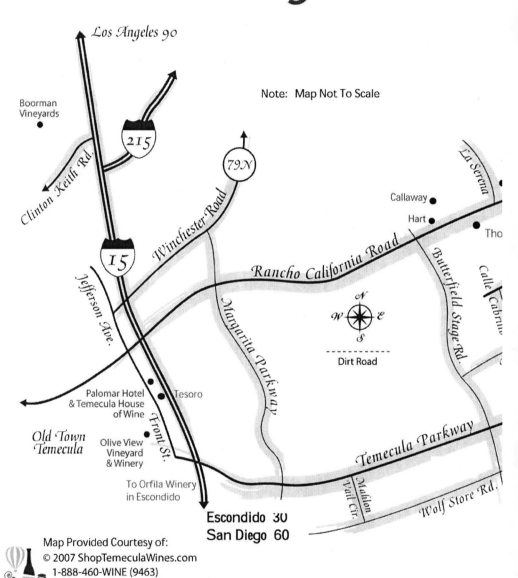

Note: Map Not To Scale

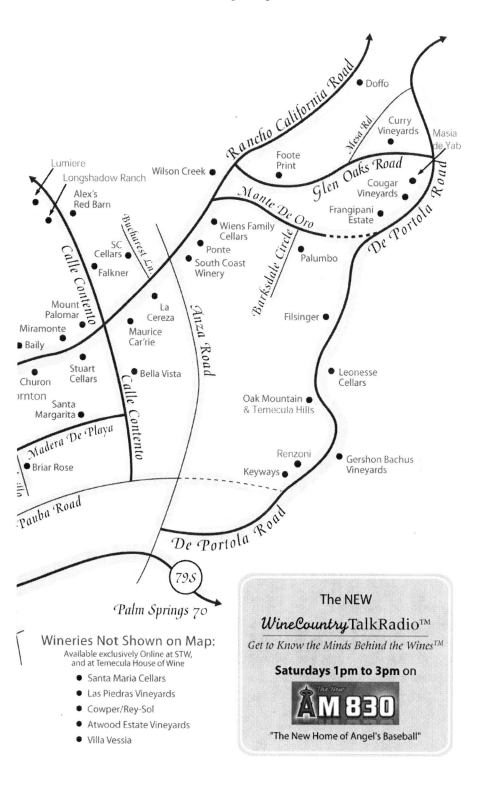

Doffo

Rancho California Road

Curry Vineyards

Mesa Rd.

Masia de Yab

Lumiere

Longshadow Ranch

Alex's Red Barn

Wilson Creek

Foote Print

Glen Oaks Road

Cougar Vineyards

De Portola Road

Monte De Oro

Frangipani Estate

SC Cellars

Bucharest Ln.

Wiens Family Cellars

Ponte

Palumbo

Falkner

South Coast Winery

Barksdale Circle

Calle Contento

Mount Palomar

La Cereza

Anza Road

Filsinger

Miramonte

Maurice Car'rie

Baily

Stuart Cellars

Bella Vista

Leonesse Cellars

Churon

Calle Contento

Oak Mountain & Temecula Hills

ornton

Santa Margarita

Madera De Playa

Renzoni

Gershon Bachus Vineyards

Briar Rose

Keyways

Pauba Road

De Portola Road

79S

Palm Springs 70

Wineries Not Shown on Map:
Available exclusively Online at STW, and at Temecula House of Wine

- Santa Maria Cellars
- Las Piedras Vineyards
- Cowper/Rey-Sol
- Atwood Estate Vineyards
- Villa Vessia

Alex's Red Barn Winery

Proprietors:	Alex and Lise Yakut
Address:	39820 Calle Contento, Temecula, CA 92591
Telephone:	(951) 693-3201
Website:	*www.redbarnwine.com*
Hours:	Sat - Sun and most holidays 11-6 (Winter 10-5)
Tasting Fees:	$7, with glass $10

Average Wine Prices: Whites: $$ Reds: $$$
Production: 1,200 cases per year

Varietals:	(Authors' Recommendations ★):
Whites:	Sauvignon Blanc ★, Riesling ★, Viognier ★, White Cabernet (New Release)
Reds:	Cabernet Sauvignon, Syrah ★
Dessert:	Solera-style Sherry ★

As part of our winery evaluation, we score each wine we tasted. Our system is simple, but more than adequate to identify the wineries that produce a menu of great wines. Rarely do we find wines that "bust" our scoring system, but we found a couple at Alex's Red Barn Winery.

Alex and Lise opened the winery in 2004, but have been active in viticulture and winemaking since Alex's retirement in 1989. Simply put, Alex produces some amazing hand-crafted wines sourced from his twenty-five acre vineyard. His Sauvignon Blanc is outstanding – a fact he attributes to his forty-year-old vines which are some of the oldest in the valley. The Riesling is another of his outstanding whites – and we know a thing or two about Rieslings, having lived in Germany for three years.

Alex's signature wine is the Cream Sherry he produces in an indoor solera which is visible just behind a large glass window as you walk into the tasting room. His Cream Sherry has been described as "candy in a glass." Not a bad description, but we prefer to think of it as liquid gold – rare, precious and oh-so delicious.

⇨ **By The Way** – A solera is a series of barrels that are used to age and blend Sherry and other dessert wines. Wine is removed for bottling from the last and "oldest" barrel in the series. When empty, this barrel is refilled from the next-to-last in the series and so on until barrels at the newer (younger) end of the series are empty. The current year's harvest is placed into the empty barrels and the process is repeated. Care is taken to ensure that the amounts of wine transferred from barrel to barrel are proportional. In this fashion, the winemaker assures a consistent and homogenous product from year-to-year.

Baily Vineyard & Winery

Proprietors:	Phil and Carol Baily
Address:	33440 La Serena Way, Temecula, CA 92591
Telephone:	(951) 676-WINE (9463)
Website:	*www.bailywinery.com*
Hours:	Sun-Fri 11- 5, Sat 10-5
Tasting Fees:	$5 to $10
Average Wine Prices:	Whites: $ Reds: $$
Production:	10,000 – 12,000 cases per year

Varietals:	(Authors' Recommendations ★):
Whites:	Chardonnay, Muscat Blanc, Rosé, Riesling, Sauvignon Blanc (Blend) ★
Reds:	Cabernet Sauvignon ★, Cabernet Franc ★, Merlot, Meritage ★, Sangiovese,
Dessert:	Port ★

If you imagine yourself a knight in armor or perhaps a princess trapped in the wrong time, then this medieval-themed winery is a must-stop-see-and-taste destination for you. As you approach the rose-encircled grounds, you will be met by the winged stone griffin that guards the entrance. Once you are safe inside the castle keep (tasting room), your gaze will be drawn to the tapestry-covered walls – and perhaps a lovely serving maiden or two, and your imaginary armor will be polished to a gleaming brilliance. What more could a knight of a royal court ask?

Might we suggest lunch for you and your Lady, Sir Knight? If you proceed past the tasting room, beneath the gargoyle perched above the doorway, you will find Carol's Restaurant. Don't forget to raise your helmet visor so they recognize you as friend and not foe. Carol's is decorated similarly to the tasting room with medieval style tapestries, shields, swords and knightly accoutrements to make you feel right at home. The food has been sampled by your royal tasters (that would be us, Sir Knight) and we pronounce the food most excellent.

And what about the wines, you ask? We are pleased to report that Phil Baily, the castle's winemaker, produces award-winning wines fit for a royal court. We most humbly urge, Sire, that you try the Montage, their Sauvignon Blanc and Sèmillon blend. But the favorites of your most humble wine tasters were the reds. They are fit for a king, if we do say so ourselves. The Cabernet Sauvignon, Cab Franc and the Meritage are all great wines, as is the Vintage Port.

⇨ **By The Way** – **Baily Vineyards won three Bronze Medals at the 2008 New World International Wine Competition – two for their Cabernet Franc and a third for their Meritage Red. They also won a Gold Medal for their 2007 Rosé and two Silver Medals for their 2003 Vintage Port and 2006 Sangiovese.**

Bella Vista Winery (formerly Cilurzo)

Proprietor:	Emery (Imre) Cziraki
Address:	41220 Calle Contento, Temecula, CA 92592
Telephone:	(951) 676-5250
Website:	*www.bellavistawinery.com*
Hours:	Daily 10-6 (Winter 10-5)
Tasting Fee:	$6
Average Wine Prices: Whites: $$ Reds: $$	
Production:	22,000 cases per year

Varietals:	(Authors' Recommendations ★):
	(**Note:** We did not sample Bella Vista's white wines.)
Whites:	Chardonnay, Fume' Blanc, Sauvignon Blanc, Riesling, Rosé, Viognier, White Cabernet
Reds:	Cabernet Sauvignon, Merlot ★, Petite Sirah, Red Blend ★, Zinfandel ★
Sparkling:	Champagne ★
Dessert:	Muscat Canelli ★, Late Harvest Petite Sirah ★

Bella Vista Winery's vineyard was part of the Vail Ranch where, in the 1960's, horticulturists were brought in to see what types of crops could best be grown here. Since the area has warm days and cool nights with moist air, it was considered perfect for growing grapes and avocados. In 1968, Vincenzo Cilurzo planted premium Petite Sirah and Chenin Blanc grapes on 40 of his 100 acres and started the first commercial vineyard business in the Temecula Valley. Five acres of the original vineyard still produce grapes used in the winery's products.

In 2004, Emery Cziraki and his wife, Gizella, purchased the winery. They changed the name to "Bella Vista" for the "beautiful view" of the surrounding valley that can be seen from the hilltop near the winery.

☞ **Authors' Tip:** *The Bella Vista Late Harvest Petite Sirah is particularly good. It is a nice sweet, fruity, non-syrupy wine that can be served over pound cake, ice cream, or cheesecake. While tasting the Petite Sirah, be sure to ask Emery to pour you one of his "specials" – a bubbly, delicious mixture of Late Harvest Petite Sirah and sparkling wine (champagne).*

The Czirakis have updated and modernized the winery. Emery (Imre) converted the old storage room into a spacious tasting area. The 45 foot-long, race-track shaped tasting bar overlooks the barrel / cask room through large, arched windows. The cask room has been renovated into a party / reception area. To make getting to the tasting room easier and more appealing for his guests, Emery has also improved the parking area and the surrounding landscaping. It is all of these special touches that have tour groups and locals flocking to this casual and friendly tasting room that has good wines and one of the lower tasting fees in the area.

⇨ **By The Way – Emery, Bella Vista's owner and winemaker, began making wine at the age of seven in Hungary under the watchful eye of his Grandfather. In honor of his roots, Emery occasionally offers visitors samples of a unique Hungarian sausage (that he imports from Chicago) to help cleanse their palates between tastings.**

If you arrive at lunch-time or need a break from sampling wines, grab some cheese, salami and crackers from the large selection offered in the Bella Vista gift shop refrigerator case and follow the brick pathway that leads up the hill behind the tasting room. Here you will find the remarkable view of the rolling hills and vineyards that inspired the winery's new name. Next to the tree-lined pond, there are lots of picnic tables under shady palapas where you can stretch-out and relax, take in the scenery, and contemplate how wonderful a life filled with wine tasting can be.

One of the reasons for the winery's popularity is Emery himself. It is obvious that Emery really enjoys meeting people. He can usually be found in the tasting room serving wine and talking to his guests. We'll let you in on a secret. Emery also enjoys a good practical joke. When working at the tasting bar, he frequently introduces himself as Jose Gonzales and tells customers he was just recently promoted from being the winery's janitor and that today is his first day serving wine. He then pleads with his customers to tell the "boss lady" out front that he is doing a good job.

Emery and his alias, Jose, are having a thoroughly good time making and serving wine in the oldest tasting room in the valley. Please stop by, introduce yourself and prepare to be entertained.

Boorman Vineyards Estate Winery

Proprietors: Todd and Rosie Boorman
Address: 21630 Ave de Arboles, Murrieta, CA   92562
Telephone: (951) 600-9333
Website: *www.boormanvineyards.com*
Hours: By Appt Only
Tasting Fee: Complimentary
Average Wine Prices: Reds: $$$
Production: 1,500 cases per year

Varietals: (Authors' Recommendations ★):
Reds: Barbera ★, Cabernet Sauvignon ★, Cabernet Franc ★, Merlot ★

One word sums up Boorman Vineyards and Winery: Passion! Located at 2,000 feet elevation at the south end of the Santa Margarita Mountains, this winery was the highest elevation we visited during our tour of the Temecula Wine Region. Because it is above the mist line, it is not a suitable area for growing white wine varietals. The decomposed granite soil and sloping hillsides are, however, perfect for growing superb red grape varietals.

Todd Boorman has studied all aspects of his three-acre vineyard's weather patterns, sun angles and humidity. He approaches wine making like an engineer, leaving no variable unnoticed, and certainly leaving nothing to chance. Quite simply, he *builds* great wines. His expertise in the vineyard and barrel room has not gone unnoticed or unappreciated. Todd manages three other vineyards in the area and consults for several local wineries.

One of the things that surprised us was the quality of his winemaking equipment. His operation is small, but he has not skimped on equipment. We think we remember Rosie telling us that she got a new crusher for her birthday. Or was it a destemmer?

The winery itself is spotless and well organized, just what you would expect from a fire-fighter / paramedic. If you are in an emergency situation and just have to have some great red wines, call Todd and Rosie. Don't even bother asking what they will be sending. It does not matter. *All* of his wines are great.

If you make it to the Temecula area, do not pass up the chance to call and schedule a visit with the Boormans. We promise you will taste some great wines and have a wonderful wine tasting experience.

⚙ *Grape Escapes Special Benefit* - Present a copy of this book and receive a free **"back-stage" tour** of the winery with the winemaker. *Advance appointment is required._*

☞ **Authors' Tip:** *If you can't make it to the Boorman Vineyards Estate Winery to try their wines, you can often find Rosie Boorman at the Temecula Farmers' Market on Saturdays. Say hello for us and pick up a bottle of their great wine to take home.*

Briar Rose Winery

Proprietors:	Les and Dorian Linkogle
Address:	41720 Calle Cabrillo, Temecula, CA 92592
Telephone:	(951) 308-1098
Website:	*www.briarrosewinery.com*
Hours:	By Appt Only
Tasting Fee:	$15 to $31
Average Wine Prices:	Whites: $$ Reds: $$$$
Production:	2,400 cases per year

Varietals:	(Authors' Recommendations ★):
Whites:	Chardonnay, Sauvignon Blanc ★, Viognier ★, Riesling ★
Reds:	Cabernet Sauvignon ★, Sangiovese, Zinfandel
Dessert:	Aleatico Port ★, Sherry, Orange Muscat

Of all the tasting rooms we have ever visited, Briar Rose is one of our all time favorites. It is unique and special for many, many reasons. The cottages are literally right out of a fairy tale. The reason for this is that the cottages that make up the Briar Rose complex were designed by an architect and set designer who worked for Disney Studios. The tasting room cottage is literally a duplicate of Snow White's cottage. When Les and Dorian Linkogle purchased the property they agreed to make no design changes. The result of this decision adds to the special magic and ambience of the wine tasting experience.

There are many words that can be used to describe Briar Rose – magical, unusual, unique, special and *exclusive*. In fact, Les has an arrangement with Harrah's Casino. When the "high-rollers" need a break they are taken to Briar Rose. After seeing some of the celebrity photos scattered about the cottages, we asked Les if he considered himself to be a winemaker to the stars. He responded, "That's a fair description." Les and Dorian fiercely guard the confidentiality of their privacy-seeking guests. We will not spill the beans either, other than to suggest you pay close attention to any limos that arrive or depart from Briar Rose. You might just see some familiar faces.

Fans of Walt Disney films will certainly enjoy this tasting room, as well as anyone who loves to taste great wines. When you arrive at your scheduled appointment, you will be greeted by one of the Briar Rose hostesses at the entrance to the property and escorted to the tasting room. Wine tasting at Briar Rose is a comfortable "sit-down" affair. There is no jostling for a position at a tasting bar. Guests are seated and served the wines in a relaxed fashion. Your visit will last 45 minutes to an hour.

While Briar Rose is exclusive, it is not by any means unwelcoming or pretentious. Les and Dorian are two of the most warm, friendly, and down-to-earth people that you are likely to meet in Wine Country, so do not hesitate to call for an appointment. The only requirement for tasting at this wonderful property is a *serious* interest in wine. As a winemaker, Les describes himself as a "cook," rather than a chef – a chef being a formally trained winemaker. All we can say is that Les is a very, very good cook.

Callaway Vineyard & Winery

Proprietors: The Lin Family
Address: 32720 Rancho California Road, Temecula, CA 92591
Telephone: (951) 676-4001
Website: *www.callawaywinery.com*
Hours: Daily 10-6 (Winter 10-5)
Tasting Fees: $7.50 to $12.50
Average Wine Prices: Whites: $ Reds: $$
Production: 25,000 cases per year

Varietals: (Authors' Recommendations ★):
                       (**Note:** We were unable to taste all of Callaway's wines.)
Whites: Chardonnay ★, Pinot Gris, Roussanne, Sauvignon Blanc,
                       Viognier, White Meritage, White Blend,
Reds: Cab Franc ★, Cabernet Sauvignon, Cab-Merlot ★,
                       Dolcetto, Merlot, Syrah, Sangiovese, Meritage, Nebbiolo,
                       Zinfandel
Sparkling: Bela Rosé
Dessert: Sweet Nancy, Port, Muscat Canelli

Callaway Vineyard and Winery is one of the oldest, largest and best known of the Temecula Valley wineries. Callaway's wines began to be known worldwide in 1976 at a New York City American Bi-Centennial Celebration when Queen Elizabeth II of Great Britain (known for not being terribly fond of wine) asked for a *second* glass of Callaway's 1974 Riesling.

Callaway Vineyard & Winery, now privately owned by the Lin Family of San Diego, was originally founded in 1969 by Ely Callaway, the man who revolutionized golf with his Big Bertha brand of clubs. Mr. Callaway believed Temecula would be a perfect spot for growing grapes. The rest, as they say, is history.

In 1974 Callaway became the first winery to open its doors in the Temecula Valley. In 2005, it was acquired by the Matthew and Patricia Lin family. Since acquiring the property, the Lin's have initiated a series of significant renovations. Their new outdoor tapas restaurant, Meritage, is open Mon - Thurs 11 AM to 4 PM; Fri - Sat 11 AM to 9 PM and Sunday 9 AM to 6 PM. Its name, which combines "merit" and "heritage" sums up the Lin's appreciation of the proud history of the winery. Callaway has always prided itself on being good stewards of the land and nature. This is a tradition the Lins plan on continuing.

The Callaway tasting bar has one of the best views in the valley. From here you are able to sample wines from one of the largest tasting menus in Wine Country. On the day we visited, there were 26 wines available for tasting. If you like to choose from a wide variety and styles of wines, this is a perfect location and a great place to start your tour of Wine Country.

☞ **Authors' Tip:** *Watch for Callaway's on-site promotions. The gift shop often offers a "Buy four (4) bottles of wine for the price of three (3)" special. In addition, the tasting room sometimes offers a free "wine-of-the-month" tasting.*

Callaway's best selling reds are the Special Selection Cab-Merlot and the Reserve Cabernet Sauvignon. Their best selling whites are the Special Selection Muscat Canelli and the Reserve Chardonnay.

✪ *Grape Escapes Discount!* - Present a copy of this book and receive a **20% discount** on all wines and tasting room merchandise purchased on the day of your visit. Also, present a copy of this book and receive **Two-for-One tasting!!!**

(Inn at) Churon Winery

Proprietors:	Ron and Judy Thomas
Address:	33233 Rancho California Road, Temecula, CA 92591

Telephone:	(951) 694-9070
Website:	*www.innatchuronwinery.com*
Hours:	Daily 10-4:30
Tasting Fee:	$10
Average Wine Prices:	Whites: $ Reds: $$$
Production:	4,000 cases per year

Varietals:	(Authors' Recommendations ★):
Whites:	Chardonnay, Riesling, Sauvignon Blanc, Viognier, White Merlot
Reds:	Cabernet Sauvignon, Merlot, Petite Sirah ★, Syrah, Vin Rouge Blend ★, Zinfandel
Dessert:	Sherry ★, Port ★

As you drive by on Rancho California Road, the French-style chateau that houses the Inn at Churon Winery will appear on a hilltop on your right. You will be excused if your first thought is "Wow"! It gets even better when you step inside. The entrance opens onto a three-story lobby where you register for the inn. As you peer downward over the attractive iron-work balcony, your eyes will be automatically drawn to the elegant spiral staircase that descends to the gift shop and tasting room. Light from the lobby atrium filters down and gives the tasting room and its rich, marble-topped wooden bar a comfortable Old World feel.

The Inn at Churon Winery has 22 rooms and if you are fortunate to get one overlooking the rolling hills and nearby vineyards, you will certainly want to stay for a few days gazing upon a landscape that is quite simply a slice of heaven.

We toured the spacious rooms at the Inn at Churon Winery and they are both elegant and well-appointed. In our opinion, the "standard" rooms in this inn are more than just comfortable – with exquisite marble baths, graceful French Provincial Furniture, plush bedding, fireplaces and lots of room to stretch out. We especially liked the rooms with patios or balconies over looking the vineyards. The Inn's rooms come with a private wine tasting and appetizer session in the evening and also include a freshly prepared gourmet breakfast. Once you have settled in, you may never want to leave.

On the day we visited, they were pouring five whites and eight reds. Our favorites were the Bronze medal-winning 2003 Vin Rouge, a blend of Cab Franc, Cabernet Sauvignon and Merlot. It is, according to Damon Prince, the Tasting Room Manager, their most popular red wine. The 2005 Zinfandel was also very nice, as was the rich and satisfying 2005 Sherry. If you are a fan of dry style wines, we suggest the 2003 Petite Syrah. Churon's White Merlot is the most popular of their white varietals.

Benny Rodriguez, Churon's winemaker, is relatively new to this winery, having only been there for approximately two years on the date we visited. He is a fan of blending and will be introducing a number of smaller lot wines. Benny is widely respected within the wine community and also produces wines under his own private label, **Santa Maria Cellars**. His Mourvèdre-Cab and Merlot-Cab blends are outstanding; consequently, we are extremely excited about his joining the Inn at Churon Winery.

Cougar Vineyard & Winery

Proprietors:	Rick and Jennifer Buffington
Address:	39870 De Portola Road, Temecula, CA 92592
Telephone:	(951) 491-0825
Website:	*www.cougarvineyards.com*
Hours:	Daily 11-6 (Winter 5 PM)
Tasting Fees:	$6

Average Wine Prices: Whites: $ Reds: $$
Production: 3,000 cases per year with plans to go to 5,000

Varietals:	(Authors' Recommendations ★):
	Note: Not all of Cougar's varietals were available for tasting on the days we visited.
Whites:	Chardonnay ★, Cortese (New Release), Malvasia Bianca (New Release), White Cab Sauvignon (Pink Cougar) ★, Vermentino
Reds:	Aglianico, Cabernet Sauvignon ★, Montepulciano, Malbec, Primitivo, Sangiovese ★, Syrah
Sparkling:	Sparkling Cougar (New Release)
Dessert:	Muscat Canelli ★

Bob declares often and robustly that in his next life he is going to be Italian. Therefore, he is especially excited about the addition of Cougar Vineyard and Winery to Temecula Wine Country. Rick and Jennifer Buffington, owners and winemakers, opened the winery and tasting room in late 2006 and it is rapidly becoming a very popular destination for both tour groups and individuals.

At the time of our visit, they had six wines on the tasting menu, including a wonderful wine called "Pink Cougar" (a 100% white Cabernet Sauvignon) and an Estate Sangiovese crafted in the more traditional, lighter to medium-bodied style. If you are a Sangio fan, the Cougar Sangiovese is not to be missed.

⇨ **By The Way – The Pink Cougar is made from grapes that come from the Boorman Vineyards and we have not found anything grown or made by Todd and Rosie Boorman that we do not like.**

One of the things about Cougar Winery that excites Bob, in addition to Sangiovese and Primitivo, is that the Buffingtons are also growing Montepulciano, Cortese, Aglianico, Pinot Grigio and Vermentino. Rick and Jennifer are proud to be bringing some different wines to the region. They are especially pleased that Italian varietals have a longer growing season and appear to do well in the Temecula climate. For genuine Italians or, like Bob, Italian-wannabes, the Cougar Winery is a must-stop-see-and-taste destination in Temecula. It is *"Semplicemente Fantastico!" (Quite simply, fantastic!!)*

If you are a fan of friendly winery dogs, you will especially like Sandi and Diego, two AKC yellow Labrador Retrievers that greet and sometimes entice customers into a game of fetch. If they are not immediately available when you arrive, shake out a few oyster crackers from the jar atop the tasting bar. We promise you will immediately make two new friends. According to Jennifer, Sandie is the huntress and lover while Diego is the relentless retriever that loves to play ball. Rick and Jennifer are committed to providing both great wines and a friendly and educational wine tasting experience. Go see them.

☞ **Authors' Tip:** *Another plus about visiting Cougar is that they have a reciprocal relationship with two other area wineries: Oak Mountain / Temecula Hills and Frangipani. Pay the tasting fee at any of these three tasting rooms and receive 50% off the tasting fee at the other two wineries.*

Falkner Winery

Proprietors: Ray and Loretta Falkner
Address: 40620 Calle Contento, Temecula, CA 92591
Telephone: (951) 676-8231
Website: *www.FalknerWinery.com*
Hours: Daily 10-5
Tasting Fees: $8 to $18
Average Wine Prices: Whites: $$ Reds: $$
Production: 7,500 cases per year

Varietals: (Authors' Recommendations ★):
Whites: Chardonnay, Riesling ★, Sauvignon Blanc ★, Viognier ★, Sweet Loretta Blend
Reds: Amante-Super Tuscan ★, Cabernet Sauvignon, Merlot, Syrah ★, Meritage ★, Red Table Wine
Dessert: Port

Falkner Winery sits atop a commanding hill. At 1,500 feet elevation, Falkner Winery's rustic redwood tasting room and vine-covered veranda offer spectacular views of the Temecula Valley below. In our opinion, the Pinnacle Restaurant next to the winery has the best panoramic view of the valley. If these are not reasons enough to visit Falkner winery, there are several more. We visited Falkner twice in the past year. Both times we were fortunate to find Bob Devon, Falkner's Tasting Room Manager, behind the tasting bar. Bob has white hair, white beard, a broad smile and a friendly, out-going personality. Wine tasting with Mr. Devon is an absolutely delightful experience. Should you see Bob behind the tasting bar, introduce yourself and tell him hello for us. He is a friend worth having and a wonderful host.

⇨ **By The Way** – **Falkner Winery won Best of Class for their 2006 Sauvignon Blanc at the 2008 San Francisco Chronicle Wine Competition.**

There are so many good things about this winery and tasting room. Where to begin? Okay, let's start with the wine quality. At the time of our visit, Falkner was the only winery in the valley to have produced a 93 point-rated wine from *Wine Spectator*. No small accomplishment! How did they do it?

Falkner has a top winemaker by the name of Steve Hagata who produces an entire menu of great wines. Most Temecula Valley winemakers excel at producing smooth, fruit-forward wines that are meant to be enjoyed early. Falkner proceeds along a slightly different path. Most of their red wines are aged at least three years before being released to the public. Another good thing about Falkner wines is that they are very affordable. On the days we visited, the average price of their wines was only $18 for whites and $20 for reds.

☞ **Authors' Tip:** *Before you visit Falkner Winery, be sure to check out their website. They frequently post coupons for half-price wine tasting and discounts for dining at the Pinnacle Restaurant.*

Filsinger Vineyards & Winery

Proprietors: Bill and Katharine Filsinger
Address: 39050 De Portola Road, Temecula, CA 92592
Telephone: (951) 302-6363
Website: *www.filsingerwinery.com*
Hours: Fri 11-4, Sat-Sun, 10-5, M-Thurs By Appt
Tasting Fee: $3 for 5 tastes
Average Wine Prices: Whites: $ Reds: $$
Production: 4,000 cases per year

Varietals: (Authors' Recommendations ★):
Whites: White Blend, Chardonnay ★, Fume Blanc, Riesling (New Release) Viognier, Gewürztraminer
Reds: Cabernet Sauvignon (Barrel Select) ★, Rosé of Cabernet, Merlot ★, Syrah, Tempranillo, Zinfandel,
Sparkling: Dry Brut (Diamond Cuvée) ★, Strawberry Rosé (Gamay-Riesling Blend)
Dessert: Orange Muscat, Sweet Zinfandel

Filsinger Vineyards and Winery is one of the longest operating wineries in the Temecula Valley. The winery, established in 1980, and its owner and winemaker, Dr. William Filsinger, have achieved a respected and iconic status. It is the fourth oldest winery in the area. The Filsinger family hails from Germany where, prior to WWII, they had a large winery in Mainz. It seems appropriate that it was the Filsinger Winery that first introduced Gewürztraminer to the Temecula Valley. In addition to the Gewürztraminer, Filsinger is also known for its Riesling.

Filsinger is one of the few wineries that does not operate a wine club. When I asked the reason for this, Eric Filsinger, son and assistant winemaker, told me that they did not want to do anything that might distract from the winemaking.

Filsinger has other points to recommend it. The wines and tasting fees are some of the least expensive in the Valley – whites average only $12 per bottle. The average price for reds is only $18. If that is not enough to attract you to this winery, Filsinger also makes an excellent Blanc de Blanc "Brut" Chardonnay which sells for only $19, or in a Magnum for $45. The Blanc de Blanc is their most popular sparkling wine and it was certainly ours. The winery also makes a dry "Brut" Rosé that contains a hint of strawberry. As for red wines, we found the "Barrel Select" Cabernet to be excellent, as was the 2005 Merlot.

The winery has an adjacent raised and covered gazebo picnic area that is set among shady trees. Should you arrive on one of those days when it rains, this is a great location to pull over and treat yourself to a glass of wine, some munchies or a picnic.

Foote Print Winery

Proprietors:	Deane and Christine Foote
Address:	36650 Glen Oaks Road, Temecula, CA92592
Telephone:	(951) 265-9951
Website:	*www.footeprintwinery.com*
Hours:	F 12-5; Sat & Sun 10-5; Weekdays by Appt. Minimum 6 persons
Tasting Fees:	$10
Average Wine Prices: Reds: $$$	
Production:	1,200 cases per year

Varietals:	(Authors' Recommendations ★):
Whites:	None
Reds:	Cabernet Sauvignon ★, Merlot ★, Red Blends ★, Syrah ★, Zinfandel,
Dessert:	Late Harvest Merlot, Late Harvest Zinfandel, Zinfandel Port ★

As you drive up the shaded lane to Foote Print Winery, you realize immediately that this is a working farm. Chances are the first thing you will notice are the horses corralled near the large metal barn that doubles as the tasting room.

Owner and winemaker, Deane Foote, does all the bottling, corking and labeling by hand. Although he did jokingly admit that his wife, Christine, is there to supervise when she thinks it necessary. Both Deane and Christine are warm and friendly people. Their goal is "to keep it simple, have some fun," and treat you to their limited production, handcrafted red wines.

Deane has a great sense of humor and told us in jest (at least we think he was joking) that he wants to expand his Foote-themed labels. Currently he has his "Red Foote" blend and a 2004 Estate "Footage," but feels that he's only scratched the surface of the potential for funny "Foote" labels. Candidate names under consideration are "Athlete's Foote," and "Foote-in-Mouth." The possibilities are endless, but thus far Christine has adamantly refused to consider expanding the tongue-in-cheek "Foote" names. Perhaps she feels that such names might somehow diminish the excellent wine her husband produces. Frankly, we're on Deane's side of this good-humored family feud. So, when you visit Foote Print Winery, please be sure to offer your own suggestions for their wines. Think of it as being a "Foote" soldier in a crusade for levity labels.

Foote Print Winery has approximately two acres of grapes planted and produces around 1200 cases of wine per year. Generally, no more than 150 cases of any particular varietal are produced. So, if you find a wine you like, buy it.

As a former military man, Deane honors the service of those currently in uniform. **Active Duty Military who show ID taste for free** and receive a **10% discount** on all purchases. We say OOHRAH!!! Heck, we were even thinking of dropping down and giving Deane twenty. For those of you non-military types, those are pushups. Still confused? Deane will explain. A final note to all the podiatrists out there. Sorry, but the free tasting does not apply to you – no matter how fancy your "Foote Work."

☞ **Authors' Tip:** *The Foote family also grows organic fruit and citrus crops which they sometimes sell in their tasting room. The day we visited, they had beautiful limes, grapefruit, and pomegranates – all at excellent prices.*

✪ *Grape Escapes Discount!* - Present a copy of this book and receive a **Two-for-One Tasting.**

Frangipani Estate Winery

Proprietor:	Don Frangipani
Address:	39750 DePortola Road, Temecula, CA92592
Telephone:	(951) 699-8845
Website:	*www.frangipaniwinery.com*
Hours:	Daily 10-5
Tasting Fees:	$10

Average Wine Prices: Whites: $ Reds: $$$
Production: 4,000 – 5,000 cases per year

Varietals:	(Authors' Recommendations ★):
Whites:	Sauvignon Blanc, Riesling, Viognier
Reds:	Cabernet Franc ★, Cabernet Sauvignon, Claret, Grenache Rosé, Grenache ★, Merlot ★, Petite Syrah ★, Sangiovese, Zinfandel
Dessert:	Late Harvest Zinfandel

Frangipani is home to "Frani" one of our favorite De Portola pooches. As you enter the tasting room, Frani will dash toward you. No worries; she's friendly. Once she's certain you have no food, she will probably turn her attention to a tennis ball which she will drop at your feet while you enjoy tasting Don Frangipani's wines.

Don't be surprised if you find yourself staring out the window and temporarily forgetting why you are there. The view from Don's "office" (tasting bar) is fantastic. If the view completely captures your attention, there are tables set up outside, just on the other side of the tasting room wall. There is even a small reach-through window from which you can be served Frangipani wines. Is this a wine-lover's paradise, or what?

Speaking of wines, may we suggest you start with the Grenache. This is an absolutely wonderful wine and our personal favorite. Don told us that the Cabernet Franc was actually even more popular and one of his best sellers. Another of Frangipani's popular wines is the Petite Syrah. This is a nice, peppery big red – perfect for pairing with a steak.

Frangipani is known for more than its wines. In conjunction with a local theater group, the winery hosts an entertainment series. The week we were there, Elvis had NOT left the building. We have it on good authority that the King was particularly fond of Don's wines. He was reportedly quoted as saying, "Thank you. Thank you very much." Okay, okay, we know. Bad joke. But work with us here, and go sample Don's wines. Then you, too, can say, "Thank you. Thank you very much."

✿ *Grape Escapes Discount!* - Present a copy of this book and receive a **30% discount** on all wines purchased on the day of your visit.

Gershon Bachus Vintners

Proprietors: Ken Falik and Christina Lesch-Falik
Address: 37750 De Portola Road, Temecula, CA92592
Telephone: (877) 458-8428
Website: *www.gershonbachus.com*
Hours: By Appt Only
Production: 800 – 1,000 cases per year
Tasting Fees: $30 for tasting only; $50 for tasting and a meal
Average Wine Prices: Whites: $$$ Reds: $$$$

Varietals: (Authors' Recommendations ★):
Whites: Duet White Blend ★, Four-Four-Two White Melange ★
Reds: Red Duet ★, Zinfandel ★, Cabernet Sauvignon ★

Gershon Bachus was the name of owner Ken Falik's European grandfather. When your family history includes a name like "Bachus," you have to assume that you are *destined to make great wines*. Gershon Bachus Vintners (GBV) provides an experience like no other – great food, great wines and great hospitality.

Ken Falik and Christina Lesch-Falik, the GBV owners, cater to prestigious and up-scale wine lovers and event clientele. They have constructed a beautiful Tuscan-style villa on a hilltop with a breathtaking 360°panoramic view of Palomar Mountain, rolling hills, ranches and the vineyards along De Portola Road. Although they describe their tasting room/event center as "rustic-elegant," we're not sure about the rustic part, but we certainly agree that the surroundings are elegant.

If you want to experience a Tuscan-style luxury wine tasting adventure that allows you the time to relax and relish exceptional, premium wines, contact GBV. Ken and Christina host private, exclusive, seated wine tastings which last approximately an hour for $30 per person with an eight person attendance minimum. For a 1 to 2-hour luncheon tasting with specially selected wine and food pairings, the fee is $50 per person. Worth it? Absolutely!

The GBV winemaker, Michael Tingley, is one of our favorite Temecula vintners and makes outstanding wines. GBV was one of our highest scoring wineries in the Temecula Valley. If you are serious about exceptional wine, you must visit this exclusive tasting room and event venue. On the day we visited, they served two exceptional white blends. The Villa Vino White Duet is 50% Chardonnay and 50% Sauvignon Blanc. The GBV "Four-Four-Two" White Melange consists of 40% Pinot Grigio, 40% Sauvignon Blanc and 20% Viognier. Our personal favorites, however, were the 100% varietal reds: the "Aquilo" is GBV's 100% full-bodied Cabernet Sauvignon and "Zephyrus" is the name of their excellent Zinfandel.

GBV provides a tasting experience of a lifetime. All tastings are By Appointment Only with a two-day advance notice. (If you or someone in your party is a vegetarian or vegan, GBV is happy to provide a special meal for that individual at no extra cost if you book the luncheon tasting.) Gershon Bachus Vintners also conducts a wide range of private and corporate functions, ranging from cocktail parties to sit-down dinners to weddings and other celebrations. The event center can accommodate up to 250 guests in their 3000 SF barrel room.

"Life is too short to drink inexpensive wine." ~ Unknown

Hart Winery

Proprietor:	Joe T. Hart
Address:	41300 Avenida Biona, Temecula, CA 92591
Telephone:	(951) 676-6300
Website:	*www.thehartfamilywinery.com*
Hours:	Daily 9 - 4:30
Tasting Fees:	$5 to $10

Average Wine Prices: Whites: $ Reds: $$
Production: 5,000 cases per year

Varietals:	(Authors' Recommendations ★):
Whites:	Viognier ★, Sauvignon Blanc
Reds:	Barbera, Cabernet Franc, Cabernet Sauvignon, Grenache ★, Grenache-Syrah ★, Merlot, Syrah, Sangiovese, Tempranillo ★, Zinfandel
Dessert:	Aleatico Port ★

Authors' Note: Not all vintages were available on the days we visited. Sadly, many were sold out. That, however, should be considered as an indication of just how good Joe Hart's wines are.

We stopped at the Hart Winery tasting room early (9:30 AM) one morning and were met by Rosalie who was just opening up. Hart is open earlier than most tasting rooms, which enabled us to get an early start on our full day of tasting. (So many wines…so little time.)

We were excited about tasting Mr. Hart's wines – not that we were unfamiliar with Hart Winery. Joe Hart is literally a legend in the local community and easily one of Temecula Valley's most admired citizens. We made it a point to ask each of the winemakers with whom we met, whose Temecula wines they admire. Joe Hart's name was voiced over and over again. In fact, his was usually the first name mentioned in answer to our question.

Joe is one of the Temecula Wine Region's original pioneers, having purchased his vineyard in 1973. He is also the area's unofficial historian. So, if you want to know something about the region, Joe is the right person to see.

Hart Winery is a must-stop-see-and-taste destination. As you sip your way through the tasting room menu of wines, you will immediately notice that his wines are incredibly smooth. We asked Joe how he manages this. His answer: "Good fruit, good equipment, better barrels and attention to detail."

Joe is extremely modest. After visiting with him for a few minutes, he almost had us convinced that the wine makes itself! We know better. This man knows the art and craft of winemaking. He is so well thought of that he serves as a wine judge at five or six major wine competitions per year. Joe says that the competitions allow him to keep in touch with what is going on in the wine industry and that, as a winemaker, it is important for him to stay in touch with what other winemakers are producing.

⇨ **By The Way** – **Hart Winery earned two Silver Medals and one Gold Medal at the 2008 New World International Wine Competition. The winners were the 2007 Sauvignon Blanc (Gold Medal) and Silver Medals for Joe's 2005 Cabernet Franc and the 2004 Zinfandel.**

Keyways Vineyard & Winery

Proprietor: Terri Pebley
Address: 37338 De Portola Road, Temecula, CA 92592
Telephone: 1-877-539-9297
Website: *www.keywayswine.com*
Hours: Daily 10-6 (Winter 10-5)
Tasting Fee: $10 - $15
Average Wine Prices: Whites: $$ Reds: $$
Production: 10,000 cases per year

Varietals: (Authors' Recommendations ★):
Whites: Amore Rosa ★, Chardonnay ★, Chenin Blanc (Ice Wine) ★, Riesling ★, Rosé of Syrah ★, Sauvignon Blanc ★,
Reds: Barbera ★, Cabernet Sauvignon, Lemberger (Frölich), Merlot ★, Petite Syrah, Rhone Blend, Syrah ★, Tempranillo ★, Zinfandel
Dessert: Late Harvest Sauvignon Blanc (Sweet Surrender) ★, Port ★

We had a phenomenal wine tasting visit at Keyways. In fact we enjoyed it so much that we invited friends who live in Orange and San Diego County to join us for one of Keyways' "sit-down" wine tastings. It was superb, in large part due to the efforts of Jamie, the Keyways Events Coordinator. Jamie took great care of our group. She informed us about each of the wines and made us all feel "at home" in the Keyways Winery.

Keyways is one of our favorite wineries – for multiple reasons. Michael Tingley is the winemaker here and he makes great wines. Keyways is also the only woman-owned and managed winery in the valley. Owner, Terri Pebley, has truly transformed the property. What was once a very, very rustic, Old West style tasting room has been converted into a very comfortable and artful property. We would describe the simple, dark wood furnished tasting room with a large field-stone fire place as masculine, but the bright spots of color and classic details could only be provided by the fairer sex. Good job, Keyways! We love what you've done with the place.

In addition to performing a $1.5M renovation of the winery, tasting room and landscaping, Ms. Pebley also tackled the vineyards. The 13 acres of Old Estate vines were removed and the vineyard replanted with Viognier, Roussanne, Tempranillo and Grenache – varieties that are proving to grow very well in the Temecula climate. All this work would probably been more than enough to occupy the average new winery owner, but not Ms. Pebley. She worked with Mr. Tingley to create the Femina Vita (Life of a Woman) series of wines with label artwork created by a female artist, of course. These delicious, fruity and complex wines, "made by women for women," include **Spellbound** (Petite Syrah), **First Crush** (Rosé of Syrah) and **Sweet Surrender** (a Late Harvest Sauvignon Blanc). In April 2008, Keyways released the fourth in this series, **Contentment**, a Rhone blend. This new wine won a Silver Medal at the 2008 New World International Wine Competition. Since 60% of the wine in the US is purchased by women, Ms. Pebley has definitely hit a home run with this concept.

We should not neglect the other wines. There are a ton of great things going on wine-wise at Keyways. Where to begin? Bob's favorite white wine is the 2005 Riesling. The Chardonnay which was slightly dry came in a close second. Cindy yielded to the late harvest Sauvignon Blanc aptly named Sweet Surrender. To say that she is fond of this wine is an understatement. If Bob even goes near it, she snarls at him.

What is on the horizon? Keyways is releasing a new Barbera in 2008. It is outstanding. Also, be sure to look for their Late Harvest Zin, a new Syrah, a Muscat and a lovely Tempranillo which we also enjoyed.

For reds, we pick the Merlot and the Syrah. The Syrah, by the way, has won both Silver and Bronze medals. And for dessert, we gave both the Port and the Krystal Ice Wine our highest scores. Just thinking about all the great wines at Keyways makes us want to go back. Since we can't go right away, you should – and tell them Bob and Cindy say "hi."

Keyways wines did very well at the 2008 New World International Wine Competition (NWIWC). Their Sauvignon Blanc took Best of Class Double Gold and their Chenin Blanc took Best of Class Gold. These are absolutely wonderful wines! Keyways' Muscat Canelli and Rosé of Syrah won Silver Medals. Congratulations, Keyways!

✪ *Grape Escapes Discount!* - Present a copy of this book and receive **Two-for-One tasting** from their "standard" tasting menu. Sorry, but offer is valid on weekdays only.

⇨ **By The Way – Keyways makes a donation to local a women's charity for each bottle of their "Femina Vita" series wines that is sold.**

La Cereza Vineyard & Winery

Proprietors:	Buddy and Cheri Linn
Address:	34567 Rancho California Road, Temecula, CA 92591
Telephone:	(951) 699-6961
Website:	*www.lacerezawinery.com*
Hours:	Daily 10-5
Tasting Fees:	$8 for 5 tastes; $12 "Passport" allows tasting at both La Cereza and Maurice Car'rie

Average Wine Prices: Whites: $ Reds: $$
Production: 15,000 cases per year

Varietals:	(Authors' Recommendations ★):
Whites:	Chardonnay, Fume Blanc, Gewürztraminer ★, Pinot Grigio ★, Viognier ★, "Girlfriends White Blend ★
Reds:	Cabernet Sauvignon, Merlot ★, Sangiovese, Shiraz ★, Tempranillo ★, Red Blend, Zinfandel
Sparkling:	Champagne ★, "Peach Girls" Champagne, Raspberry Champagne

La Cereza is another of our favorite wineries and tasting rooms. There are a ton of things going on here that make this award-winning Spanish-style winery and tasting room worth a lengthy visit. Gus Vizgirda, the winemaker, is one of the most passionate vintners we have ever met. His enthusiasm reminds us of the wonderful sparkling wines available from La Cereza and its sister winery, Maurice Car'rie. Gus's enthusiasm naturally bubbles to the surface.

Gus loves to share information about his craft. He's been known to empty the tasting room of its patrons by announcing excitedly that "You just have to come see what we're working on in the winery." Gus told us that the tasting bar staff find this particular habit of his to be a bit disconcerting, but that the patrons love learning about the wine making process. Gus enjoys working for the Linns and shares the owners' philosophy of making good wine at affordable prices. Their wines are, according to Gus, priced significantly lower than comparable wines in the area.

Pay special attention to the antique bar in the tasting room. This beautiful, hand-carved piece of history dates back to the 1680's. It might be easy to overlook, especially if you have just been served the Viognier, Gewürztraminer, or the "Girlfriends." These were some of our top-scoring white wines. The 2006 Gewürztraminer was named the Best Wine of Temecula Valley. Not too shabby for a wine that sells for under \$15. It also won a Gold medal at the San Diego International Competition in 2006.

⇨ **By The Way – "Gewurzt" is the German word for spicy.**

The red wines are no slouches either. The 2005 Tempranillo and Sangiovese won Silver Medals at the 2006 San Francisco Chronicle International Wine Competition. Our favorite was the Shiraz which was aged in oak barrels for 30 months before its release.

The tasting room is filled with interesting gift items and the walls are adorned with artwork from local artists. The art does not stop at the walls, but extends to the wine labels as well. Many are taken from original paintings. Each label comes with its own story which the Linns have thoughtfully included on the back label of the bottles. Our favorite label is the cigar-smoking and "mature" woman featured on the "Girlfriends" label.

Speaking of cigars, we have to tell you about one of the best features of La Cereza. It is **Hemingway's Wine and Cigar Lounge** which is located about seventy-five yards south of the tasting room. Even if you are not a fan of cigars, this is a great place to enjoy a glass of La Cereza wine and perhaps a loaf of their Brie-filled sourdough bread. We gotta tell you, sitting by one of the fire-rings within the covered courtyard and sampling the bread and wine while gazing at the cigar-themed Cuban art was one of the highlights of our trip. Oh, and did we mention that you can purchase hand-rolled custom cigars blended specifically for Hemingway's. All we can say is that Hemingway's is *Smokin'!*

In addition to great wines, wonderful art and ambience, La Cereza has one of the friendliest tasting room staffs in Temecula. Keep an eye out for Don who works behind the bar. He will be the guy with the warm, friendly smile. If you get to taste in the VIP or wine club area on a weekend, say "Hi" to Delphina who will tell you that Gewürztraminer is not really a German grape, but that it was taken to Germany from its original home in Italy.

⇨ **By The Way** – **La Cereza earned two Bronze Medals at the 2008 New World International Wine Competition for their Rojo Novato Red Table Wine and their 2007 Viognier.**

❂ *Grape Escapes Discount!* - Present a copy of this book and receive a **10% discount** on all wines and tasting room merchandise purchased on the day of your visit. Sorry, but offer is not valid on weekends.

Leonesse Cellars

Proprietors:	Mike Rennie and Gary Winder
Address:	38311 DePortola Road, Temecula, CA 92592
Telephone:	(951) 302-7601
Website:	*www.leonessecellars.com*
Hours:	Daily 10-5
Tasting Fees:	$10 to $20: Private Group Tastings (15 persons or more) $20 - $30

Average Wine Prices: Whites: $$ Reds: $$$
Production: 15,000 cases per year

Varietals:	(Authors' Recommendations ★):
Whites:	Chardonnay, Pinot Grigio, Riesling, Sauvignon Blanc, White Merlot
Reds:	Cabernet Sauvignon ★, Cab Franc-Merlot, Merlot ★, Meritage ★, Syrah, Zinfandel ★,
Dessert:	Cinsault Dessert Wine (formerly called Port) ★, Muscat Canelli

Now we're probably going to sound somewhat like proud parents of this winery. We're not, but we are certainly a little nostalgic. We first visited Leonesse immediately after they opened in 2003. They were operating out of the metal-fab building that now serves as the winery building and barrel room. The enthusiasm the Leonesse folks had for what they were creating was electric. Over the next couple of years, we went back often – many times introducing friends to "the wonderful little winery" we had discovered.

We're proud of what Leonesse has become: an incredibly sophisticated winery with some of the best wines in the valley and an elegant tasting room. We do, however, somewhat miss that earlier time when it seemed like it was "just us and them."

Oh, well, if your winery "kids" have to grow up, you can't do much better than wishing for them to turn out like Leonesse. By the way, Leonesse means "village of dreams," and reflects their desire to create the finest wines in the Temecula Valley. We can't help but suspect that a lot of their dreams have truly been realized.

Tim Kramer, Leonesse's winemaker, went out of his way to explain his winemaking operations – which he described as "painstaking." One of the things Leonesse Cellars does is keep each wine lot separate throughout the aging process. This requires racking each lot separately every four months or so. Leonesse's wine lots can range from as small as two barrels to a group of 50. Since 50 barrels contains almost 12 tons of wine, the task of racking is a large undertaking.

⇨ **By The Way – Racking is the process of removing the wine from one container and placing it in another in order to remove the sediment. Removing the sediment has a couple of advantages; it serves as a natural method for clarifying the wine and can also remove unwanted flavors that might result from the sediment.**

Almost all of our favorite winemakers speak of the importance of treating the grapes and their juice gently. Gentle treatment of the wine throughout the winemaking process results (in our opinion and that of many professionals) in better wine. Tim uses Nitrogen gas instead of a traditional mechanical pump – all in order to be "easier on the wine." A mechanical wine pump, while very efficient at moving wine from one container to another, puts the wine through a harsh blender-like mechanism. This is hard on the wine. By using Nitrogen gas to propel the wine, Leonesse avoids the harsh treatment the wine would normally experience if it were processed through a traditional pumping mechanism.

Leonesse consistently produces good wines. For whites, we liked their Pinot Grigio. For Reds, the Cabernet Sauvignon is outstanding, as is their Zinfandel. We also liked the Meritage. Each of these wines sells for between $35 and $38. One of their most popular wines is the Cinsault (pronounced "san-so") Port-style Dessert Wine. This wine has won three gold medals within the last few years.

Speaking of medals, Leonesse did well in the 2007 San Diego International Wine Competition. It took two Silver medals, one for the Vista Del Monte Vineyard Syrah and one for "Three" which is one of their Limited Selection series wines. Their 2004 Cabernet received a Bronze medal. Their 2004 Merlot received a Silver Medal in the 2007 Riverside International. And one of their 2004 Rhone-style blends received a Gold Medal at this same competition. *Wine Enthusiast* gave their 2004 Syrah a 90 point score. The list of accolades goes on and on.

One final note. If you have the opportunity to try Tim Kramer's Signature Selection wines, please do. We tried both the Meritage and the Merlot. Simply put, these are fantastic wines and some of the best of what Temecula has to offer. Bottom line, these wines are exactly what wine is meant to be – wonderful and truly outstanding. You will remember these wines long after the bottles are empty.

Okay, it is now time to stop reading and get moving to Leonesse Cellars.

☞ **Authors' Tip:** *While at Leonesse, be sure to stop in at the winery's Block Five Restaurant and try their wonderfully tender fried Calamari; it is some of the best fried Calamari we have ever tasted.*

Longshadow Ranch Vineyard & Winery

Proprietors:	John and Susan Brodersen
Address:	39847 Calle Contento, Temecula, CA 92591
Telephone:	(951) 587-6221
Website:	*www.longshadowranchwinery.com*
Hours:	M-F 12-5, Sat 10-4 (Sat Night Bonfire 5-9 April - Oct), Sun 10-5
Tasting Fees:	$7 to $10

Average Wine Prices: Whites: $ Reds: $$$
Production: 15,000 cases per year

Varietals:	(Authors' Recommendations ★):
Whites:	Sauvignon Blanc, Chardonnay ★, White Merlot
Reds:	Cab-Franc, Merlot ★, Red Blend, "Reata" Red Blend ★, Syrah ★, Zinfandel
Dessert:	Solera-style Syrah, Zin Port ★

Perhaps no winery or tasting room in the Temecula Wine Region captures the spirit of Old Temecula better than the very popular Longshadow Ranch Winery. In a perfect world, we would live just a quarter-mile down the road from them. With this vineyard's wonderful entertainment venue, they would be the ideal neighbor. Many must agree since their wine club is one of the largest in the region.

The entertainment that takes place at this winery is incredible. This fact probably speaks to owner / winemaker John Brodersen's music and entertainment background. We're told that it is not unusual for John, who used to be in a Punk Rock band in the 80's, to climb up on the stage and play with the guest bands that are featured at their Saturday Night Bonfire and Live Music parties. Although this event is open only to wine club members, you can sometimes get a free "guest pass" at the tasting room.

All of the events John presents are "family friendly." This is one of the reasons they are so popular with locals. The events normally start around 5:30 PM. At around 6:45 PM, the kids head for the barn which doubles as a movie theater – complete with popcorn and snacks. Festivities end by around 9 PM – just, according to John, in time to put the kids to bed.

⇨ **By The Way** – **Longshadow Ranch was a name developed by John's wife, Susan. Just before sunset, when standing on the hilltop of their property, she and the kids cast a very long shadow that reached hundreds of yards to the roadway.**

In addition, when you make reservations in advance, you can also enjoy an evening horse-drawn wagon ride through the vineyard. If the wagon ride seems a little too tame for you, then you can always try your hand at riding their mechanical bull. As for us – no thanks, although we did try to "tame" a bottle of John's very nice Reata Red during our most recent visit. We also liked the 2005 Merlot, as well as the 2005 Syrah. We enjoyed the 2006 Chardonnay. This was one of the better Chards we found during our research visits.

When we last spoke with John, we asked him if there was anything else he wanted to tell us about his winery. His answer: "Nope. We're the best. That's all there is to it." Well there you have it, pardner. We think you should saddle-up and mosey on down to Longshadow Ranch.

☺ *Grape Escapes Discount!* - Present a copy of this book and receive a **10% discount** on all wines purchased on the day of your visit.

Maurice Car'rie Winery

Proprietors:	Buddy and Cheri Linn
Address:	34225 Rancho California Road, Temecula, CA 92591
Telephone:	(951) 676-1711
Website:	*www.mauricecarriewinery.com*
Hours:	Daily 10-5
Tasting Fees:	$8 for 5 Tastes; $12 Passport for Tasting at both Maurice Car'rie and La Cereza

Average Wine Prices: Whites: $ Reds: $

Production: 25,000 cases per year

Varietals:	(Authors' Recommendations ★):
Whites:	Chardonnay, Chenin Blanc, "Heather's Mist" White Blend ★, Riesling ★, Sauvignon Blanc ★, White Cabernet, White Zinfandel
Reds:	Cabernet Sauvignon, Merlot ★, "Cody's Crush" Red and White Blend, Pinot Noir ★, Syrah, Sangiovese ★
Sparkling:	Pineapple Champagne ★, Champagne
Dessert:	Late Harvest Chardonnay, Cream Sherry, Muscat Canelli ★

If someone were to draft a set of Cardinal Rules for wine tasting, the Maurice Car'rie philosophy that "Wines should be fun and affordable" covers two of the most important. To this we say "Amen, and Thank you Buddy and Cheri Linn." One of the ways the Linns do this is by focusing on producing wines that are approachable and enjoyable at an early age. We can tell you that the Maurice Car'rie winemaker, Gus Vizgirda, is very good at doing just this. Check out the tremendous number of medals and awards that they have earned.

Maurice Car'rie was founded in 1986. The old Victorian style farm house (now tasting room) with its wrap-around veranda is a local landmark. Its peaceful setting amid well-manicured lawns just seems to pull people into the winery.

⇨ **By The Way – If you are looking for more than fine wines, this is one of our favorite shopping locations. On weekends, Maurice Car'rie hosts an outdoor craft fair that features art, jewelry, food items and various types of handcrafts. Different vendors are featured each week.**

The fact that Maurice Car'rie is one of the older wineries in the valley is interesting, but more important to us is the fact that they still maintain some of the oldest vineyards in the Valley. Call us traditionalists, but there is something to be said for "old vine" wines. According to Gus, unlike in prior years when many of Temecula's visitors were looking for sweet wines, now more and more customers are looking for fine and more complex wines. Gus likes the fact that Maurice Car'rie produces lower alcohol wines. (Higher alcohol content can disguise flaws in a wine.) It is much more of a challenge to bring out the character in a lower alcohol wine. Gus told us that, in the future, they hope to create more wines that have 12% or less alcohol by volume.

Maurice Car'rie produces fourteen different varietals plus several blends. The winemaker's favorite is the Pinot Noir. We liked the Non Vintage Heather's Mist. This wine won a Gold Medal at the 2006 California State Fair and sells for less than $11 per bottle. It was one of our higher scoring white wines. Their 2005 Merlot (a Silver Medal winner) was also outstanding. But our favorite was the 2005 Sangiovese. We will admit that we have a weakness for Italian varietals. For us, Sangiovese is top of that particular list. Both the Merlot and the Pinot Noir are slightly dry and are wonderful wines to pair with a meal. For dessert, we recommend Maurice Car'rie's Gold Medal-winning sweet dessert wine, the Muscat Canelli – another great value at around $13 per bottle.

⇨ **By The Way – Maurice Car'rie won a Silver Medal for their 2007 Premium Blend Sauvignon Blanc and a Bronze Medal for their 2007 White Cabernet at the 2008 New World International Wine Competition. Congratulations, Gus, Buddy and Cheri!**

✪ *Grape Escapes Discount!* - Present a copy of this book and receive a **10% discount** on all wines and tasting room merchandise purchased on the day of your visit. Sorry, but offer is not valid on weekends.

Miramonte Winery / Celebration Cellars

Proprietor: Cane Vanderhoof
Address: 33410 Rancho California Road, Temecula, CA 92591
Telephone: (951) 506-5500
Website: *www.miramontewinery.com*
Hours: Daily 11-6 (Live music 5:30-8:30, Fri & Sat)
Tasting Fees: $6 - $8
Average Wine Prices: Whites: $$ Reds: $$$
Production: 5,000 cases per year

Varietals: (Authors' Recommendations ★):
                     Note: Regrettably, due to temporary closure of the tasting room, we
                     did not have the opportunity to taste all of Miramonte's wines.
Whites: Chardonnay, Sèmillon, Riesling, Sauvignon Blanc,
                     Viognier, White Rhapsody Blend, Numero Uno Garnacha
                     Rosé, Numero Uno Sauvignon Blanca
Reds: Numero Uno Cabernet Sauvignon ★, Merlot, Opulente,
                     Syrah, Sangria ★, Zinfandel,
Sparkling: Grand Reserve Brut, Grand Reserve Blanc de Noirs

The first things we noticed upon entering the tasting room of Miramonte Winery were the rows of etched and brilliantly painted "Celebrity" wine bottles behind the counter. It was a "Whoa!" moment in which we tried to take in all the labels. Madonna, Kiss, The Stones, Celine, Bon Jovi and the Police were all there. These collector bottles are works of art in and of themselves and played a primary role in the creation of Miramonte Winery.

Winemaker and owner, Cane Vanderhoof, is also the owner of Celebration Cellars which makes the etched wine bottles. The success of this business provided Cane the means to develop the Miramonte brand of wines. The winery was founded in 2001 and actually features wines under two labels: the Miramonte label for their more distinctive wines and the Numero Uno label which might best be described as affordable every-day wines.

The fun does not stop with the Numero Uno wines. Miramonte's tasting room has become a prime weekend entertainment destination. Fridays and Saturdays are not only the end of the work week, but at Miramonte they are "Flamenco Fridays" and "Saturday Night Blues Jam" events. Beginning at 5:30 PM on Friday, for a nominal cover charge of $6 to $8, you get to enjoy

Rumba, Latin Jazz and Flamenco music. Local chefs prepare tapas and dinner meals that you can enjoy for an additional charge. Miramonte Club members get in free.

Saturday night is "Blues Jam Night." Food, prepared by local chefs, is sold and, of course, wine tasting is available. As with Flamenco Fridays, the cover charge is $6 to $8. Seating is limited for both of these events, so we recommend arriving early.

Mount Palomar Winery

Proprietor: Louidar LLC since September 2006
Address: 33820 Rancho California Road, Temecula, CA 92591
Telephone: (951) 676-5047
Website: *www.mountpalomar.com*
Hours: Mon-Thurs 10-6, Fri-Sun 10-7 (Winter – Closed Mon-Tue; Wed-Thur 10-5, Fri-Sun 10-6)
Tasting Fees: $8 to $14
Average Wine Prices: Whites: $$ Reds: $$
Production: 12,000 – 30,000 cases per year

Varietals: (Authors' Recommendations ★):
Whites: Chardonnay, Cortese ★, Riesling, Sauvignon Blanc, Viognier,
Reds: Cabernet Franc, Cabernet Sauvignon ★, Merlot (New Release), Meritage / Red Blends ★, Sangiovese ★
Sparkling: Muscato di Amore (Frizzante)
Dessert: Late Harvest Sèmillon, Riesling Desert Wine, Solera-Style Cream Sherry ★, Port

The road up to Mount Palomar is fairly steep until it crests the hill and drops gently down to the parking lot. From there it is an easy walk past the juniper trees down to the Mediterranean-style landscaping and courtyard patios just outside the winery and tasting room entrance. The adoption of a Mediterranean theme for the winery was no accident. Temecula's climate closely matches that part of the world. The courtyard is filled with statuary: winged cherubs and other angel-like creatures are everywhere. Perhaps this hints at the "little slice of heaven" waiting inside the tasting room.

Our appointment was with Craig Boyd, Mount Palomar's winemaker. There is a lot going on at this winery and not just the extensive remodeling by the new owners. A hotel is planned, as is a major restaurant. The winery also plans to increase annual production to 30,000 cases per year. The owners are actively shopping for new vineyards. Their goal is to eventually make Mount Palomar Winery into a destination resort.

What attracted Craig to accept the position at Mount Palomar and relocate from the Sierra Foothills was the pioneering spirit he finds in Temecula. He sees Temecula as an exciting wine region and is especially enthusiastic about the increase in Italian varietals being planted in the area. He believes that for many years Temecula's wine quality suffered as a result of the region having planted the wrong varietals in the wrong places. He is proud of the fact that Mount Palomar was the first to plant Sangiovese and Syrah.

Speaking of Sangio, Mount Palomar's is absolutely excellent. In fact, the red wines were excellent across the board. We tried the Cab Franc, the Castelletto Travato, the Meritage, and the Solera Sherry. These are all very, very good wines, as is the Cortese. (The Cortese is a somewhat obscure grape from the Piedmont region of Italy.) Very, very few vineyards grow it. If you would like to try this excellent Gold Medal-winning white wine, we strongly urge that you visit Mount Palomar Winery.

✪ *Grape Escapes Discount!* - Present a copy of this book and receive a **Two-for-One tasting!!!**

Oak Mountain Winery and Temecula Hills Winery

Proprietors: Valerie and Steve Andrews
Address: 36522 Via Verde, Temecula, CA 92592
Telephone: (951)699-9102
Website: *www.oakmountainwinery.com*
Hours: Daily 11- 5
Tasting Fees: $6 to $8
Average Wine Prices: Whites: $ Reds: $$$
Production: 6,500 cases per year

Varietals: (Authors' Recommendations ★):
Whites: Chardonnay, Rosé of Cabernet, Muscat Canelli, Sauvignon Blanc, Viognier ★, White Merlot ★, Mourvèdre / Viognier Blend
Reds: Barbera, Cabernet Sauvignon, Grenache ★, Merlot, Meritage ★, Mourvèdre ★, Syrah, Red Blends ★, Tempranillo ★, Zinfandel ★
Sparkling: Brut ★, Raspberry Champagne ★
Dessert: Port ★

If folks could only visit one tasting room in the Temecula Valley, this very well might be the one we recommend. Why? Oak Mountain Winery and Temecula Hills Winery are the ultimate twofer. The two wineries share the same tasting room address, winemaker and owners. When we visited, Annie Austin (close friend of owner Valerie Andrews) provided us one of the best tasting experiences we've ever had. Annie is a wonderful hostess, knowledgeable and passionate about wine. And let us tell you, Oak Mountain and Temecula Hills have some great, award-winning wines.

We were initially confused as to why the Andrews have two different wine labels. Valerie explained that the wines come from two different vineyards. Oak Mountain makes Bordeaux style wines, whereas Temecula Hills' wines are Rhone style.

According to Valerie, she and her husband, Steve, became winery owners as a result of a hobby that went flying out of control. Flying out of control? Maybe, but these folks certainly brought their creation to a smooth landing! We are absolutely delighted we had the chance to visit and taste their wines. Speaking of which, let's talk about a few of our favorites.

The medal-winning 2005 White Merlot is a really, really nice wine. It sells for an incredibly low $14 per bottle. If you like white wines, this one is a real winner. Sticking in the Merlot column, their 2004 Merlot won a Silver Medal in the Riverside Wine Competition. This is a very, very big Merlot, but surprisingly smooth. We didn't think we could find anything we liked better than the Merlot until we tried the 2004 Meritage – another medal-winning wine. This one is 40% Cabernet Sauvignon, 20% Cabernet Franc and 40% Merlot. We awarded this wine our "Wow!" award. If you are a Port fan, then you must try Oak Mountain's incredible Port. It also received our "Wow!" award and "busted" our humble wine ranking system.

If you are beginning to get the impression that Oak Mountain is a winning winery, then we have done our job. But we're not done yet. As we mentioned, Temecula Hills makes Rhone style wines and, boy, do they ever make good ones! Their Viognier and Barbera have captured Bronze medals at the prestigious New World International Wine Competition (NWIWC), but we thought the 2005 Mourvèdre and the 2005 Grenache were equally as good. The Temecula Hills 2004 Zinfandel is another medal-winning wine, as is the Zinfandel which we decided to christen as our favorite – until we tried the 2005 Tempranillo which was simply outstanding. Get the picture? Your last wine at Oak Mountain / Temecula Hills will probably be your favorite – until, that is, you try the next one on their tasting room menu.

✪ *Grape Escapes Discount!* - Present a copy of this book and receive a **10% discount** on all wines purchased on the day of your visit. Also, present a copy of this book and receive **Two-for-One tasting** for up to four guests. Offer does not include the souvenir logo glass.

⇨ **By The Way – Temecula Hills Winery won two Bronze Medals at the 2008 New World International Wine Competition, one for their 2005 Red Wine and another for their 2005 Sangiovese.**

Orfila Vineyards & Winery

Proprietor:	Ambassador Alejandro Orfila
Winemaker:	Leon Santoro
Address:	13455 San Pasqual Road, Escondido, CA 92025
Telephone:	(760) 738-6500 or 1-800-868-9463
Website:	*www.orfila.com*
Hours:	Open 7 Days, 10 AM – 6 PM
Tasting Fee:	One taste free; $6 for 5 additional tastes. Tasting is free for Wine Club Members.
Production:	15,000 cases per year

Average Wine Prices: Whites: $$ Reds: $$

Varietals:	(Authors' Recommendations ★):
Whites:	Chardonnay, and various Blends ★, Gewürztraminer ★, Riesling ★
Reds:	Cabernet Sauvignon, Merlot ★, Pinot Noir, Sangiovese ★, Syrah ★, Zinfandel ★
Dessert:	Muscat Canelli, Port

Distance from Temecula: A little over 30 miles; directions given below.

Set among beautifully landscaped lawns and gardens, Orfila Vineyards & Winery has a lovely flag-draped tasting room in Escondido, which is about a forty-five minute drive from Temecula on Highway 15 South. Orfila is one our "Road Trip" wineries and is easy to find. Take the I-15 south toward San Diego for 32 miles and exit onto Via Rancho Parkway. Turn right onto the parkway and follow it for one mile. Via Rancho becomes Bear Valley Parkway. Turn Right onto San Pasqual Road. Orfila's tasting room is only a mile further along this road.

Once at Orfila, you are in for a true treat. Leon Santoro, General Manager and Winemaker, has a wonderful selection of wines that include Chardonnay, Sangiovese, Riesling, Marsanne, Roussanne, Merlot, and Cabernet.

Leon's great wines are no accident. After immigrating to the US from Italy, he worked at some of the top Northern California wineries, including: Louis Martini, Stag's Leap, and Quail Ridge. Upon his arrival at Orfila, he was not satisfied with the quality of grapes and ultimately grafted and planted a total of seventeen different varietals before identifying the ones that grow best on the vineyard's forty acres.

"Good fruit equals good wine," according to Leon, and it all begins in the vineyard. The Orfila Vineyard is at 700 feet elevation and is only twelve miles from the Pacific Ocean – a bit closer than the Temecula Valley vineyards. You should enjoy comparing Leon's wines to Temecula Valley wines and identifying how the wines from these two areas differ in taste and characteristics.

It is not only flags that hang from the tasting room walls and ceilings. Orfila has done extremely well on the competition circuit and their ribbons and awards are also proudly on display. Their 2005 "Gold Rush" Zinfandel won Gold at the 2008 San Francisco Chronicle Wine Competition – as did their 2006 White Riesling. The 2004 Estate Sangiovese "Di Collina" won Gold and Best of Glass in the 2007 SF Chronicle Wine Competition and their 2004 Estate Syrah took Double Gold and Best of Class at the Florida State Fair International Wine Competition.

⇨ **By The Way – Only about 5% of wines submitted in a wine competition earn a Gold Medal.**

If there are those in your group who believe Southern California wines cannot compete with the wines of Napa and Sonoma, you only have to take them to Orfila to put a pleasant end to this particular argument.

⇨ **By The Way – Orfila Vineyards & Winery won four Bronze Medals at the 2008 New World International Wine Competition. Their winners were: the "Lot 34" Coastal Cuvée, the 2006 White Riesling, the 2006 Chardonnay and the 2005 Sangiovese. In addition, their 2005 Coastal Cuvée Merlot won Gold at the 2008 Monterey Wine Competition. Congratulations, Leon!**

✪ *Grape Escapes Discount!* - Present a copy of this book and receive **free tasting** for up to four people in your party. In addition, you will also receive a **15% discount** on all wines purchased (except the Ambassador Reserve Merlot), plus a **10% discount** on all tasting room merchandise purchased on the day of your visit. Present a copy of this book and receive an additional **5% discount** (total of 20%) on a case or more of wine. Also, present a copy of this book and receive a **free "back-stage" tour** of the winery. Appointment required.

⇨ **By The Way – As of Spring of 2008, Orfila Vineyard & Winery had earned a total of 1,231 medals for its wines over the past 14 years.**

Palumbo Family Vineyards & Winery

Proprietors: Nick and Cindy Palumbo
Address: 40150 Barksdale Circle, Temecula, CA 92591
Telephone: (951) 676-7900
Website: *www.palumbofamilyvineyards.com*
Hours: Fri 12-5; Sat & Sun 10-5; Weekdays By Appt. (Limos & Shuttles By Appt due to limited space)
Tasting Fees: $7 to $10
Average Wine Prices: Whites: $$ Reds: $$$
Production: 2,400 cases per year

Varietals: (Authors' Recommendations ★):
Whites: Viognier ★
Reds: Syrah, Shiraz (Australia Clone 04) ★, Merlot ★, Meritage (Tre Fratelli)★, Sangiovese ★, Shiraz-Cabernet Blend
Dessert: Port

Palumbo Family Vineyards & Winery holds a special place in our hearts since we were fortunate enough to visit the very first week the winery opened. Nick's Mom, who did not know us, was at the tasting room that day and she promptly invited us for dinner. That's the kind of people the Palumbos are. Warm, friendly – simply the best. And that is exactly how we would describe their cozy tasting room as well.

At Palumbo Family Vineyards & Winery, it is all about making high quality wines that age well. Many, if not most, of the Temecula Valley wineries focus on producing wines that are meant to be consumed while young. Nick (winery owner and winemaker) takes a different approach. By the time his wines get to the tasting room, they are very good. But if you leave them in your cellar for awhile, they will age and improve.

Nick and Cindy Palumbo, in our humble opinion, represent the heart and soul of "old" Temecula Wine Country. They have no plans to establish a destination style resort. They simply want to make great wines and take great care of their loyal customers. Most of Palumbo's wines go directly to their cadre of fiercely loyal wine club members. The remainder is sold through the tasting room. Nick Palumbo told us straight out that his goal is not to be the best winemaker in Temecula, but rather to make the best wines in all of California. Bravo, Nick!

On the day we visited, there were five wines on the tasting menu and we were lucky to sample one that was not. (Nick let us try his Sangiovese. Wonderful!) We had a hard time deciding which of the Palumbo wines was our favorite. For a long time, the Tre Fratelli Meritage, their signature wine, has been our Number One choice, but we think the 2005 Shiraz, made from an Australian Clone, may just have moved into first place. We're not entirely certain. What we are certain of is that no visit to Temecula is complete without a visit to this excellent winery.

Nick is normally open only on the weekend. However, if you are serious about wine and can only visit them during the week, please give them a call and schedule an appointment. Be sure to ask Nick if he has any new wines hidden in back that he might be willing to share. Who knows? You may get lucky. We sure did.

☺ *Grape Escapes Complimentary Tasting!* - Present a copy of this book and receive a **complimentary tasting for two people** in your party.

Ponte Family Estate Winery

Proprietors: Claudio Ponte and Roberto Ponte
Address: 35053 Rancho California Road, Temecula, CA 92591
Telephone: 951-694-8855
Website: *www.pontewinery.com*
Hours: Daily   10-5
Tasting Fees: $10
Average Wine Prices: Whites: $$ Reds: $$$
Production: 15,000 cases per year

Varietals: (Authors' Recommendations ★):
Whites: Chardonnay, Moscato NV ★, Pinot Grigio, Riesling ★, Viognier, White Blends ★,
Reds: Barbera, Dolcetto, Merlot, Meritage, Nebbiolo ★, Petite Syrah, Super Tuscan, Red Blends ★, Tempranillo
Sparkling: Rosé Spumante
Dessert: Sherry, Zin Port

The interior of the barn-style Ponte tasting room and gift shop is warm and welcoming. The open-beamed ceilings and the light that filters in from the upper windows simply make this a very spacious and comfortable place to taste wines. If you are a shopper, this winery has the largest and possibly the best gift shop in the area. And if you are hungry, the **Smokehouse Restaurant** is our personal favorite of the winery restaurants. Both the food and service are truly excellent.

One of the things we liked about tasting at Ponte is that they have a range of wines: reds, whites, sparkling and dessert wines. The wines range in style from lighter to heavier and from dry to sweet, so this is an especially good stop for beginning wine tasters to get a sense of the types and styles of wine that they like. If you are a more experienced taster, not to worry. Ponte has wines for you, as well. You may want to try their private tour which includes barrel tasting. Reservations are required, as is a minimum of four people per tour. More information is included in our ***Winery Tours and Tastings*** chapter.

On the day we tasted, Ponte's tasting room menu contained fifteen wines, from which you can choose any six wines. We tried the Graciela (named after Claudio Ponte's mother) and the Riesling. Both were very good. On the red side, we liked the Nebbiolo, the Super Tuscan, and our personal favorite, the Beverino (Red Blend). We also liked the slightly sweeter Moscato NV.

The Ponte philosophy is that a good wine is one you like. We certainly agree with that. Please note, however, unlike other wineries in the area, **Ponte wines are only available through their tasting room or online store.** If you are a fan of wine clubs, Ponte's has some unusual and excellent benefits. In addition to free tastings for you and a guest each time you visit, you will also receive a 10% discount off your bill at the Smokehouse Restaurant, AND a 20% discount on all gift items sold in The Marketplace or their online store. Not bad… Good wines and perks. What more can you ask for?

✪ ***Grape Escapes Discount!*** - Present a copy of this book and receive a **Two-for-One tasting**!!! Offer valid Monday Through Thursday, excluding holidays.

Robert Renzoni Vineyards

Proprietors: Robert and Fred Renzoni
Address: 37350 De Portola Road, Temecula, CA 92592
Telephone: (951) 302-8466
Website: *www.robertrenzonivineyards.com*
Hours: Daily 11-6
Tasting Fees: $10
Average Wine Prices: Whites: $$ Reds: $$$
Production: 6,000 to 15,000 cases per year

Varietals: (Authors' Recommendations ★):
                      Note: Only a few of the Renzoni wines were ready for sampling at the
                      time of our visit.
Whites: Chardonnay, La Rosa ★, Malvasia Bianca, Pinot Grigio
Reds: Cabernet Sauvignon, Sangiovese, Red Blends, Super
                      Tuscan, Zinfandel ★
Dessert: Port

We met with Fred (father) and Robert (son) Renzoni just a couple of months before they opened their new winery. We had the best time walking the ground and hearing about their exciting plans for this Italian-themed winery. The plans include a Tuscan-style tasting room and gift shop with antiqued plaster façade and a fifty-foot bell tower. The gift shop will feature all Italian goods, such as ceramics, and glassware with Italian music in the background…. *Certamente!* One would expect nothing less.

The Renzoni's goal for their new winery is to make you feel as if you've stepped into the central plaza of a small Italian village after leaving De Portola Road. In addition to the Tuscan Tasting Room, they will also have a Tratoria (planned for 2010), and picnic grounds with a gazebo and benches from which you can gaze out over one of the best views of the valley and Mount Palomar. The Renzonis certainly believe their property has the *best* view.

Robert and Fred are genuinely nice people who are descended from a long line of winemakers that stretches all the way back to the Old Country in the late 1800s. Robert, owner and vintner, has literally spent his entire working career involved in some aspect of the wine business. They plan on using their twelve-acre vineyard to produce Bordeaux and Italian grape varieties.

Only two of the Renzoni wines, the Zinfandel and the La Rosa were available for tasting before our book went to press. We enjoyed both and are anxiously looking forward to a return visit to Temecula where we can try all of the Renzoni wines.

✪ *Grape Escapes Discount!* - Present a copy of this book and receive a **10% discount** on all wines and tasting room merchandise purchased on the day of your visit. Also, present a copy of this book and receive an additional **10% discount** (total of 20%) on a case or more of wine.

South Coast Winery, Resort & Spa

Proprietor: Jim Carter
Address: 34843 Rancho California Road, Temecula, CA 92591
Telephone: 1-866-994-6379 or (951) 587-9463
Website: *www.wineresort.com*
Hours: Daily 10-6
Tasting Fee: $10
Average Wine Prices: Whites: $ Reds: $$
Production: 30,000 - 50,000 cases per year

Varietals: (Authors' Recommendations ★):
Note: Due to the size of the wine list at South Coast, we were unable to sample all of their wines.
Whites: Chardonnay, Gewürztraminer (New Release), Pinot Grigio (New Release), Sauvignon Blanc, Riesling, Viognier,
Reds: Cabernet Sauvignon (Wild Horse Peak) ★, Grenache, Meritage, Merlot Rosé, Merlot, Red Table (Romanza), Sangiovese, Syrah (Rolling Hills) ★, Tempranillo,
Sparkling: Brut (Pinot / Chard) ★, Extra Dry Sparkling (Pinot / Chard), Ruby Cuvée ★
Dessert: Muscat Canelli ★, Late Harvest Zinfandel, Black Jack Port ★, Sweet Maggie

As we began organizing all of our data on the amazing South Coast Winery, Resort & Spa, Cindy remarked that, "We're going to need a bigger book." No kidding. There is a lot going on this $36 million dollar luxury resort. Perhaps no other winery symbolizes Temecula's on-going evolution to a destination resort area more than South Coast.

Everything about South Coast is big – the beautifully landscaped grounds; the 12,000 square foot, 160-seat top-end restaurant; the three-floor spa; the seventy-six villas; and the wine list itself. It is literally possible to have a great wine tasting experience at South Coast over multiple days without ever leaving the property! On the day we visited, there were *twenty-nine* wines on the tasting menu. Of the twenty-nine wines, nineteen have won numerous medals in national and international wine competitions. Here is an amazing fact for you. South Coast wines won 203 medals – in 2007 alone!

The only thing about this winery that doesn't scream "first class luxury" is the price of the wines. The average price of the wines on the tasting room menu was under $22. They actually had fifteen wines on the menu that were priced under $15.

⇨ **By The Way – South Coast makes two wines that are bottled exclusively for Olivia Newton-John. The first is a Viognier which is fermented in stainless steel tanks and aged in French oak. The second is the medal-winning Olivia Newton-John Merlot. When we visited South Coast, these wines were listed on the tasting menu and available for sampling.**

As we traveled around the valley meeting with Temecula's winemakers and asking them whose wines they respected, Jon McPherson's and Javier Flores' names came up over and over again. Their names were almost always spoken in tandem, sort of like "Batman and Robin," and always with the same amount of reverence and awe that true super heroes receive.

We caught up with McPherson and Flores in the South Coast tank room. We could tell by the way they fielded our questions that they are a team – and the teamwork extends throughout the winemaking process. They went to great lengths to credit the vineyard manager and his staff for making their jobs much easier. We spoke for some time about what it takes to make good wines. The phrase "attention to detail" came up and we asked if they could give us an example of what that means. McPherson and Flores told us that they personally taste the wines every day and that they sample each barrel before it goes into the bottle. Jon said, "You never know. Things can go wrong in the barrel." They want to catch any problems before the wine is bottled and the South Coast label is applied.

As for our favorites, we liked the Ruby Cuveé, South Coast's sparkling Syrah. Their Brut Sparkling Wine was one of our highest scored sparkling wines. The 2003 Wild Horse Peak Cabernet Sauvignon is simply an amazing wine. We also liked the 2005 Rolling Hills Estate Syrah. If you are a fan of Ports, you must try South Coast's Black Jack Port. This one has won a total nine medals at last count.

⇨ **By The Way – South Coast won an incredible twelve medals at the 2008 New World International Wine Competition. Their 2004 Wild Horse Peak Cabernet Sauvignon, the 2006 Sauvignon, the 2006 Grenache, the 2006 Riesling, the 2004 Sangiovese, and the NV Port all earned Silver Medals. The 2004 Meritage Red, the 2006 Muscat Canelli, the NV Sparkling Syrah, and the 2005 Late Harvest Zinfandel won Bronze Medals. Wow!**

Stuart Cellars

Proprietor:	Marshall Stuart
Address:	33515 Rancho California Road, Temecula CA 92591
Telephone:	(951) 676-6414 or 888-260-0870
Website:	*www.stuartcellars.com*
Hours:	Daily 10-5
Tasting Fees:	$10
Average Wine Prices: Whites: $ Reds: $$$	
Production:	26,000 cases per year

Varietals: (Authors' Recommendations ★):
Whites: Chardonnay, Pinot Grigio, Riesling, Sauvignon Blanc, Viognier, White Blend (Callista®) ★, White Merlot
Reds: Cabernet Franc ★, Cabernet Sauvignon ★, Malbec, Merlot, Pinot Noir, Red Blend (Tatria®) ★, Sangiovese ★, Tempranillo, Zinfandel ★
Dessert: Muscat (New Release), Zin Port ★

Stuart Cellars is another of the fine Temecula wineries that make wine the "Old-World" way – and we absolutely love it. Their aim is to achieve richer flavors and they do this by numerous methods, starting in the vineyard where the grapevine rows run north to south so that the fruit matures more evenly. In addition, many of the red wines they produce are unfiltered – which translates into more flavor. Stuart Cellars also crafts wines that have the potential for aging – something that appeals to us, as well.

One of the things we like about Stuart Cellars is their commitment to education. A lot of wineries talk about educating folks about wine, but Stuart actually carries through on this pledge. Click on their website and we promise you will learn something. Same thing with their Vine Press publication which, by the way, contains some great recipes and wine pairing tips.

We think of Stuart Cellars as champions of the "Slow Wine" Movement. (We were not even sure if there was such a thing as a "Slow Wine" Movement until we verified it with a Google search.) Stuart's philosophy that some things should not be rushed – the enjoyment of wine being one of them – is the basis of the "Slow Wine" Movement. Slow down… take your time… and enjoy.

We found lots of wines that we liked at Stuart Cellars. Their award-winning 2002 Vintage Port is outstanding. We also liked their Sangiovese, the Long Valley Red®, the Estate Tatria®, and the Viognier. However, our personal favorite was the Zinfandel. Although we did not get a chance to taste it, we were told that the 2005 Viognier was awarded a 90-point rating by *Wine Enthusiast Magazine*. Way-to-go, Stuart!

If you have wine-snob friends that believe Temecula wineries are unable to compete with the wineries of Northern California, we say, "Take them to Stuart Cellars and prove them wrong."

⇨ **By The Way – Stuart Cellars won three Bronze and one Silver Medal at the 2008 New World International Wine Competition. Bronze winners were: the 2006 Zinfandel, the 2004 Port, the 2005 Long Valley Red® Meritage and the 2005 Cabernet Franc. Stuart's White Merlot took the Silver. Congratulations, Stuart!**

Tesoro Winery Tasting Room

Proprietors:	Kimberly and Buzz Olson
Address:	28475 Old Town Front Street, Temecula, CA 92590
Telephone:	(951) 308-0000
Website:	*www.tesorowines.com*
Hours:	Daily 10-5 (Later hours during Old Town special events)
Tasting Fees:	$10 for 5 out of 7 wines
Average Wine Prices: Whites: $$ Reds: $$$	
Production:	1,000 to 5,000 cases per year

Varietals:	(Authors' Recommendations ★): **Note:** We were unable to taste all Tesoro wines since some were still being bottled at the time we went to press.
Whites:	Riesling, White Blend (Dolce Innoncenza – Sweet Innocence) ★
Reds:	Cabernet Sauvignon ★, Merlot, Sangiovese ★, Trinità (Super Tuscan-Style Red) ★, Zinfandel

Step over the threshold of this new tasting room and you are magically transported from the Old West into Tuscany. Located near Mad Madeline's Grill and the Farmer's Market in Old Town Temecula, Tesoro Winery's Tasting Room is truly an Italian "Treasure." From the wood beamed ceiling to the hand-painted trompe l'oeil Tuscan scene on the mural behind the 19-foot tasting bar, every item has been specially selected to enhance its "Old World" charm and the tranquil, simple-life atmosphere. However, the luxury Mediterranean style wines served in the tasting room are anything but simple.

Tesoro Winery, which opened their new downtown tasting room in March of 2008 (right as we were going to press) almost slipped beneath our radar. Thankfully, **Le Roy Guilford** of *ShopTemeculaWines.com*, let us know about this wonderful new winery. We contacted Kimberly Olson, Managing Partner for Tesoro, and she promptly sent us two of their wines to sample: the Trinità (a Super Tuscan style red blend) and the Dolce Innocenza (Sweet Innocence), a white blend.

We really liked the "Sweet Innocence," but fell completely in love with the Trinità. We were so enamored of this wine that we contacted Ms. Olson and begged to be adopted. She politely declined our request, but did agree to send us two more wines: their Cabernet Sauvignon and the Sangiovese. All we can say is - wonderful! Simply wonderful. The Sangiovese is one of the best Sangios we have had.

What a great addition Tesoro Winery will make to the Temecula Valley. For more information on Tesoro's future plans for their winery, vineyard and Tuscan-style Villa Inn, turn to our *Coming Attractions* chapter.

After tasting Tesoro wines, we suspect you will be asking anxiously about their wine club, "Treasure Chest." Club benefits were not finalized at the time we went to press, but here is what we know. You will receive a two-bottle shipment (one red and one white) every other month. Prices for the shipment will range from $25 to $65 depending upon the wines selected by the winemaker. Club members will receive a 20% discount off the regular prices on wine purchases, to include wine club shipments. Club members will also receive a 15% discount on merchandise purchased from the Tesoro gift shop.

✪ *Grape Escapes Discount!* - Present a copy of this book and receive a **Two-for-One tasting** for up to four people in your party!!! Present a copy of this book and receive a **10% discount** on all wines and tasting room merchandise purchased on the day of your visit.

Thornton Winery

Proprietors: The Thornton Family
Address: 32575 Rancho California Road, Temecula, CA 92591
Telephone: (951) 699-0099
Website: *www.thorntonwine.com*
Hours: Daily 10-5
Tasting Fees: $10 - $15
Average Wine Prices: Whites: $ Reds: $$$
Production: 40,000 - 50,000 cases per year

Varietals: (Authors' Recommendations ★):
Whites: Chardonnay, Moscato, Sauvignon Blanc, Viognier
Reds: Cabernet-Merlot, Cabernet Sauvignon, Nebbiolo ★, Sangiovese, Syrah ★, Rhone Red Blend ★, Zinfandel ★
Sparkling: Brut Reserve ★, Non-Vintage Brut, Blanc de Noir, NV Cuvée Rouge
Dessert: Late Harvest Zinfandel Brut Reserve ★, Non-Vintage Brut, Blanc de Noirs

Thornton Winery is the first winery on your right as you enter Temecula Wine Country along Rancho California Road. You might be tempted to keep driving past in order to get more into the heart of Wine Country. *Don't!* Stop and turn around if necessary, but do not pass up this outstanding wine tasting opportunity. The winery is French-chateau in style and offers a well-appointed gift shop and an outstanding award-winning restaurant, Café Champagne. Seriously, don't pass up Thornton.

Temecula is changing and so are Thornton wines. Until 1993, their production was all sparkling wines. This is no longer the case. Winemaker Don Reha was kind enough to give us an informative tour of the winery and discuss his plans for the future. Thornton is in the process of procuring and installing new wine-making equipment to match Don's winemaking style, as well as increasing the number of red wines produced. While Thornton produces some outstanding sparkling wines, we were particularly impressed with their reds. But more on that later.

Don has been at Thornton for about five years and is tremendously excited, not just about the changes at Thornton, but the overall potential for winemaking in the Temecula Valley. He is especially enthusiastic about the new and, he thinks, better suited varietals that are now being planted in the region.

Don's focus as a winemaker is on emphasizing the distinctive characteristics of each individual wine varietal in an effort to create a menu of unique and appealing wines. He has succeeded. In 2007, the 2005 Estate Syrah was voted the "Best Red Wine in Temecula."

One of the things that we most like about this winery is that they are "employee friendly." What do we mean by this? We asked why certain steps in the winemaking process were not automated and were told that automation would cost someone their job – and that the owners did not want to do this. Thornton's employees stay with the winery for years and, as a result, are considered to be extended members of the Thornton family. We believe Thornton's commitment to its employees translates into good wine and good service.

Thornton's approach to wine tasting is very *civilized* and unrushed. No jostling for a position at the tasting bar. You are seated very comfortably in either the tasting room or the larger outside covered patio. Once seated, you choose from a menu of wine flights: reds, whites, sparkling. We sampled a couple of mixed flights and were served some superb appetizers prepared by Café Champagne.

As for the wines, we promise you will not be disappointed. We started with Thornton's sparkling wines and loved the Brut Reserve and the non-vintage Brut. The Reserve Reds were, however, our favorite. The 2005 Nebbiolo is fantastic, as are the 2005 Estate Syrah and Old Vine Zinfandel. When we say "Old Vine," we're not kidding. These vines are in Amador County and are 120 years old. And the Late Harvest Zin, well… it is best described with one of those technical wine tasting terms, "Wow!" Yep, that's it. Wow! Some things are just perfect!

Our wine tasting experience at Thornton was just that – Perfect! We urge everyone to sample Thornton's wonderful wine tasting experience.

Wiens Family Cellars

Proprietors: The Wiens Family
Address: 35055 Via Del Ponte, Temecula, CA 92592
Telephone: (951) 694-9892
Website: *www.wienscellars.com*
Hours: Daily 10-5
Tasting Fees: $10
Average Wine Prices: Whites: $$ Reds: $$$
Production: 10,000 - 15,000 cases per year

Varietals: (Authors' Recommendations ★):
Whites: Chardonnay, Malvasia Bianca, Pinot Gris, Viognier, White Blend
Reds: Cabernet Sauvignon, Cab-Franc, Merlot ★, Petite Syrah, Pinot Noir, Primitivo, Syrah ★, Zinfandel ★, Red Blends
Sparkling: Amour De L'Orange
Dessert: Ruby Port ★, White Port ★

From humble beginnings (fourteen acres in Lodi and Doug Wiens' garage), can spring big things – like Wiens Family Cellars. Winemaking became a family affair when Doug, winemaker and viticulturist, asked his relatives to help plant and harvest the grapes when they were ready. No one at that time had any idea that this home winemaking hobby would literally turn into a large and successful family winery business in Temecula, California.

Wiens' unofficial motto flies on a banner outside their large, country-style tasting room. "Big Reds" is what the sign promises. Once inside, Wiens delivers. They presently farm sixty vineyard acres in the Temecula area and bring in about 10% to 15% of their fruit from the Lodi / Amador County areas. The Wiens have high standards. If a wine fails to meet their criteria, it is sold off.

⇨ **By The Way – Wiens won a Bronze Medal at the 2008 New World International Wine Competition for their 2005 Zinfandel.**

Operating under the old axiom of "grapes that struggle make good wine," Doug is purposefully hard on his grapes. They are given very little fertilizer and low levels of irrigation. The result is smaller berries, but ones that possess a more intense fruit flavor. It must be true since Wiens has won and continues to win an impressive array of medals at prestigious regional and international competitions.

Wiens is an extremely popular tasting spot – especially on weekends. The winery does a good job of managing the large number of weekend visitors by opening an outdoor tasting area. If you like their wines, buy while you are at the tasting room. Wiens' wines are sold only in the tasting room, although they are starting to appear in a few area restaurants.

Not content with just making great wine, Doug is also the founder and number one instructor for the **California Wine School**. Give them four weeks and they will, if not make you a wine expert, certainly put you on the path to becoming one. You cannot do much better than having Doug Wiens as your teacher.

✪ *Grape Escapes Discount!* - Present a copy of this book and receive **Two-for-One** wine tasting, plus a **10% discount** on all wines purchased on the day of your visit. Also, present a copy of this book and receive a free "back stage" tour of the winery with the winemaker. *Advance appointment is required*. Phone (951) 694-9892 to schedule.

Wilson Creek Winery & Vineyards

Proprietors: The Wilson Family
Address: 35960 Rancho California Road, Temecula, CA 92591
Telephone: (951) 699-9463
Website: *www.wilsoncreekwinery.com*
Hours: Daily 10-5
Tasting Fees: $10 to $20
Average Wine Prices: Whites: $$ Reds: $$$
Production: 30,000 cases per year

Varietals: (Authors' Recommendations ★):
Whites: Chardonnay, Sauvignon Blanc ★, Muscat Canelli, White Cabernet Sauvignon ★, Riesling,
Reds: Cabernet Sauvignon (Legacy) ★, Merlot, Petite Sirah ★, Syrah, Zinfandel ★
Sparkling: Champagne ★, Almond Champagne
Dessert: Duet (Late Harvest Cab & Zin Blend) ★, Cream Sherry ★, Chocolate Port ★

There is so much great info to tell you about Wilson Creek that it is hard to know where to begin. Let us state up front that this is one of our long-time favorite wineries – for so, so many reasons. It takes a lot of courage to bring a winery to successful fruition. (Pardon the pun.) Setbacks along the way are not uncommon. The Wilson family had a developer walk out on them, taking with him a significant amount of monies that were to be used for their winery and tasting room. According to Rosie Wilson, the family matriarch, they ate peanut butter sandwiches for over a year in order to meet their financial obligations and keep the winery going. Their sacrifices have paid off handsomely and they are adding a soon-to-be completed event center and restaurant to their winery.

If ever there was a winery that perfectly captures what wine tasting should be about, it is Wilson Creek. One Sunday afternoon after completing our third "research" visit to this wonderful establishment, we looked out upon the Wilson Creek grounds and observed a perfect "Norman Rockwell" moment. People were strolling the landscaped grounds, picnicking by the small stream, and tasting wine in the gazebo. Kids were frolicking on the playground while parents and others were simply sitting on nearby benches, chatting while enjoying some of Wilson Creek's outstanding wines. The setting could not have been more idyllic.

Wilson Creek Winery & Vineyards is another of the "Family Affair" wineries that have become both hugely popular and successful in the Temecula Valley. In our first winery guidebook on the Paso Robles Wine Region, we said about the Tobin James Winery – "If you can't have a good time at Tobin James, you probably can't have a good time." Well, the same axiom applies to Wilson Creek Winery &Vineyards. This is a fun stop.

The Wilson Creek Winery opened in 2000 and it is already producing 30,000 cases annually. Eight family members work in the winery – not counting their five Retrievers: Chianti, Cabbie (short for Cabernet) Cristal, AJ, and Jazz. In addition, the winery has a huge list of entertainment activities that range from charity fund raisers to cigar nights, to concerts, to spa days…to name just a few.

⇨ **By The Way** – **For you military buffs, Wilson Creek is the unofficial "official" wine of the US Navy. Wilson Creek has designed personalized wine labels for over fifty navy ships and other military units. Pretty cool, huh? (If you are not humming the theme song to Top Gun, you should be.) Wilson Creek wines are served aboard at least seven aircraft carriers. Not to worry, they don't serve it when the pilots are flying. The wines are only for special functions or when the ships host functions with Allied Navies. Consequently, the Wilsons are considered very special people by the Navy – so don't mess with them. They were even invited to experience a "trap" landing and catapult launch from a carrier. The Navy doesn't just let anyone do that. We're talking 0 to 160 MPH in about two seconds. It is almost as much fun as drinking their Decadencia Port!**

All the Wilson family members have killer senses of humor. In the movie *Cast Away* with Tom Hanks, you may remember "Wilson," the Volleyball who was Tom's sole companion on the otherwise deserted island. Well, the Wilsons have a "Wilson" (complete with bloody hand print) mounted on their trophy wall. Like we said, if you can't have fun at Wilson Creek, you probably just can't have fun.

As for their wines, there is a lot to like and a lot to choose from. Our favorites were the 2005 Sauvignon Blanc, called Quartet. This was one of our highest scoring white wines. The sweeter Golden Jubilee also scored very well, as did the White Cabernet. For reds, we liked the Wilson Family "Legacy" which is a Bordeaux blend of Merlot, Cabernet Sauvignon, Petit Verdot, Cabernet France and Malbec. Whew! Now that's a blend. We also liked the 2004 Estate Cab and loved the Angelica Cream Sherry. And we already talked about the Decadencia Port. This particular wine has won both the Chairman's Award and Gold Medal (Riverside International Wine Competition). Go, Wilson!!!

⇨ **By The Way** – Wilson Creek won an amazing seven Bronze Medals at the 2008 New World International Wine Competition. Winners were: the 2005 Cabernet Sauvignon, the Merlot, the Meritage Red, the 2006 Sauvignon Blanc, the Non-Vintage Mourvèdre / Pinot Noir and a White Blend. Wilson Creek's 2005 Estate Zinfandel took Double Gold and their Petite Sirah also earned a Gold Medal. Their Sherry earned the Silver Medal. See? We told you. Wilson Creek Rocks!

❂ *Grape Escapes Discount!* - Present a copy of this book and receive **Two-for-One tasting** for up to four guests (a $20 value). PLUS, present a copy of this book and receive a **10% discount** on all wines purchased on the day of your visit. Offers good Monday – Friday only, except on holidays. And if this is not reason enough to visit one of our favorite wineries, present a copy of *The Grape Escapes 2* and receive a **free glass of Almond Champagne** for up to four guests (one glass per entrée) with your purchase of an entrée at the **Creekside Grille** located at Wilson Creek Winery. This is a $28 value and is valid Monday – Friday only, except on holidays.

"God made only water, but man made wine." ~Victor Hugo

TEMECULA'S HIDDEN GEMS
(Wineries Without Tasting Rooms or Not Open to the Public)

Not all of Temecula's outstanding wineries are open to the public. Sad, but true. A number of the area's top winemakers have what we refer to as "private label" wines. However, being the intrepid, daring and ultra-dedicated wine researchers that we are, we sought out these hidden wines.

We would like to say that we moved heaven and earth to obtain samples of these wines, but we didn't. Actually, Le Roy Guilford of **ShopTemeculaWines.com** did all the work collecting and shipping us the "private label" wines. But, but, but … We want you to know that we did do all the tasting and that part was *lots and lots* of *work*. Yeah, right! Thanks, Le Roy. We had a blast.

ShopTemeculaWines.com

Proprietor:	Le Roy Guilford
Telephone:	1-888-460-WINE (9463)
Hours:	Online 24 hours
Address:	LP Guilford Companies, Inc.
	c/o 2466 Cavalcade Court
	Perris, CA 92571
Wines:	All Temecula Wines

The great thing about *ShopTemeculaWines.com* is not just that you can arrange to have Temecula wines shipped to your door, but you can also use Le Roy as your own personal wine advisor. He is constantly in Temecula Wine Country discovering new gems and is rapidly becoming the "go-to" guy for all things associated with Temecula Wine Country and its wines. As the host of **Wine Country Talk Radio**, he is also up-to-date on the latest happenings in Temecula Wine Country. Call or Email him and tell him what you like and he will put together a shipment of the latest or best releases, so you never have to worry about buying blind. Think of Le Roy and *ShopTemeculaWines.com* as the perfect companion resource to this book. Le Roy can also help you capture the latest award-winning wines or prized micro-boutique wines, such as the **Atwood Syrah** discussed below.

☞ **Authors' Tip:** *Even if you are not within reception range of Wine Country Talk Radio, located at AM830, you can still hear Le Roy's weekly programs by visiting www.WCTRonline.com*

★ = Authors' Recommendation

Atwood Estate Vineyard

Winemaker:	Tim Kramer
Production:	~ 100 cases
Hours:	Not open to the public
	Wines are available at the *Temecula House of Wine* in Old Town and online via *ShopTemeculaWines.com*

Wine:	Syrah ★
Price:	$25 to $30

The Atwood label wine is made for a private client by a super winemaker, **Tim Kramer**, of **Leonesse Cellars**. Only a small amount of the wine (a Syrah) is produced each year. We had the 2004 Syrah and it was truly exceptional – one of the best Syrahs we have tasted. In fact, it was one of our favorite Temecula wines, period.

If you are a Syrah fan, we urge you to go online to *ShopTemeculaWines.com* or call / visit Carlos at *Temecula House of Wine* and order a few bottles before they are all gone. One positive note, however, by the time this book hits the shelves, the 2005 vintage should also be available. According to Tim, the 2005 "is equally as nice" as the 2004 vintage.

○ *Grape Escapes Discount!* - Present a copy of this book at the **Temecula House of Wine** (28522 Front Street) in Old Town Temecula and receive a **10% discount** on all wines purchased on the day of your visit. If you purchase a case or more of wine during your visit, you will receive an additional **5%** (total 15%) **discount**. Tel: 951-699-0929 ◆ Hours: 10 AM to 8 PM weekdays and 10 AM to 10 PM on weekends ◆ Website: *www.palomarinntemecula.com*

Cowper Family Vineyards – Rey Sol Wines

Winemaker:	Etienne Cowper
Production:	Very Limited
Telephone:	(858) 654-4651
Hours:	Not open to the public
	Wines are available at the *Temecula House of Wine* in Old Town and online via *ShopTemeculaWines.com*

Wine:	2001 Barbera ★
Price:	~$25

Etienne Cowper is another of the Temecula Valley's outstanding winemakers. Prior to joining **Wilson Creek** in 2007, Etienne was the winemaker at **Mount Palomar** for sixteen years. He is an extremely well-regarded winemaker.

Etienne is a quiet man, perhaps believing that his wines should speak for themselves. And his wines, especially his private label, Rey Sol wines, speak volumes. If you are a fan of Barbera, or simply appreciate fine, hand-crafted red wine, then we highly recommend you visit *Temecula House of Wine* or order a few bottles of his "private label" Rey Sol Barbera from *ShopTemeculaWines.com*

✪ *Grape Escapes Discount!* - Present a copy of this book at the *Temecula House of Wine* (28522 Front Street) in Old Town Temecula and receive a **10% discount** on all wines purchased on the day of your visit. If you purchase a case or more of wine during your visit, you will receive an additional **5%** (total 15%) **discount**. Tel: 951-699-0929 ♦ Hours: 10 AM to 8 PM weekdays and 10 AM to 10 PM on weekends ♦ Website: *www.palomarinntemecula.com*

Curry Vineyards

Winemaker:	Charlie Curry
Production:	~ 300 Cases
Telephone:	(909) 821-1282 or (951) 302-5647
Hours:	Not open to the public
	Wines are available directly from the winemaker, at the *Temecula House of Wine* in Old Town or via *ShopTemeculaWines.com*

Wines:	Syrah★, Cabernet Sauvignon, and Cabernet Franc
Price:	~ $20 per bottle

Sadly, Curry Vineyards is not open to the public. The good news, however, is that Charlie Curry produces some excellent red wines from the grapes grown on his 16-acre vineyard. Charlie Curry, like his neighbors Nick Palumbo and Don Frangipani, is a former professional chef turned wine-maker. There is a lot to be said about winemakers who possess both wine-making and gourmet food skills. Charlie's 2005 Syrah is one the best we tasted.

✪ *Grape Escapes Discount!* - Present a copy of this book at the *Temecula House of Wine* (28522 Front Street) in Old Town Temecula and receive a **10% discount** on all wines purchased on the day of your visit. If you purchase a case or more of wine during your visit, you will receive an additional **5%** (total 15%) **discount**. Tel: 951-699-0929 ♦ Hours: 10 AM to 8 PM weekdays and 10 AM to 10 PM on weekends ♦ Website: *www.palomarinntemecula.com*

Doffo Winery

Winemaker:	Marcelo Doffo
Production:	Limited
Telephone:	(951) 676-6989
Website:	*www.doffowines.com*

Address:	36083 Summitville
	Temecula, 92592

Hours: Not open to the public. Wines are available via the **Doffo website**, at the *Temecula House of Wine* in Old Town and via *ShopTemeculaWines.com*

Wines: Cabernet Sauvignon, Mistura Blend ★
                 Shiraz, NV Port, Viognier, Malbec
Prices: $27 to $60

☞ **Authors' Tip:** *Although the winery is not open to the public at this time, Marcelo Doffo is hoping to reopen his tasting room in the near future. Be sure to phone and stop by.*

We were unable to visit in person with Mr. Marcelo Doffo, owner and winemaker for Doffo wines, but our friend, Le Roy Guilford of *ShopTemeculaWines.com* arranged to have some of Marcelo's wines shipped to us. We sampled the 2002 Mistura and the 2004 Cabernet Sauvignon. We recommend decanting both wines before drinking, but decanting the 2002 is an absolute must to fully appreciate this aged wine.

Marcelo, as you may have guessed, is of Italian descent, but grew up in Argentina where he had the opportunity to learn first-hand about farming, ranching and winemaking. Marcelo certainly learned his lessons well.

Las Piedras Vineyards

Winemaker:	Steve Hagata
Production:	~ 400 Cases
Hours:	Not open to the public, but wines are available at the *Temecula House of Wine* in Old Town and online via *ShopTemeculaWines. com*

Wines:	Sangiovese ★, Syrah ★
Price:	~ $15 - $18

Steve Hagata is the award-winning winemaker at the well known and popular **Falkner Winery**. He also makes wine under his own private label, **Las Piedras**. The wines are produced from his personal vineyard which is located on the northeast slope of Palomar Mountain in Warner Springs. In case you are curious, "Piedras" is Spanish for "Stones." Something we know Steve found a lot of as he cleared the land that became his vineyard.

Steve's Sangiovese is very, very good, but our personal favorite is his big, earthy Syrah.

✪ *Grape Escapes Discount!* - Present a copy of this book at the ***Temecula House of Wine*** (28522 Front Street) in Old Town Temecula and receive a **10% discount** on all wines purchased on the day of your visit. If you purchase a case or more of wine during your visit, you will receive an additional **5%** (total 15%) **discount**. Tel: 951-699-0929 ✦ Hours: 10 AM to 8 PM weekdays and 10 AM to 10 PM on weekends ✦ Website: *www.palomarinntemecula.com*

(Barrett Bird's) Santa Margarita Winery

Winemaker:	Barrett Bird
Production:	~ Very Limited
Hours:	Not open to the public, but wines are available at the *Temecula House of Wine* in Old Town and online via *ShopTemeculaWines.com*
Wines:	Cabernet Sauvignon, Chardonnay ★, Viognier
Prices:	Approx. $10 per bottle

Barrett Bird, owner and founder of Santa Margarita Winery, is one of the Temecula Valley's original pioneers. Barrett planted his first grapes in 1974 and produced his first crush in 1985. A self-taught winemaker and something of a maverick, Barrett has strong feelings about how wine should be made and how it should be priced.

In the mid 80's, we would drive out on weekends to purchase his Chardonnay. It was, in our humble opinion, one of the best Chards in the Temecula Valley and was incredibly priced at only $4 per bottle. We need more "mavericks" like Barrett!

What we recall most about Barrett's wines is that they were extremely "smooth and buttery," a fact we attribute to his using highly-aged cooperage. Some of his barrels actually predate World War II! These aged barrels no longer introduce tannins into the wine. The result is very smooth wines.

Unfortunately, this iconic winery is no longer open to the public. Le Roy Guilford is, however, committed to keeping alive the memory of Barrett's winery and his contribution to the Temecula Valley. Limited quantities of Barrett's classic wines are available at the locations listed above. Like always, they are priced amazingly low – less than many *tasting fees* in the valley.

✪ *Grape Escapes Discount!* - Present a copy of this book at the *Temecula House of Wine* (28522 Front Street) in Old Town Temecula and receive a **10% discount** on all wines purchased on the day of your visit. If you purchase a case or more of wine during your visit, you will receive an additional **5%** (total 15%) **discount**. Tel: 951-699-0929 ✦ Hours: 10 AM to 8 PM weekdays and 10 AM to 10 PM on weekends ✦ Website: *www.palomarinntemecula.com*

Santa Maria Cellars

Winemaker:	Benny Rodriguez
Production:	Limited
Hours:	Not open to the public, but wines are available at the *Temecula House of Wine* in Old Town and online via *ShopTemeculaWines. com*

Wines:	Mourvèdre-Cabernet ★, Merlot-Cabernet ★
Prices:	~ $20 per bottle

Santa Maria Cellars is the private label wine of Benny Rodriguez, the wine-maker for the **Inn at Churon Winery**. We arranged with Le Roy Guilford of *ShopTemeculaWines.com* to taste Benny's wines. We can tell you, without a doubt, at the special purchase price of $12.95 for both the Mourvèdre-Cab and the Merlot-Cab that these wines represent *the best red wine bargain in Temecula!*

You can order these wines from *ShopTemeculaWines.com* or taste and pur-chase them at Carlos Palma's *Temecula House of Wine*. According to Car-los, the Santa Maria Mourvèdre-Cabernet is one his top selling wines, so the public must agree with our assessment.

✪ *Grape Escapes Discount!* - Present a copy of this book at the ***Temecula House of Wine*** (28522 Front Street) in Old Town Temecula and receive a **10% discount** on all wines purchased on the day of your visit. If you purchase a case or more of wine during your visit, you will receive an additional **5%** (total 15%) **discount**. Tel: 951-699-0929 ◆ Hours: 10 AM to 8 PM weekdays and 10 AM to 10 PM on weekends ◆ Website: *www.palomarinntemecula.com*

Villa Vessia Vineyard

Proprietor:	Franco Vessia
Winemaker:	Todd Boorman
Telephone:	(951) 676-8040
Production:	Limited
Address:	Frankie's Steak and Seafood Restaurant
	41789 Nicole Lane (Creekside Center) Temecula, CA 92591
Hours:	**Dining Room**: 5-10 PM Daily; **Bar**: 4-11 PM (12 midnight Fri-Sat)
Websites:	*www.frankies-restaurant.com* and *www.vessia.com*
Wine:	Cabernet Sauvignon ★
Price:	Approximately $30

☞ **Authors' Tip:** *If you happen to live in Orange County, California, you can also find the Villa Vessia Vineyard Cabernet Sauvignon at Franco's Italian restaurant, Vessia Ristorante, which is located at 3966 Barranca Parkway in Irvine, CA. Phone (949) 654-1155; Website:www.vessia.com*

The absolute best place to enjoy **Villa Vessia** wine is at **Frankie's Steak and Seafood** restaurant. **Frankie's** is located in the Creekside Center, at the corner of Overland and Nicole Lane (across the street from the Temecula Costco). Owner Franco Vessia has created a sophisticated dining venue in Temecula that provides five-star food and service with a California Casual dress code. Frankie's Steak and Seafood also has a modern walk-in wine cellar with a long list of fine California and Italian wines. Our favorite is his own Villa Vessia Vineyard Cabernet Sauvignon which is made by Todd Boorman.

If you are unable to visit Frankie's in Temecula or Villa Vessia Ristorante in Irvine, the outstanding Villa Vessia Vineyard Cabernet Sauvignon is also available at the *Temecula House of Wine* in Old Town and online via *ShopTemeculaWines.com*.

⇨ **By The Way** – In addition to great food and wine at his Frankie's Steak and Seafood Restaurant, Franco Vessia also offers customized cooking demonstration classes at his home, Villa Vessia, in Temecula. If you have a group of eight or ten people, give Franco a call to arrange for a fun, entertaining and educational dining experience. For more information on his cooking class program, contact him by phone (949) 654-1155 or Email Franco@vessia.com.

COMING ATTRACTIONS...

Lumière Winery (Opening mid 2008)

Proprietor:	Andrew Kleiner
Production:	~ 1,500 cases
Address:	39555 Calle Contento, Temecula, CA 92591
Telephone:	(951) 972-0585
Website:	*www.lumierewinery.com*
Hours:	To Be Opened on Weekends and Weekdays by Appt

Varietals:	(Authors' Recommendations ★):
	(Note: We were only able to taste one of Lumière's wines, the Sauvignon Blanc which is a very nice, fruity and sweeter-style wine.)
Whites:	Sauvignon Blanc ★
Reds:	Cabernet Sauvignon, Merlot, Petit Verdot
Dessert Wines:	Late Harvest Sauvignon Blanc
Prices:	Whites: $$ Reds: $$$

Lumière is the French word for "light." When we spoke with the owner / winemaker Andrew Kleiner about the reason for choosing this as the name of his winery, he told us that all life springs from light and that he wants his winery to be a celebration of both light and life. We suspect that is the reason his **Sauvignon Blanc** is bottled in clear glass. And to be honest, it is the color of golden sunshine.

Located next door to Longshadow Ranch and overlooking the Maurice Car'rie Winery, the Lumière tasting room will be housed in an old barn that is being completely refurbished but will have a "country rustic" feel. A picnic area is planned and they will have a covered patio / gazebo area where wine club events, weddings and private parties will be held.

☞ **Authors' Tip:** *While at Lumière, be sure to ask about any purchase discounts they might be offering such as "Buy one case and get a second case at half-price."*

Masia de Yabar Vineyard (Anticipated opening 2009)

Proprietor:	Wilmer Yabar
Production:	1,000+ cases per year
Address:	39788 Camino Arroyo Seco, Temecula, CA 92592
Telephone:	(951) 316-4714
Website:	None
Hours:	Daily; Hours Not Yet Established (as of Spring 2008)
Varietals:	(Authors' Recommendations ★):
	(Note: We did not have the opportunity to taste any of Masia de Yabar's wines.)
Whites:	Viognier, Muscat Canelli
Prices:	Range from $15 to $50
Reds:	Cabernet Sauvignon, Syrah, Tempranillo

Roughly translated, the Vineyard name means "Yabar Farm or Ranch." Wilmer Yabar hopes to open his winery tasting room in early 2009. He presently has been granted his growers license from the state and is in the process of going through Riverside County's approval process.

Once Wilmer's wines are produced, you should be available to purchase them through the *Temecula House of Wine* or via the internet at *www.ShopTemeculaWines.com*

✪ *Grape Escapes Discount!* - Present a copy of this book at the ***Temecula House of Wine*** (28522 Front Street) in Old Town Temecula and receive a **10% discount** on all wines purchased on the day of your visit. If you purchase a case or more of wine during your visit, you will receive an additional **5%** (total 15%) **discount**. Tel: 951-699-0929 ◆ Hours: 10 AM to 8 PM weekdays and 10 AM to 10 PM on weekends ◆ Website: *www.palomarinntemecula.com*

Tesoro Winery & Inn (Future Plans)

Proprietors:	Kimberly and Buzz Olson
Production:	1,000 - 5,000 cases
Address:	28475 Old Town Front Street, Temecula, CA 92590
Telephone:	(951) 308-0000
Website:	*www.tesorowines.com*
Hours:	Daily 10-5
Tasting Fees:	$10 for 5 out of 7 wines

Average Wine Prices: Whites: $$ Reds: $$$

Varietals: (Authors' Recommendations ★):
Note: We were not able to taste all of Tesoro's wines.

Whites: Dolce Innocenza (White Blend) ★, Riesling
Reds: Cabernet Sauvignon ★, Merlot, Sangiovese ★, Trinità ★
(A Super Tuscan-style wine)

Tesoro Winery has big plans for the future. They are building a Tuscan-style winery at the corner of Monte de Oro and Rancho California Road. They have twenty-two acres, enough to accommodate the winery, vineyard and a 16-18 room Tuscan Villa (inn).

Tesoro's winemaker is Etienne Cowper – and if you know anything at all about Temecula winemakers, you know that Etienne makes great wines. Tesoro will be featuring primarily Mediterranean wines. In the future, they will be expanding their vineyards to include Cortese, Dolcetto, Tempranillo and Viognier.

In the meantime, you are free to taste Tesoro's other wines at their Old Town Temecula tasting room. The Trinità (a Super Tuscan style wine) is outstanding, as is the Sangiovese and Cabernet Sauvignon. They also have a Merlot and a Riesling which we are looking forward to trying as well.

❂ *Grape Escapes Discount!* - Present a copy of this book and receive a **Two-for-One tasting** for up to four people in your party!!! Present a copy of this book and receive a **10% discount** on all wines and tasting room merchandise purchased on the day of your visit.

FOR BEGINNERS ONLY – 101
(A "Glass" Act)

We had our friend, John, over for an evening of wine tasting. John drinks wine occasionally, but would certainly not describe himself as an experienced wine taster. We sampled three wines before dinner, the 2003 Mourvèdre-Cabernet from **Santa Maria**, the 2003 **Santa Maria** Merlot-Cabernet, and the 2005 **Orfila** Gold Medal-winning "Gold Rush" Zinfandel.

We served the wines right out of the bottle immediately after opening. We sampled them multiple times over a period of 45 minutes – just so John could appreciate the difference in taste as the wines "opened up" after exposure to air.

We also played something of trick on John. We served him one of the red wines in a white wine glass. Then we served him the same wine in a red wine glass. John was absolutely convinced he had been served two different wines.

Just prior to dinner, we asked John to pick his favorite wine. He selected Santa Maria's 2003 Merlot-Cab. We also poured him a glass of the Orfila Zinfandel and asked him to try both during the meal, even though he had preferred the Merlot-Cab when tasted alone.

For dinner we served a spicy pepper and rice dish with chicken. About half-way through the meal, John announced, in a somewhat surprised voice, that he thought the Zinfandel was the better pairing wine for the meal.

Lessons Learned:

Wine glasses can make a big difference in the taste of your wine. Red wine glasses usually have a wider bowl and are narrower at the top than at the

bottom to concentrate the wine's aromas. Except in extreme emergencies
– such as an unwanted in-law coming to stay for a week – white wine
glasses should never be used to serve red wine.

Red wines "open up" after exposure to air and generally become "rounder"
and smoother. If a wine is more than three years old, we uncork the bottle
at least a half hour or more before serving it with a meal.

A great "cocktail" (stand-alone) wine, and Santa Maria's Merlot-Cab is
certainly a great wine, may not be the best wine for pairing with a meal.
Zinfandels are great wines for serving with spicy foods such as Mexican,
Barbecue or Italian.

⇨ **By The Way – A single grapevine can produce up to six bottles of
wine.**

CREATE YOUR OWN WINE TASTING ADVENTURE ...

**"It's impossible to separate
a great wine from a great experience.
~ Dorothy Gaiter & John Brecher**

"Solitude is often the best society." ~ Unknown

FAR FROM THE MADDENING CROWD

Let's face it. Sometimes we want to be in the middle of the crowd, soaking up the energy that only one of the "power" wineries can provide. But at other times, we're thinking, "a little wine, a low-key spot without a lot of chatter. Yep, that's the ticket."

So, what's a girl (or guy) to do to avoid the crowds? It's easy. Simply turn to your handy-dandy *Grape Escapes 2* Temecula Wine Country reference and the solution is at hand. If you're looking for a more relaxed and quieter wine tasting adventure, here are the spots we recommend:

Alex's Red Barn Winery
39820 Calle Contento, Temecula, CA 92951 ◆ Tel: 951-693-3201 ◆ Hours: Sat-Sun and most holidays 11-6, Winter 10-5 ◆ Website: *www.redbarnwine.com*

Briar Rose Winery
41720 Calle Cabrillo, Temecula, CA 92592 ◆ Tel: 951-308-1098 ◆ Hours: By Appointment Only ◆ Website: *www.briarrosewinery.com*

Foote Print Winery
36650 Glen Oaks Road, Temecula, CA 92592 ◆ Tel: 951-265-9951 ◆ Hours: Fri 12-5, Sat-Sun 10-5, Mon-Thurs By Appointment ◆ Website: *www.footeprintwinery.com*

✪ *Grape Escapes Discount!* - Present a copy of this book and receive a **Two-for-One tasting!!!**

Frangipani Estate Winery
39750 De Portola Road, Temecula, CA 92592 ◆ Tel: 951-699-8845 ◆ Hours: Daily 10-5 ◆ Website: *www.frangipaniwinery.com*

✪ *Grape Escapes Discount!* - Present a copy of this book and receive a **30% discount** on all wines purchased on the day of your visit.

Hart Winery
41300 Avenida Biona, Temecula, CA 92591 ♦ Tel: 951-676-6300 ♦ Hours: Daily 9-4:30 ♦ Website: *www.thehartfamilywinery.com*

Longshadow Ranch Vineyard & Winery
39847 Calle Contento, Temecula, CA 92591 ♦ Tel: 951-587-6221 ♦ Hours: Mon-Fri 12-5, Sat 10-4 (Sat Bonfire 5-9 PM April through October), Sun 10-5 ♦ Website: *www.longshadowranchwinery.com*

✪ *Grape Escapes Discount!* - Present a copy of this book and receive a **10% discount** on all wines purchased on the day of your visit.

Oak Mountain Winery / Temecula Hills Winery
36522 Via Verde, Temecula, CA 92592 ♦ Tel: 951-699-9102 ♦ Hours: Daily 11-5 ♦ Website: *www.oakmountainwinery. com*

✪ *Grape Escapes Discount!* - Present a copy of this book and receive a **10% discount** on all wines purchased on the day of your visit. Also, present a copy of this book and receive **Two-for-One tasting** for up to four guests. Offer does not include the souvenir logo glass.

Palumbo Family Vineyards & Winery
40150 Barksdale Circle, Temecula, CA 92591 ♦ Tel: 951-676-7900 ♦ Hours: Fri 12-5, Sat-Sun 10-5, Mon-Thurs By Appointment ♦ Website: *www.palumbofamilyvineyards.com*

✪ *Grape Escapes Complimentary Tasting!* - Present a copy of this book and receive a **complimentary tasting for two people** in your party.

Robert Renzoni Vineyards
37350 De Portola Road, Temecula, CA 92592 ♦ Tel: 951-302-8466 ♦ Hours: Daily 11-6 ♦ Website: *www. robertrenzonivineyards.com*

✪ *Grape Escapes Discount!* - Present a copy of this book and receive a **10% discount** on all wines and tasting room merchandise purchased on the day of your visit. Also, present a copy of this book and receive an additional **10% discount** (total of 20%) on a case or more of wine.

"I always say shopping is cheaper than a psychiatrist."
~ Tammy Faye Bakker

SHOP TILL YOU DROP!

One of the best aspects of Temecula area wineries is that most are not overly commercialized. Each has a unique character which makes visiting it a fun experience. Although the majority of winery gift shops sell bar-related items and T-shirts, most do not contain extensive gift shopping areas. However, Temecula does have a few wineries that offer a variety of unique gift and home décor items, as well as art, books and food items. In many cases, we found the tasting room gift items to be less expensive than similar items found in many of the gift and specialty shops throughout the Temecula area.

Buying gifts in a winery tasting room (whether for yourself, a loved one, a co-worker, or a friend) lets you share the winery experience. Merchandise is constantly changing and many items are stocked only in limited quantities and for limited times, so if you see something you like, *buy it!*

So…, sharpen up your multi-tasking skills – while you are savoring that delicious glass of wine, pull out your credit card, and help the local economy!

Callaway Vineyard & Winery
32720 Rancho California Road, Temecula, CA 92591 ♦ Tel: 951-676-4001 ♦ Summer Hours: Daily 10-6, Winter Hours: 10-5 ♦ Website: *www.callawaywinery.com*

Spacious and inviting, Callaway's airy gift shop overlooking the vineyards is a showcase of beautifully displayed merchandise that strives to help you recreate the "wine country lifestyle" in your own home. Distinctive goblets and barware, decanters, candles, serving pieces, table linen, and dining décor are elegantly displayed in beautiful Mediterranean-inspired cabinets, atop strategically placed wine barrels, and in specially crafted glass-topped tables with grapevine pedestals. Wine racks and beautiful Tuscan tapestries adorn the walls.

If you are yearning to learn more about wine and wine tasting, the gift shop carries a wide range of books, cards and games to quench your thirst for knowledge. In addition, Callaway Winery offers an outstanding assortment of seasonal gourmet food products (flavored oils, mustards, dips, grilling sauces, condiments, etc.).

For a unique and playful gift, surprise your friends with a jar of "Frog Balls" (pickled Brussels sprouts) or marinated "Hearty-Chokes." Callaway Winery also specializes in distinctive personalized gifts. The gift shop staff can help you create a customized wine label, select an elegant or dramatic hand-painted bottle of Callaway wine, or fashion a basket filled with gourmet foods and Callaway wines.

✿ *Grape Escapes Discount!* - Present a copy of this book and receive a **20% discount** on all wines and tasting room merchandise purchased on the day of your visit. Also, present a copy of this book and receive **Two-for-One tasting**!!!

Cougar Vineyard & Winery
39870 De Portola Road, Temecula, CA 92592 ◆ Tel: 951-491-0825 ◆ Hours: Daily 11-6, Winter 11-5 ◆ Website: *www.cougarvineyards.com*

Cougar Winery's gift area features unique, hand-thrown pottery and collectable artwork signed by the creators. The winery also carries small, hand-made purses / handbags made out of Cougar's wine corks that Cindy loves! Cougar is presently in the process of constructing a new Early California / Spanish-style tasting room which will also house an expanded gift shop area.

La Cereza Vineyard & Winery
34567 Rancho California Road, Temecula, CA 92591 ◆ Tel: 951-699-6961 ◆ Hours: Daily 10-5 ◆ Website: *www.lacerezawinery.com*

The first things you notice about the interior of the Spanish-style La Cereza Winery are the warm, dark red and golden walls that are filled with original paintings and artwork by talented artists. *(Many of the beautiful and vibrant Spanish, primitive, and music-themed paintings have been made into labels for their specialty wines.)* Next, your glance is quickly drawn to the amazing hand-crafted, lead-free pewter home décor and serving pieces that are elegantly displayed throughout the gift shop. All the winery's pewter ware, in addition to being beautiful, is food-friendly, oven-safe, and can also be used in the refrigerator. *How great is that?* The shopping area is filled with colorful ceramic serving dishes, wine accessories and dramatic decorative items, including Old World mirrors, candelabras, crosses, and urns. In tribute to Temecula's equestrian lovers, one of the display tables is filled with "horse country" themed items – platters, dishes, statuary, barware and accessories.

La Cereza also has a playful side – its "Girlfriends" products are a sight you won't soon forget! They feature a white-haired woman with big black glasses dressed in pink, red and yellow, wearing tennis shoes. Lounging in a stone doorway, this "girlfriend" is smoking a big, fat Cuban cigar (a la George Burns). The "Girlfriends" theme is also featured on bottles of La Cereza's wine. Its "Girlfriends" vintage is a special blend of white wines filled with citrus, melon and papaya flavors. Don't leave without a gift for your own special "girlfriends" – La Cereza offers *Girlfriends*-decorated hats, tee-shirts (with bling!), and jewelry.

✪ *Grape Escapes Discount!* - Present a copy of this book and receive a **10% discount** on all wines and tasting room merchandise purchased on the day of your visit. Sorry, but offer is not valid on weekends.

Longshadow Ranch Vineyard & Winery
39847 Calle Contento, Temecula, CA 92591 ♦ Tel: 951-587-6221 ♦ Hours: Mon-Fri 12-5, Sat 10-4 (Sat Bonfire 5-9 PM April through October), Sun 10-5 ♦ Website: *www.longshadowranchwinery.com*

We have to say that this winery and gift shop is unlike any we have ever seen! The winery's down-home, "cowboy-country" atmosphere does not stop at the horse corrals outside. It extends into the small combination tasting room and gift shop. Longshadow Ranch offers Western wear for children and adults, including cowboy hats, hand-crafted western leather wallets and handbags, and not-to-be-overlooked leather belts with plenty of "bling." Everything in the gift shop is geared to having fun – wooden wall plaques with humorous sayings, whimsical picture frames, and other home décor items every "cowboy" needs to have.

✪ *Grape Escapes Discount!* - Present a copy of this book and receive a **10% discount** on all wines purchased on the day of your visit.

Maurice Car'rie Winery
34225 Rancho California Road, Temecula, CA 92591 ◆ Tel: 951-676-1711 ◆ Hours: Daily 10-5 ◆ Website: *www.mauricecarriewinery.com*

The Maurice Car'rie Winery was founded in 1986 and was designed to reflect a Victorian-style farmhouse. The inviting, warm, country-casual atmosphere of the tasting room also fills the gift shop. The Maurice Car'rie shopping area carries items for the informal and fun-loving home, such as brilliantly colored porcelain roosters, vividly painted serving ware, and uniquely shaped dishes. In addition, they offer a wide range of country-style accessories that are sure to add a special charm to your home. The gift shop also carries an assortment of frilly or humorous bib aprons that will bring a chuckle to your friends and family.

If you are looking for picnic items, Maurice Car'rie features special, all-inclusive picnic backpacks (including wine) that will serve two or four. The shop also offers large picnic hampers that you can fill with all sorts of goodies from their selection of private label gourmet olives and vinegars. If your gift needs run more to the classical side, Maurice Car'rie displays an extensive collection of elegant wall tapestries, crystal bottle stoppers in a rainbow of colors, and fine linen napkin sets.

✪ *Grape Escapes Discount!* - Present a copy of this book Monday through Friday and receive a **10% discount** on all wines and tasting room merchandise purchased on the day of your visit. Sorry, but offer is not valid on weekends.

Ponte Family Estate Winery
35053 Rancho California Road, Temecula, CA 92591 ◆ Tel: 951-694-8855 ◆ Hours: Daily 10-5 ◆ Website: *www.pontewinery.com*

As you enter the Ponte Winery tasting room and gift area, the first thing you notice is how large and spacious it is. The barn-like design, complete with open beam-work and a pitched roofline, allows the sun to filter downward. This provides dramatic lighting for the glassware, mirrors, and the silver, gold, and frosted decorative ferns, feathers, and branches that adorn displays. The merchandise actually seems to shine and sparkle as it catches the sun's rays! Color-coordinated merchandise is artistically and casually arranged on the floor and tables: blue and silver items for a sea-themed display; black and red pottery, lamps, vases, and glassware create a dramatic scene; a tall pyramid of sherbet-colored pillar candles creates a virtual rainbow, etc. Everything is situated and designed to reinforce the classical, casual elegance of the tasting room.

This is Cindy's favorite shopping area for gifts because of the distinctive, unique items Ponte displays. Plus, its prices are very competitive with other specialty and gift shops in the Temecula area, as well as the other wineries. Ponte stocks a large selection of gourmet food items (herb-infused oils and vinegars, sauces, mustards, flavored syrups and baking mixes). The gift shop also showcases specialty items such as vases, ornate candle holders, lamps, serving dishes, ceramic and metal animals, and decorative wall art in displays that will give you great ideas for your own home.

Need some personal items? They also have lotions, soaps, perfumes, clothing, books, and beautiful enamel butterfly gifts adorned with colorful crystals. Best of all (Cindy's downfall) – they have gourmet *chocolate* candy, dessert sauces, and cookies.

Once home, if you run out of that "must have" gourmet item or need a special wedding or birthday gift, go to Ponte's website. It features a wide selection of wonderful merchandise and food items, as well as specially designed, unique "theme" gift baskets and boxes.

☺ *Grape Escapes Discount!* - Present a copy of this book and receive a **Two-for-One tasting**!!! Offer valid Monday Through Thursday, excluding holidays.

☞ **Authors' Tip:** *A few times each year, Ponte hosts an after-hours "Shopping Night" and offers wine club members and guests 30% off everything – wine, gourmet foods, books and gift items! Not only do you get great discounts on some of the best merchandise in the Temecula area, they also serve you complimentary wine and hors d'oeuvres while you shop.*

South Coast Winery
34843 Rancho California Road, Temecula, CA 92591 ✦ Tel: 951-587-9463 ✦ Hours: Daily 10-6 ✦ Website: *www.wineresort.com*

At the entrance to the gift shop, you are met by joyous Bella Donna, the life-sized "statuesque" plaster signora who is busily stomping grapes in a wine barrel. Be sure to take advantage of this photo op! Then continue to the shopping area where intricate wrought iron racks and honey-toned wooden tables and cabinets display South Coast Winery's wide variety of high-quality gift and home décor items.

The sales area features Intrada brand Italian ceramics, wine racks of all shapes and sizes (some accommodating up to 60 bottles of wine), Sonoma brand serving ware and dishes, San Remo bedding items, and elegant tapestry wall hangings with Tuscan motifs. It also carries a wide selection of unique clocks ranging from small, distinguished desk-sized timepieces to ornate wall and floor models. If you are looking for just the right ornamentation for your garden or courtyard, South Coast Winery carries whimsical birdhouses and angel-themed statuary.

For the "foodies" in your life, purchase some of the winery's gourmet salsas, oils, jams, dips, and yummy chocolates. Still undecided? A personal gift is always appreciated and South Coast Winery offers a wide range of resort wear and unique custom, handmade jewelry with precious stones. Once you are home, if you remember something you cannot live without, go to South Coast Winery's website. You will find multiple pages of the store's merchandise that can be shipped directly to you or a loved one.

Wilson Creek Winery & Vineyards
35960 Rancho California Road, Temecula, CA 92591 ✦ Tel: 951-699-9463 ✦ Hours: Daily 10-5 ✦ Website: *www.wilsoncreekwinery.com*

As guests enter the tasting room doors at Wilson Creek Winery, they often say "What is that wonderful scent?" Not only does Wilson Creek produce wonderful wines that please your palate, they also stock a special line of "cabernet" candles from Scentations that will delight your nose. For your eyes, the antiqued plaster walls of the sun-filled 2000 square foot tasting room are decorated with Italian wine-scene tapestries and trompe l'oeil grapevines. You can go to Wilson Creek Winery and be totally surrounded by the sight, scent, and taste of wonderful wine. How cool is that!

The gift shop area offers a wide variety of wine-related items, such as wine barrel "lazy susans," vineyard-scene stained glass, "character" wine holders, wrought iron wine and grape-themed wall décor, cookbooks, and grape decorator lights. Their hand-painted wine and martini glasses are some of Wilson Creek's best sellers. In addition, they feature a variety of unique "bling-bling" rhinestone T-shirts and soft-soled slippers adorned with humorous slogans and artwork for both adults and children.

For that lovable canine in your life, the gift shop area features dog collars and leashes with many wine designs. They also carry a book called *"Wine Dogs"* which contains photos of the dogs at North American wineries. The second edition will be released in Fall 2008 and it will include Wilson Creek's five Golden Retrievers! The dogs are considered to be an important part of the Wilson family – as you can see from their presence in the family portrait that is the focus of the tasting room bar and in many of the winery newsletters.

Feeling hungry and need a break from all that heavy duty sipping? The gift shop offers a variety of packaged food items that can be taken out to picnic tables by the creek, such as salami, cheese, sauces / spreads, crackers, and olives loaded with blue cheese or almonds.

For a more personalized gift, Wilson Creek will help you customize a label for a bottle of its Almond Champagne. Don't know what to say or create? Don't worry. Wilson Creek's in-house graphic artist is on hand to help. This unique gift is a perfect way to celebrate a birthday, wedding, holiday, birth, promotion, graduation, or to say "thank you" to a special friend.

☞ **Authors' Tip:** *Being a dedicated, un-reformed chocoholic, Cindy loves Wilson Creek's Dutch Chocolate "shot glass." Not only can you fill it with their award-winning chocolate port, but it can also be used for a very unique dessert when frozen and filled with chocolate mousse or slightly softened ice cream. It never fails to get a "Wow!" from our friends. Wilson Creek sells 12 shot glasses in a gold foiled box for approximately $20. (A word of caution: If you use a liquid, fill the shot glass to just below the rim and "sip first, then nibble." If you bite too aggressively, you will be wearing the contents – so take it slow and savor the flavor.)*

✪ *Grape Escapes Discount!* - Present a copy of this book and receive **Two-for-One tasting** for up to four guests (a $20 value). PLUS, present a copy of this book and receive a **10% discount** on all wines purchased on the day of your visit. Offers good Monday – Friday only, except on holidays. And if this is not reason enough to visit one of our favorite wineries, present a copy of **The Grape Escapes 2** and receive a **free glass of Almond champagne** for up to four guests (one glass per entrée) with your purchase of an entrée at the **Creekside Grille** located at Wilson Creek Winery. This is a $28 value and is valid Monday – Friday only, except on holidays.

"Winemaking is part art and part science.
Given the same grapes from the same vineyard and the same facilities, no
two winemakers will make the same wine."
~ Lewis Perdue, *The Wrath of Grapes*

WE'RE OFF TO SEE THE WIZARDS
(Favorite Wineries for Meeting the Winemaker)

We're off to see the wizards, the wonderful wizards of wines!

We know who the real wizards are – and they are not Harry Potter or Merlin. They are the passionate and driven men and women who cast their magic and create the red and golden elixirs we enjoy so much. We like to be in the presence of wizards, hanging on their every word and waiting for the magical secrets of winemaking to be revealed. If you like getting up close and personal with wizards and learning how they produce the potions we so enjoy, these are the wineries and tasting rooms we recommend you visit.

Boorman Vineyards Estate Winery
**21630 Ave de Arboles, Murrieta, CA 92562 ◆ Tel: 951-600-9333 ◆
Hours: By Appointment Only ◆ Website:** *www.boormanvineyards.com*

✪ *Grape Escapes Special Benefit* - Present a copy of this book and receive a **free "back-stage" tour** of the winery with the winemaker. *Advance appointment is required.*

Briar Rose Winery
**41720 Calle Cabrillo, Temecula, CA 92592 ◆ Tel: 951-308-1098 ◆
Hours: By Appointment Only ◆ Website:** *www.briarrosewinery.com*

Cougar Vineyard & Winery
**39870 De Portola Road, Temecula, CA 92592 ◆ Tel: 951-491-0825 ◆
Hours: Daily 11-6, Winter 11-5 ◆ Website:** *www.cougarvineyards.com*

Foote Print Winery
36650 Glen Oaks Road, Temecula, CA 92592 ♦ Tel: 951-265-9951 ♦ Hours: Fri 12-5, Sat-Sun 10-5, Mon-Thurs By Appointment ♦ Website: *www.footeprintwinery.com*

✪ *Grape Escapes Discount!* - Present a copy of this book and receive a **Two-for-One tasting!!!**

Frangipani Estate Winery
 39750 De Portola Road, Temecula, CA 92592 ♦ Tel: 951-699-8845 ♦ Hours: Daily 10-5 ♦ Website: *www.frangipaniwinery.com*

✪ *Grape Escapes Discount!* - Present a copy of this book and receive a **30% discount** on all wines purchased on the day of your visit.

Hart Winery
41300 Avenida Biona, Temecula, CA 92591 ♦ Tel: 951-676-6300 ♦ Hours: Daily 9-4:30 ♦ Website: *www.thehartfamilywinery.com*

Maurice Car'rie Winery
34225 Rancho California Road, Temecula, CA 92591 ♦ Tel: 951-676-1711 ♦ Hours: Daily 10-5 ♦ Website: *www.mauricecarriewinery.com*

✪ *Grape Escapes Discount!* - Present a copy of this book and receive a **10% discount** on all wines and tasting room merchandise purchased on the day of your visit. Sorry, but offer is not valid on weekends.

Palumbo Family Vineyards & Winery
40150 Barksdale Circle, Temecula, CA 92591 ♦ Tel: 951-676-7900 ♦ Hours: Fri 12-5, Sat-Sun 10-5, Mon-Thurs By Appointment ♦ Website: *www.palumbofamilyvineyards.com*

✪ *Grape Escapes Complimentary Tasting!* - Present a copy of this book and receive a **complimentary tasting for two people** in your party.

"We are the Champions – My Friends…" Queen (1977)

FAVORITE "HEAVY MEDAL" WINNING WINERIES

(Sampling the Award-Wining Wines)

There's Gold and Silver in them thar Temecula Hills. And Bronze, too.

We're going to get into a lot of trouble for this one. We just know it.

A large number of our readers enjoy seeking out wines that have earned the Gold, Silver, or Bronze medals. For the record, we know there are a lot more medal-winning wineries in the Temecula area than just the ones we recommend below.

So how did we arrive at the list? It wasn't easy. First, we researched data from over a half-dozen recent major regional and international wine competitions – the 2007 California State Fair, the 2007 San Francisco Chronicle Wine Competition, and the 2007 Riverside International Wine Competition, the 2007 and 2008 "Jerry D. Mead's" New World International Wine Competition (NWIWC), to name just a few.

What we were looking for were the Temecula Valley wineries that *consistently* did well in these competitions. With this data in hand, we went back to the tasting menus and checked to see which of these wineries actually had their award-winning wines *available for tasting*. With these criteria in mind, here are the wineries we recommend you visit to sample award-winning wines.

⇨ **By The Way – The hands-down winner for tasting award-winning wines is the South Coast Winery. According to Crystal Magnon, Marketing Director, South Coast's wines won an incredible 203 medals in 2007.**

Baily Vineyard & Winery
33440 La Serena Way, Temecula, CA 92591 ♦ Tel: 951-676-9463 ♦ Hours: Sun-Fri 11-5, Sat 10-5 ♦ Website: *www.bailywinery.com*

La Cereza Vineyard & Winery
34567 Rancho California Road, Temecula, CA 92591 ♦ Tel: 951-699-6961 ♦ Hours: Daily 10-5 ♦ Website: *www.lacerezawinery.com*

✿ *Grape Escapes Discount!* - Present a copy of this book Monday through Friday and receive a **10% discount** on all wines and tasting room merchandise purchased on the day of your visit. Sorry, but offer is not valid on weekends.

Mount Palomar Winery
33820 Rancho California Road, Temecula, CA 92591 ♦ Tel: 951-676-5047 ♦ Summer Hours: Mon-Thurs 10-6, Fri-Sun 10-7; Winter Hours: Closed Mon & Tues; Wed-Thur 10-5, Fri-Sun 10-6 ♦ Website: *www.mountpalomar. com*

✿ *Grape Escapes Discount!* - Present a copy of this book and receive a **Two-for-One tasting!!!**

Oak Mountain Winery / Temecula Hills Winery
36522 Via Verde, Temecula, CA 92592 ♦ Tel: 951-699-9102 ♦ Hours: Daily 11-5 ♦ Website: *www.oakmountainwinery. com*

✿ *Grape Escapes Discount!* - Present a copy of this book and receive a **10% discount** on all wines purchased on the day of your visit. Also, present a copy of this book and receive **Two-for-One tasting** for up to four guests. Offer does not include the souvenir logo glass.

South Coast Winery
34843 Rancho California Road, Temecula, CA 92591 ♦ Tel: 951-587-9463 ♦ Hours: Daily 10-6 ♦ Website: *www.wineresort.com*

Wiens Family Cellars
35055 Via Del Ponte, Temecula, CA   92592 ♦ Tel: 951-694-9892 ♦ Hours: Daily 10-5 ♦ Website: *www.wienscellars.com*

✪ *Grape Escapes Discount!* - Present a copy of this book and receive **Two-for-One wine tasting**, plus a **10% discount** on all wines purchased on the day of your visit. Also, present a copy of this book and receive a **free "back-stage" tour** of the winery with the winemaker. *Advance appointment is required.* Phone (951) 694-9892 to schedule.

Wilson Creek Winery & Vineyards
35960 Rancho California Road, Temecula, CA 92591 ♦ Tel: 951-699-9463 ♦ Hours: Daily 10-5 ♦ Website: *www.wilsoncreekwinery.com*

✪ *Grape Escapes Discount!* - Present a copy of this book and receive **Two-for-One tasting** for up to four guests (a $20 value). PLUS, present a copy of this book and receive a **10% discount** on all wines purchased on the day of your visit. Offers good Monday – Friday only, except on holidays. And if this is not reason enough to visit one of our favorite wineries, present a copy of *The Grape Escapes 2* and receive a **free glass of Almond Champagne** for up to four guests (one glass per entrée) with your purchase of an entrée at the **Creekside Grille** located at Wilson Creek Winery. This is a $28 value and is valid Monday – Friday only, except on holidays.

"There are no secrets to success. It is the result of preparation, hard work, and learning from failure." ~ Colin Powell

WINERY TOURS AND TASTINGS

Do you ever wonder how grapes are miraculously turned into hundreds of different wines? Did you know that many wine labels are personally designed by the winemaker or a family member and that each label generally has an intriguing story behind it?

One of the fun aspects of visiting wineries and vineyards is learning interesting and educational facts about the craft of cultivating grapes and the art of making wine. If you enjoy learning about the steps your favorite wine went through from the "grape to the bottle," we recommend taking a tour at any of the wineries listed below. Don't be afraid to ask questions. Most tour guides and winery staff are excited about their wines and love to share their knowledge, experiences, and humorous stories. You'll be surprised at what you learn!

☞ **Authors' Tip:** *Most of the smaller wineries do not offer scheduled or formal tours. Since these tasting rooms are usually run by the winemaker and / or owner, you may be able to get a quick "behind-the-scenes" tour if they are not busy with other guests.*

COMPLIMENTARY (FREE) WINERY TOURS
RESERVATIONS NOT REQUIRED

Note: The information contained in this guidebook was current at the time of publication, but is subject to change. Telephone numbers and website addresses are provided to assist the reader in obtaining up-to-date information.

Callaway Vineyard & Winery

32720 Rancho California Road, Temecula, CA 92591 ♦ Tel: 951-676-4001 ♦ Summer Hours: Daily 10-6, Winter Hours: 10-5 ♦ Website: *www.callawaywinery.com*

Callaway Vineyard and Winery is one of the largest and best known Temecula wineries that offers free public tours. Public tours (excluding tasting) last approximately 30 minutes and are conducted on weekends hourly between 11 AM to 4 PM. During the week, you can take tours at 11 AM, 1 PM, and 3 PM. (Reservations are required for groups of 20 or more.) *Be sure to arrive early* because this interesting tour is limited to 30 people and it fills up quickly on weekends and in summer.

Since Callaway was Temecula's first estate vineyard, the tour offers glimpses into the winery's history and vineyard practices. The tour visits the demonstration vines, crush pad, fermentation tanks, and barrel room. You will learn all about the winemaking process (from harvesting to bottling), as well as the vineyard management and conservation practices Callaway uses to sustain the land and nature.

☞ **Authors' Tip:** *If you want to know more about different styles of wine and wine tasting, make a reservation for the "Callaway Experience Tour and Wine Tasting." This tour is open to the public only on weekends following the 2 PM tour. See the "Callaway" entry under the "Winery Tours - Reservations Required" portion of this chapter for information on cost and reservation details.*

❂ *Grape Escapes Discount!* - Present a copy of this book and receive a **20% discount** on all wines and tasting room merchandise purchased on the day of your visit. Also, present a copy of this book and receive **Two-for-One tasting!!!**

Cougar Vineyard & Winery

39870 De Portola Road, Temecula, CA 92592 ♦ Tel: 951-491-0825 ♦ Hours: Daily 11-6, Winter 11-5 ♦ Website: *www.cougarvineyards.com*

Jennifer and Rick Buffington are the owners and winemakers at this small, friendly winery with very good wines. They are passionate about their wines and interested in educating others about the winemaking process.

Per Jennifer, they are generally willing to give individuals and small groups an impromptu tour of the equipment, tanks, and barrels, as well as explaining the activities going on at the winery on the day of your visit. They will probably do a sample "tank tasting" if they have wine in the tanks. When they are in the middle of bottling, they might be able to take you to see the process and perhaps give you a sample of what is being bottled.

Orfila Vineyards & Winery
13455 San Pasqual Road, Escondido, CA 92025 ♦ Tel: 760-738-6500 ♦ Hours: Daily 10-6 ♦ Website: *www.orfila. com*

Orfila Vineyards & Winery offers free winery tours at 2 PM daily. Leon Santoro, Orfila's winemaker, loves to educate people about the process of winemaking. The fun and interesting tour lasts approximately 30 minutes and takes guests through the vineyards, crush pad, production area and cellar (barrel room). Afterward, return to the Tasting Room where you can taste a sample of many of the wines you learned about for only $6. *Note: Since a portion of the tour includes walking outside in the vineyard over uneven ground, you should wear comfortable shoes.*

✪ *Grape Escapes Discount!* - Present a copy of this book and receive **free tasting** for up to four people in your party. In addition, you will also receive a **15% discount** on all wines purchased (except the Ambassador Reserve Merlot), plus a **10% discount** on all tasting room merchandise purchased on the day of your visit. Present a copy of this book and receive an additional **5% discount** (total of 20%) on a case or more of wine.

⇨ **By The Way – In 2003, Leon Santoro, Orfila's Winemaker and General Manager, was named Winemaker of the Year by the California Travel Industry Association.**

Thornton Winery
32575 Rancho California Road, Temecula, CA 92591 ♦ Tel: 951-699-0099 ♦ Hours: Daily 10-5 ♦ Website: *www.thorntonwinery.com*

Known world-wide for its award-winning sparkling wines ("champagne"), Thornton Winery strives to provide its guests with an elegant, unique tasting experience. Thornton's free guided winery tour lasts approximately 20-30 minutes. The tours are conducted only on weekends at 11 AM, 12:30 PM, 2 PM and 4 PM by specially trained Thornton staff.

The tour visits the crush pad where grapes are delivered and crushed, the tank room where wine is blended and processed, and the champagne caves (barrel room) where the aging process is explained. The tour concludes in the production area where the hosts describe the final steps of the méthode champenoise process used for sparkling wines (champagne).

Wiens Family Cellars
35055 Via Del Ponte, Temecula, CA   92592 ◆ Tel: 951-694-9892 ◆ Hours: Daily 10-5 ◆ Website: *www.wienscellars.com*

Free public 45 minute tours are conducted by the Wiens winemaker, Doug Wiens, each Saturday and Sunday at 2 PM and 4 PM and are offered on a "*first come, first served*" basis. Filled with interesting facts and stories about the winery's history and winemaking process, the tour takes guests to visit the vineyard, crush pad, tank room, and the production area. The last stop on the tour is the barrel room where lucky guests occasionally get to sample wines directly from the barrel before they are bottled.

✪ *Grape Escapes Discount!* - Present a copy of this book and receive **Two-for-One wine tasting**, plus a **10% discount** on all wines purchased on the day of your visit. Also, present a copy of this book and receive a free "back stage" tour of the winery with the winemaker. *Advance appointment is required*. Phone (951) 694-9892 to schedule.

WINERY TOURS
PARTICIPATION FEE & RESERVATIONS REQUIRED

Note: *Prices and times listed were accurate at the time of publication, but are subject to change.*

Bella Vista Winery
41220 Calle Contento, Temecula, CA 92592 ◆ Tel: 951-676-5250 ◆ Hours: Daily 10-6, Winter 10-5 ◆ Website: *www.bellavistawinery.com*

Private Tour and Tasting – $7 per person. Tours of the Bella Vista Winery operations are conducted *only on weekends*. Advance reservations are required for groups of 10 or more. The tour visits the winery grounds, crush pad, tank room, barrel room, and concludes in the tasting room where you sample five of Bella Vista's wines.

Callaway Vineyard & Winery
32720 Rancho California Road, Temecula, CA 92591 ♦ Tel: 951-676-4001 ♦ Summer Hours: Daily 10-6, Winter Hours: 10-5 ♦ Website: *www.callawaywinery.com*

Private Tour and Tasting – $15 per person. This fun and informative tour is conducted only for groups of 20 or more. The tour begins with an in-depth look at the winery and winemaking process, including the demonstration vines, crush pad, fermentation tanks, and barrel room. Next, you are taken to the Chardonnay Room for a personal one-on-one, sit-down tasting with a specially trained wine host. The host will guide you through wine tasting techniques and the styles and nuances of six specially selected wines.

⇨ **By The Way – Callaway's wines began to be known worldwide in 1976 at a New York City American Bi-Centennial Celebration when Queen Elizabeth II of Great Britain, who has a reputation for not being fond of wine, asked for a second glass of Callaway's 1974 White Riesling.**

Callaway Experience Tour & Wine Tasting – $15 per person. Want to experience a private tasting, but don't have a group? Make a reservation for this personalized tasting session that is offered only on weekends *following* the 2 PM public tour. After the tour, you are taken to the Chardonnay Room for a comfortable, intimate, seated wine sampling where the hosts explain various aspects of winemaking, wine styles and the wine tasting process. You will be given a taste of an unfinished wine from a fermentation tank and samples of five specially selected wines. This tour is limited to a total of 30 people and it fills up quickly.

Callaway's "Walk About the Barrel Room" – $65 per person. This event is held periodically throughout the year and gives guests the opportunity to taste their way through tanks and barrels with the Callaway Winemaker, Bela Varga. In addition, you get to experience the art of food and wine pairing with six different hors d'oeuvres (ranging from seafood to vegetables to dessert) specially designed by the Executive Chef of Callaway's Meritage Restaurant, Michael Henry.

During the tasting, Chef Henry explains how he designs menus based upon the wines being served. Occasionally, guests receive the opportunity to taste a soon-to-be-released wine and submit their ideas for a name.

✪ *Grape Escapes Discount!* - Present a copy of this book and receive a **20% discount** on all wines and tasting room merchandise purchased on the day of your visit. Also, present a copy of this book and receive **Two-for-One tasting!!!** The Two-for-One tasting discount does not apply to tours.

Falkner Winery
40620 Calle Contento, Temecula, CA 92591 ◆ **Tel: 951-676-8231** ◆ **Hours: Daily 10-5** ◆ **Website:** *www.falknerwinery.com*

Public guided tours – $3 per person. These one-hour tours are open to individuals and small groups (less than 10 people) and are conducted on the weekends at 11 AM and 2 PM. The tour takes you through the winemaking process as you visit the vineyards, crush pad, production area and the barrel room. You also get "up close and personal" with the equipment used in harvesting, processing, and winemaking. If you want to taste some of the great wines you learned about, samples are available in the Falkner Tasting Room for a small fee.

Private tours – $13 per person. Tours for larger groups (10 or more persons) are conducted by appointment during the week. In addition to the activities in the guided tour described above, the private tour also includes samples of at least six wines (including two of Falkner's premium wines). Many times, guests are offered wine tastes directly out of the barrels or holding tanks. Private tours last 60 – 90 minutes depending on the guests' interests / questions and the number of wines sampled.

Keyways Vineyard & Winery
37338 De Portola Road, Temecula, CA 92592 ◆ **Tel: 1-877-539-9297** ◆ **Hours: Daily 10-6, Winter 5** ◆ **Website:** *www.keywayswine.com*

Private tours – $20 per person. Keyways staff conducts tours of their winery for individuals, as well as groups. Tours are generally conducted on *weekends* and require reservations, especially for groups with 12 or more. The tour lasts approximately one hour.

During this fun and educational tour, you are escorted through many of the winery's operational areas, including the crush pad, production area, tank site, and the barrel room. The tour concludes in a private tasting area where your host will guide you through seven samples, (including a few of their premium wines, as well as port and ice wine,) and explain the fascinating history behind each varietal.

✪ *Grape Escapes Discount!* - Present a copy of this book and receive **Two-for-One tasting** from their "standard" tasting menu. Sorry, but offer is valid on weekdays only.

Leonesse Cellar
38311 De Portola Road, Temecula, CA 92592 ◆ Tel: 951-302-7601 ◆ Hours: Daily 10-5 ◆ Website: *www.leonessecellars.com*

Winery Tour and Tasting – $15 per person. This tour visits the crush pad in the production facility. You learn about the processes involved in harvesting, crushing, and fermenting the grapes. Then, it is on to the barrel room where the host discusses barrels and the effect they have on wine. All tours end in the tasting room where you are guided through a fun and educational wine-by-wine tasting filled with interesting facts about each varietal sampled. The basic tour lasts approximately 1 hour and 15 minutes.

VIP Tasting – $20 per person. This tasting orientation is conducted in the Leonesse VIP room. Your group will be shown a video presentation about winemaking that includes interviews with the winemaker and the owners of Leonesse. The VIP Tasting includes delicious cheeses and chocolates that are specially selected for pairing with Leonesse's Cellar Selection (CS) wines. The VIP Tasting lasts approximately 1 hour and 30 minutes.

VIP Winery Tour and Tasting – $25 per person. This two-hour tour is a combination of the Winery Tour and the VIP Tasting (described above). *It is well worth the extra $5!!!*

Winery Tour with VIP Tiered Tasting – $40 per person. This tour package not only combines the Winery Tour and the VIP Tasting, but it also features all three tiers of Leonesse's award-winning wines: Cellar Selection (CS), Vineyard Selection (VS), and Signature Selection (SS). The VS and SS wines are exclusive, limited production wines not available anywhere else for public tasting. Tim Kramer, Leonesse's winemaker was kind enough to share with us two of his Signature Selection Wines. *Simply put, these wines are what wines are supposed to be. This is a "must-see-taste-and-do" tour for wine lovers and aficionados!!*

Maurice Car'rie Winery
34225 Rancho California Road, Temecula, CA 92591 ◆ Tel: 951-676-1711 ◆ Hours: Daily 10-5 ◆ Website: *www.mauricecarriewinery.com*

Tours are offered by reservation only *for groups of 15 or more* and require a non-refundable deposit. *The winery does not conduct small group tours.* Visit the winery's website for the reservation form.

Winery Tour and Tasting – $15 per person. Each tour lasts approximately 30-45 minutes and includes sampling in the tasting room at the end of the tour. During the week, if the winemaker, Gus Vizgirda, is available, he will personally conduct your tour through the vineyard, crushing and tank areas, and barrel room.

☞ **Authors'Tip:** *In January 2008, we met with Gus and had a fantastic time learning about the sister wineries (Maurice Car'rie and La Cereza) and sampling their award-winning wines. We recommend you schedule your tour on a weekday. Weekends can be crowded at this popular winery and you may not get the personalized attention that is available during the week.*

✺ *Grape Escapes Discount!* – Present a copy of this book and receive a **10% discount** on all wines and tasting room merchandise purchased on the day of your visit. Sorry, but offer is not valid on weekends.

Mount Palomar Winery
33820 Rancho California Road, Temecula, CA 92591 ◆ Tel: 951-676-5047 ◆ Summer Hours: Mon-Thurs 10-6, Fri-Sun 10-7; Winter Hours: Closed Mon & Tues; Wed-Thur 10-5, Fri-Sun 10-6 ◆ Website: *www.mountpalomar. com*

Mount Palomar offers four levels of private tours *for groups of 15 or more.* The tours last approximately one hour and end with wine samples served on one of the patios or in the barrel room. Reservation and payment instructions are located on the winery's website.

Tour with Traditional Tasting – $10 per person. The basic tour includes a private tour and a tasting of six wines from the Traditional menu. You can purchase additional refreshments, such as dips, salads, sandwiches, or dessert for an extra charge.

Tour with Traditional Tasting and Snacks – $15 per person. For those who want a little something extra, this tour includes the private tour and wines from the traditional menu, plus crackers, Palomar port jelly, and chocolate kisses.

Tour with Premier Tasting – $15 per person. Wine lovers should try this tour which includes the private tour and samples of eight wines from the Premier menu. Refreshments are available for an extra charge.

Tour with Premier Tasting and Snacks – $20 per person. If you are interested in wine and cheese pairings, this tour is for you. It includes the private tour, plus eight Premier wines and a platter of assorted cheeses and crackers.

✪ **Grape Escapes Discount!** - Present a copy of this book and receive a **Two-for-One tasting**!!! The Two-for-One discount does not apply to tours.

Ponte Family Estate Winery
35053 Rancho California Road, Temecula, CA 92591 ♦ Tel: 951-694-8855 ♦ Hours: Daily 10-5 ♦ Website: *www.pontewinery.com*

Private Tour & Tasting – $15. Ponte conducts its private tours for groups of *four people or more*. The tour lasts approximately 45 minutes (excluding the tasting) and reservations are required. Tours are conducted during normal tasting room hours Monday thru Friday. However, *on the weekend, private tours are only conducted before 12 noon.*

Guests are taken on a fun and educational tour of the winery and its equipment (including the crush pad, the production and tank areas, and the barrel room). Hosts explain the part each plays in the winemaking process. Those taking this tour are in for a treat – hosts routinely offer guests tastes of wine straight out of the huge fermentation tanks and / or the giant oak barrels. The tour concludes in the Tasting Room where guests sample five specially selected Ponte Vineyard wines and its famous Port.

☞ **Authors' Tip:** *Ponte offers a unique feature with its private tour – After the tour and tasting, guests obtain a 10% DISCOUNT on wine and / or gift purchases in the Ponte Marketplace!*

✪ *Grape Escapes Discount!* - Present a copy of this book and receive a **Two-for-One tasting**!!! Offer valid Monday - Thursday, except holidays. The Two-for-One discount does not apply to tours.

Robert Renzoni Vineyards
37350 De Portola Road, Temecula, CA 92592 ♦ Tel: 951-302-8466 ♦ Hours: Daily 11-6 ♦ Website: *www. robertrenzonivineyards.com*

Private Tour & Tasting – $15 per person. Reservations are required for the private tours of this newly opened winery. The small, intimate tours last approximately 30 minutes and are usually lead by the winemaker. If weather permits, the tour begins with a short hike up the hill to a scenic overlook of the property. Next, you walk through a portion of the vineyard and the winemaking facility (crush pad, production and tank areas, and barrel room).

If you are lucky and your visit coincides with the harvest or production cycle, you might be offered a block grape sampling, a tank / barrel taste, or some other unique activity involved in the winemaking process! The tour concludes in the tasting room with a sampling of five of the Robert Renzoni Vineyard wines.

☞ **Authors' Tip:** *Since a portion of the Renzoni tour includes walking outside over uneven ground and up a small hill, you should wear comfortable shoes. Special arrangements can be made for visitors who are unable to participate in the outside walking portions of the tour.*

✪ *Grape Escapes Discount!* - Present a copy of this book and receive a **10% discount** on all wines and tasting room merchandise purchased on the day of your visit. Also, present a copy of this book and receive an additional **10% discount** (total of 20%) on a case or more of wine. The discounts do not apply to tour prices.

South Coast Winery, Resort & Spa
34843 Rancho California Road, Temecula, CA 92591 ♦ Tel: 951-587-9463 ♦ Hours: Daily 10-6 ♦ Website: *www.wineresort.com*

Prepare to be pampered! South Coast Winery offers specially designed tours and tastings for individuals and small groups.

Behind the Scene Tour and Private Tasting – $20 per person. These tours are limited to 20 people and are conducted once daily, Monday thru Friday at 10:30 AM and twice on Saturday and Sunday at 10:30 AM and 12:30 PM. The walking portion of the tour lasts approximately 30-45 minutes and is lead by South Coast's wine specialists.

You visit the vineyard, the crush pad, and the production area. You may even get a chance to sample wine right out of the barrels! Once you understand how the magic happens, you are then escorted to a private area where you are guided through a sit-down tasting of five specially selected wines, along with a fruit and artisanal cheese plate chosen to complement the wine.

Stuart Cellars
33515 Rancho California Road, Temecula, CA 92591 ♦ Tel: 951-676-6414 ♦ Hours: Daily 10-5 ♦ Website: *www.stuartcellars.com*

Tour and Tasting – $15 per person. Guided, public tours are offered on *weekends* at 11 AM, 2 PM, and 4 PM. During the week, call to schedule a specific time. Nathan, the "official" tour guide, leads you through an entertaining visit to the vineyards, crush pad, tank yard, barrel room, bottling line, and the lab / testing room. This is one of the few wineries that generally allows the public to view the laboratory area. The tour ends with a sampling of five wines in a souvenir glass.

Thornton Winery
32575 Rancho California Road, Temecula, CA 92591 ♦ Tel: 951-699-0099 ♦ Hours: Daily 10-5 ♦ Website: *www.thorntonwinery.com*

Private Tour and Tasting – $15. The tour visits the crush pad where grapes are delivered and crushed, the tank room where wine is blended and processed, and the champagne caves (barrel room) where the aging process is explained. The final stop is in the production area where the host describes the various steps in the méthode champenoise process used to make sparkling wines (champagne).

Then, it is on to the tasting room where guests are seated at a private table and treated to a sample of three specially selected still wines and one sparkling wine (champagne), along with artisan bread and a delicious goat cheese / cream cheese spread.

"...if I could win the admiration of my peers,
I could do anything." ~ Lou Ferrigno (The Hulk)

SURVEY SAYS...
(Temecula Winemakers' Favorites)

One of the best things about doing the research for this book was talking to dozens of winemakers and attempting to extract their secrets. While most kept mum about their unique winemaking techniques, they were willing to share the names of the winemakers and wineries whose wines they most admire.

The envelope, if you please. ...... *(Dramatic pause to allow the suspense to build.)*

1ST PLACE: Okay, the winner is.... in First Place, Joe Hart and **Hart Winery**. Yaaay! Congratulations, Joe. Your peers think you and your wines are simply the best.

Hart Winery
41300 Avenida Biona, Temecula, CA 92591 ♦ Tel: 951-676-6300 ♦ Hours: Daily 9-4:30 ♦ Website: *www.thehartfamilywinery.com*

2ND PLACE: **South Coast Winery** (Jon McPherson and Javier Flores, winemakers) and **Leonesse Cellars** (Tim Kramer, winemaker) finished second in a photo-finish.

Leonesse Cellars
38311 De Portola Road, Temecula, CA 92592 ♦ Tel: 951-302-7601 ♦ Hours: Daily 10-5 ♦ Website: *www.leonessecellars. com*

South Coast Winery
34843 Rancho California Road, Temecula, CA 92591 ♦ Tel: 951-587-9463 ♦ Hours: Daily 10-6 ♦ Website: *www.wineresort.com*

3RD PLACE: Nick Palumbo, owner and winemaker, **Palumbo Family Vineyards & Winery**.

Palumbo Family Vineyards & Winery
40150 Barksdale Circle, Temecula, CA 92591 ✦ **Tel: 951-676-7900** ✦ **Hours: Fri 12-5, Sat-Sun 10-5, Mon-Thurs By Appointment** ✦ **Website:** *www.palumbofamilyvineyards.com*

✪ *Grape Escapes Complimentary Tasting!* - Present a copy of this book and receive a **complimentary tasting for two people** in your party.

4TH PLACE: **Ponte Family Estate Winery, Stuart Cellars, and Wilson Creek Winery** were the fourth most-recommended wineries in our informal survey.

Ponte Family Estate Winery
35053 Rancho California Road, Temecula, CA 92591 ✦ **Tel: 951-694-8855** ✦ **Hours: Daily 10-5** ✦ **Website:** *www. pontewinery.com*

✪ *Grape Escapes Discount!* - Present a copy of this book and receive a **Two-for-One tasting!!!** Offer valid Monday Through Thursday, excluding holidays.

Stuart Cellars
33515 Rancho California Road, Temecula, CA 92591 ✦ **Tel: 951-676-6414** ✦ **Hours: Daily 10-5** ✦ **Website:** *www. stuartcellars.com*

Wilson Creek Winery & Vineyards
35960 Rancho California Road, Temecula, CA 92591 ✦ **Tel: 951-699-9463** ✦ **Hours: Daily 10-5** ✦ **Website:** *www. wilsoncreekwinery.com*

✪ *Grape Escapes Discount!* - Present a copy of this book and receive **Two-for-One tasting** for up to four guests (a $20 value). PLUS, present a copy of this book and receive a **10% discount** on all wines purchased on the day of your visit. Offers good Monday – Friday only, except on holidays. And if this is not reason enough to visit one of our favorite wineries, present a copy of *The Grape Escapes 2* and receive a **free glass of Almond Champagne** for up to four guests (one glass per entrée) with your purchase of an entrée at the **Creekside Grille** located at Wilson Creek Winery. This is a $28 value and is valid Monday – Friday only, except on holidays.

⇨ **By The Way** – Temecula's population in 1980 was less than 10,000. Today it is has over 100,000 residents.

"…wine [is] a constant proof that God loves us
and loves to see us happy." ~ Benjamin Franklin

THE PRICE IS RIGHT
(Wines Under $15)

If you are a person who says, "I'm-not-gonna-pay-a-lot-for-my-wine," or
if you simply cannot resist a great bargain, we recommend stopping by the
wineries listed below. Their tasting rooms offer good, but inexpensive
wines. Some are even award winners.

WHITE WINES…

Baily Vineyard & Winery
33440 La Serena Way, Temecula, CA 92591 ◆ Tel: 951-676-9463 ◆
Hours: Sun-Fri 11-5, Sat 10-5 ◆ Website: *www.bailywinery.com*

Bella Vista Winery
41220 Calle Contento, Temecula, CA 92592 ◆ Tel: 951-676-5250 ◆
Hours: Daily 10-6, Winter 10-5 ◆ Website: *www.bellavistawinery.com*

La Cereza Vineyard & Winery
34567 Rancho California Road, Temecula, CA 92591 ◆ Tel: 951-699-
6961 ◆ Hours: Daily 10-5 ◆ Website: *www.lacerezawinery.com*

✪ *Grape Escapes Discount!* - Present a copy of this book and receive a
10% discount on all wines and tasting room merchandise purchased on
the day of your visit. Sorry, but offer is not valid on weekends.

Maurice Car'rie Winery
34225 Rancho California Road, Temecula, CA 92591 ◆ Tel: 951-676-
1711 ◆ Hours: Daily 10-5 ◆ Website: *www. mauricecarriewinery.com*

✪ *Grape Escapes Discount!* - Present a copy of this book and receive a **10% discount** on all wines and tasting room merchandise purchased on the day of your visit. Sorry, but offer is not valid on weekends.

Oak Mountain Winery / Temecula Hills Winery
36522 Via Verde, Temecula, CA 92592 ✦ **Tel: 951-699-9102** ✦ **Hours: Daily 11-5** ✦ **Website:** *www.oakmountainwinery. com*

✪ *Grape Escapes Discount!* - Present a copy of this book and receive a **10% discount** on all wines purchased on the day of your visit. Also, present a copy of this book and receive **Two-for-One tasting** for up to four guests. Offer does not include the souvenir logo glass.

Orfila Vineyards & Winery
13455 San Pasqual Road, Escondido, CA 925025 ✦ **Tel: (760) 738-6500** ✦ **Hours: Daily 10-6** ✦ **Website:** *www.Orfila. com*

✪ *Grape Escapes Discount!* - Present a copy of this book and receive **free tasting** for up to four people in your party. In addition, you will also receive a **15% discount** on all wines purchased (except the Ambassador Reserve Merlot), plus a **10% discount** on all tasting room merchandise purchased on the day of your visit. Present a copy of this book and receive an additional **5% discount** (total of 20%) on a case or more of wine. Also, present a copy of this book and receive a **free "back-stage" tour** of the winery. Appointment required.

South Coast Winery
34843 Rancho California Road, Temecula, CA 92591 ✦ **Tel: 951-587-9463** ✦ **Hours: Daily 10-6** ✦ **Website:** *www. wineresort.com*

RED WINES…

Filsinger Vineyards & Winery, Inc.
39050 De Portola Road, Temecula, CA 92592 ✦ **Tel: 951-302-6363** ✦ **Hours: Fri 11-4, Sat-Sun 10-5** ✦ **Website:** *www. filsingerwinery.com*

South Coast Winery
34843 Rancho California Road, Temecula, CA 92591 ✦ **Tel: 951-587-9463** ✦ **Hours: Daily 10-6** ✦ **Website:** *www. wineresort.com*

SPARKLING WINES...

South Coast Winery
34843 Rancho California Road, Temecula, CA 92591 ◆ Tel: 951-587-9463 ◆ Hours: Daily 10-6 ◆ Website: *www. wineresort.com*

Wilson Creek Winery & Vineyards
35960 Rancho California Road, Temecula, CA 92591 ◆ Tel: 951-699-9463 ◆ Hours: Daily 10-5 ◆ Website: *www. wilsoncreekwinery.com*

✪ *Grape Escapes Discount!* - Present a copy of this book and receive **Two-for-One tasting** for up to four guests (a $20 value). PLUS, present a copy of this book and receive a **10% discount** on all wines purchased on the day of your visit. Offers good Monday – Friday only, except on holidays. And if this is not reason enough to visit one of our favorite wineries, present a copy of *The Grape Escapes 2* and receive a **free glass of Almond Champagne** for up to four guests (one glass per entrée) with your purchase of an entrée at the **Creekside Grille located** at Wilson Creek Winery. This is a $28 value and is valid Monday – Friday only, except on holidays.

ROAD TRIP... ROAD TRIP ...
ROAD TRIP!!!

If the refrain "ROAD TRIP... ROAD TRIP... ROAD TRIP" creates a mental image of John Belushi, of ***Animal House*** fame, crushing a beer can against his forehead, this is not exactly what we were aiming for with this title.

We like the enthusiasm, though. There is nothing like a "road trip" to get the juices flowing. Even if you arrived in Temecula by car, there's nothing that says you cannot take a mini-road trip while in Temecula Wine Country. We have two great road trips for you to take:

Boorman Vineyards Estate Winery
Distance from Temecula: 20 Miles
Proprietors:	Todd and Rosie Boorman
Telephone:	(951) 600-9333
Hours:	By Appt Only
Website:	*www.boormanvineyards.com*
Address:	21630 Ave de Arboles, Murrieta, CA 92562
Production:	1,200 cases per year
Tasting Fee:	Complimentary
Varietals:	(Authors' Recommendations ★):
Reds:	Barbera ★, Cabernet Sauvignon ★, Cabernet Franc ★, Merlot

Average Wine Prices: Reds: $$$

The Boormans are great people who produce great wines. In fact, should Todd or Rosie call you up and tell you they would like to send you some wine, don't ask questions. Don't ask about the types of red wines they are sending; just dig out the credit card. *All* their wines are outstanding.

By day Todd Boorman is a paramedic / fireman. When not working at the fire department, he spends his days managing three vineyards, including his own. His winery produces some amazing red wines. And he makes them the old fashion way: with care, attention to detail and *extreme* winemaking.

What do we mean by *extreme* winemaking? Todd may be the most intense winemaker we've ever met. He studies everything – the angle of the sun, the temperature profile, the soil, the best barrels for his varietals and on and on. His goal is to get the absolute most out of his grapes and we think he succeeds tremendously by making some of the best wines we have sampled.

Call for an appointment. It is only 20 miles from Temecula Wine Country and the drive to their 2000-foot elevation winery is a very pretty one. Here are the directions, so you have no excuse not to go.

> **Directions to Boorman Vineyards Estate Winery:** Exit the I-15 Freeway in Murrieta at Clinton Keith Road and go west 3.8 miles to Avenue La Cresta. Turn Right. Go 0.2 miles and Avenue La Cresta turns to the right. Go past the guard station (no need to stop) and continue for an additional 2.8 miles until you hit Calle Centro. Turn right. Go 200 yards to Avenida de Arboles and turn right. Go 0.7 miles to 21630 Avenida de Arboles which will be on your left. You've arrived at one of our favorite wine tasting destinations.

✪ *Grape Escapes Special Benefit* - Present a copy of this book and receive a **free "back-stage" tour** of the winery with the winemaker. *Advance appointment is required.*

* * *

The second "Road Trip" winery we recommend is **Orfila Vineyards & Winery** located in Escondido.

Orfila Vineyards & Winery
Distance from Temecula: 36 miles (40 minutes)
Proprietor: Ambassador Alejandro Orfila
Telephone: (760) 738-6500 or 1-800-868-9463
Hours: Open 7 Days, 10 AM - 6 PM
Website: *www.orfila.com*
Address: 13455 San Pasqual Road, Escondido, CA   92025
Production: 15,000 cases per year

Tasting Fee: Free for wine club members. For non-wine club members, the first taste is free and then it is $6 for five additional tastes.

Varietals: (Authors' Recommendations ★):

Whites: Chardonnay, Gewürztraminer ★, Riesling ★, Viognier, and various Blends ★
Reds: Cabernet Sauvignon, Merlot ★, Sangiovese, Syrah ★, Zinfandel ★

Average Wine Prices: Whites: $$ Reds: $$

Set among beautifully landscaped lawns and gardens, **Orfila Vineyards & Winery** has a lovely flag-draped tasting room in Escondido, which is about a forty minute drive from Temecula on Highway 15 South. Orfila is easy to find.

> From Temecula, take the I-15 south toward San Diego for 32 miles and exit onto Via Rancho Parkway. Turn right onto the parkway and follow it for one mile where Via Rancho becomes Bear Valley Parkway. Turn Right onto San Pasqual Road. Orfila's tasting room is only a mile further along this road.

Once at Orfila, you are in for a true treat. Leon Santoro, General Manager and Winemaker, has a wonderful selection of wines that includes Chardonnay, Sangiovese, Riesling, Marsanne, Roussanne, Merlot, and Cabernet.

Leon's great wines are no accident. After immigrating to the US from Italy, he worked at some of the top Northern California wineries, including Louis Martini, Stag's Leap, and Quail Ridge. Upon his arrival at Orfila, he was not satisfied with the quality of grapes and ultimately grafted and planted a total of seventeen different varietals before identifying the ones that grow best on the vineyard's forty acres.

"Good fruit equals good wine," according to Leon and it all begins in the vineyard. The Orfila Vineyard is at 700 feet elevation and is only twelve miles from the Pacific Ocean – a bit closer than the Temecula Valley vineyards. You should enjoy comparing Leon's wines to Temecula Valley wines and identifying how the wines from these two areas differ in taste and characteristics.

It is not just flags that hang from the tasting room walls and ceilings. Orfila has done extremely well on the competition circuit and their ribbons and awards are also proudly on display. Their 2005 "Gold Rush" Zinfandel won Gold at the 2008 San Francisco Chronicle Wine Competition – as did their 2006 White Riesling. The 2004 Estate Sangiovese "Di Collina" won Gold and Best of Class in the 2007 SF Chronicle Wine Competition and their 2004 Estate Syrah took Double Gold and Best of Class at the Florida State Fair International Wine Competition.

⇨ **By The Way – Only about 5% of wines submitted in a wine competition earn a Gold Medal.**

If there are those in your group that believe Southern California cannot compete with the wines of Napa and Sonoma, you only have to take them to Orfila to put a pleasant end to this particular argument.

⇨ **By The Way – Orfila Vineyards & Winery won four Bronze Medals at the 2008 New World International Wine Competition. Their winners were: the "Lot 34" Coastal Cuvée, the 2006 White Riesling, the 2006 Chardonnay and the 2005 Sangiovese. In addition, their 2005 Coastal Cuvée Merlot won Gold at the 2008 Monterey Wine Competition. Congratulations, Leon!**

☘ *Grape Escapes Discount!* - Present a copy of this book and receive **free tasting** for up to four people in your party. In addition, you will also receive a **15% discount** on all wines purchased (except the Ambassador Reserve Merlot), plus a **10% discount** on all tasting room merchandise purchased on the day of your visit. Present a copy of this book and receive an additional **5% discount** (total of 20%) on a case or more of wine. Also, present a copy of this book and receive a **free "back-stage" tour** of the winery. Appointment required.

"Whatever women do they must do twice as well as men to be thought half as good. Luckily this is not difficult."
~ Charlotte Whitton

CHICKS RULE!!!

The following recommended wineries are run almost exclusively by women or have female winemakers. Now relax guys. We know what you are thinking. Your ladies are going to try and drag you to some *froufrou* places. Right? Wrong! What you will find at the following wineries are great wines, friendly people, and the fine attention to detail that only the fairer sex can bring to wine tasting. We think after you visit these great establishments that even guys will agree, *Chicks Rule!!!* However, chances are the men will never admit it publicly.

Cougar Vineyard & Winery
39870 De Portola Road, Temecula, CA 92592 ◆ Tel: 951-491-0825 ◆ Hours: Daily 11-6, Winter 11-5 ◆ Website: *www.cougarvineyards.com*

Keyways Vineyard & Winery
37338 De Portola Road, Temecula, CA 92592 ◆ Tel: 1-877-539-9297 ◆ Hours: Daily 10-6, Winter 5 ◆ Website: *www.keywayswine.com*

✪ *Grape Escapes Discount!* - Present a copy of this book and receive **Two-for-One tasting** from their "standard" tasting menu. Sorry, but offer is valid on weekdays only.

☞ **Authors' Tip:** *Many of the wineries conduct fun and exciting bridal information events where "brides-to-be" learn about and tour the winery's ceremony / reception facilities and services; get information on floral, photography, bakery, and music vendors; and find out about wedding trends and "insider" tips for planning the perfect ceremony and reception. Contact each winery's Events Coordinator and check their websites for more information.*

Oak Mountain Winery / Temecula Hills Winery

36522 Via Verde, Temecula, CA 92592 ◆ **Tel: 951-699-9102** ◆ **Hours: Daily 11-5** ◆ Website: *www.oakmountainwinery.com*

✪ *Grape Escapes Discount!* - Present a copy of this book and receive a **10% discount** on all wines purchased on the day of your visit. Also, present a copy of this book and receive **Two-for-One tasting** for up to four guests. Offer does not include the souvenir logo glass.

⇨ **By The Way** – "Woofs and Purrs in the Vines" is an annual charity food and wine event hosted by "Cause for Paws" and Oak Mountain Winery. The event raises money to cover the medical expenses of animals with diabetes.

WINERY ACTIVITIES AND WINES DESIGNED WITH "CHICKS" IN MIND

Even "Ruling" Chicks need a little pampering and special attention now and then.

Keyways Vineyard & Winery

37338 De Portola Road, Temecula, CA 92592 ◆ **Tel: 1-877-539-9297** ◆ **Hours: Daily 10-6, Winter 5 PM** ◆ Website: *www.keywayswine.com*

Femina Vita (Life of a Woman) Festival – Each year Keyways hosts it famous two-day arts and crafts festival to celebrate its "Femina Vita" series wines – "wines created by women for women." In addition to getting the opportunity to enjoy some of Keyways' fabulous food, wine, and music – you also get to meet local artisans who will be demonstrating and displaying their crafts. But perhaps the most important reason for attending Keyways' *Femina Vita Festival* is to help others. Keyways owner, Terri Pebley, always donates a portion of the proceeds from each *Femina Vita Festival* to a local charity.

✪ *Grape Escapes Discount!* - Present a copy of this book and receive **Two-for-One tasting** from their "standard" tasting menu. Sorry, but offer is valid on weekdays only.

La Cereza Vineyard & Winery

34567 Rancho California Road, Temecula, CA 92591 ◆ Tel: 951-699-6961 ◆ Hours: Daily 10-5 ◆ Website: *www.lacerezawinery.com*

La Cereza is another winery that has created a series of special wines that focuses on women's distinctive tastes. (If you want to know why women and men seem to prefer different style wines, see our *Wine Tasting for Beginner's 102 – A Difference Between the Sexes?* chapter.)

Michelle's Place Series Wine – In 2007, La Cereza created two "Michelle's Place" wines. "Hope" and "Miracles Happen" are special blends of Syrah, Grenache, and Chenin Blanc. This series of lighter wines with some berry and melon characteristics is dedicated to Michelle Watson for whom Temecula Valley's breast cancer center, Michelle's Place, is named. A portion of the proceeds from each bottle sold is donated to the center in honor of Michelle Watson and her family.

Girlfriends Wine – Per Cheri Linn, co-owner of the La Cereza Winery, samples of this special blend of white wines were tested on many of her girlfriends until just the right combination was reached. This lighter style white wine has flavors of citrus, melon and papaya. Another fun thing about this wine is its label. It features a "mature," white-haired and bespectacled woman lounging in a doorway of a stone building – smoking a big cigar. The "Girlfriends" wine has been such a hit at La Cereza that they have introduced a line of "Girlfriends" clothing and jewelry – and a "Girlfriends" cigar which is specially sized to fit a woman's smaller hand. The cigar is 6.5 inches long and has a "smooth creamy taste with buttery overtones." We'll let you in on a secret – the winery sells a whole lot of these to men who also enjoy the "Girlfriends" Corona Light cigar.

Peach Girls Sparking Wine – Ladies, if you are in the mood to celebrate, you simply must try La Cereza's "Peach Girls" peach-flavored sparkling wine (champagne). You can't help but smile when you see the label of this non-vintage wine – three colorfully dressed, and very rotund, ladies are shown with their champagne glasses held high overhead and huge peach colored bubbles float in the background.

✪ *Grape Escapes Discount!* - Present a copy of this book on and receive a **10% discount** on all wines and tasting room merchandise purchased on the day of your visit. Sorry, but offer is not valid on weekends.

South Coast Winery
34843 Rancho California Road, Temecula, CA 92591 ♦ Tel: 951-587-9463 ♦ Hours: Daily 10-6 ♦ Website: *www. wineresort.com*

Women's Wine and Wellness Weekend – South Coast Winery, Resort, & Spa has developed a weekend getaway designed especially for "chicks" who are ready to *relax, be pampered, and get de-stressed!* This special women's wellness event is an "all inclusive" weekend that is held annually. Not only does it include two nights' stay in one of South Coast Resort's luxury villas, some wine, and all your meals, but you also get two signature spa treatments at South Coast Resort's famous Grape Seed Spa, multiple Wellness Sessions, and a winery tour. Some of the Wellness Sessions focus on yoga, meditation, and healthy cooking. So, get together with your girlfriends or relatives and treat yourself to a wonderful experience – you deserve it!

⇨ **By The Way – In 2006, South Coast Winery unveiled Ruby Cuvée, a sparkling light and fruity Shiraz wine, as its first wine developed especially for women. The wine was created at the request of Jim Carter, South Coast's owner, as a tribute to his Aunt Ruby.**

Wilson Creek Winery & Vineyards
35960 Rancho California Road, Temecula, CA 92591 ♦ Tel: 951-699-9463 ♦ Hours: Daily 10-5 ♦ Website: *www.wilsoncreekwinery.com*

Spring Spa Day – Wilson Creek sponsors an extravagant day of pampering for ladies at the Pala Casino Resort & Spa a few times each year. The special event begins at Wilson Creek where the ladies sample Almond Champagne mimosas and enjoy a continental breakfast. Then guests are taken to the Pala Spa aboard a luxury shuttle from *The Grapeline®*. In addition to lounging around the pool in private cabanas stocked with fruit and cheese platters (and Wilson Creek wines), you and your gal-pals get to unwind with massages, facials, and pedicures.

✪ *Grape Escapes Discount!* - Present a copy of this book and receive **Two-for-One tasting** for up to four guests (a $20 value). PLUS, present a copy of this book and receive a **10% discount** on all wines purchased on the day of your visit. Offers good Monday – Friday only, except on holidays. And if this is not reason enough to visit one of our favorite wineries, present a copy of *The Grape Escapes 2* and receive a **free glass of Almond Champagne** for up to four guests (one glass per entrée) with your purchase of an Entrée at the **Creekside Grille** located at Wilson Creek Winery. This is a $28 value and is valid Monday – Friday only, except on holidays.

"I need that on stage. I need a burst of life.
That's entertainment for me." ~ Tina Turner

"NOW, THAT'S ENTERTAINMENT!"

It's the weekend – you are bored and have nothing to do. Where should you go for some unique entertainment? Head for the wineries in Temecula! Want to attend a concert? They have it. Want to dance? They have that, too. Looking for theater? Ditto. One of the wineries even offers you a chance to ride a mechanical bull! What more could you ask for?

Here's a look at the Temecula wineries that offer a **recurring series** of entertainment programs.

☞ **Authors' Tip:** *Many wineries host unique programs that are offered only one time each season. However, more wineries are beginning to host multiple programs during the Summer and early Fall. For more information on the following special programs and other events, check out the websites for the individual wineries, as well as the websites listed in our Internet Links chapter in the back of this guidebook.*

Falkner Winery
40620 Calle Contento, Temecula, CA 92591 ◆ Tel: 951-676-8231 ◆ Hours: Daily 10-5 ◆ Website: *www.falknerwinery.com*

Jazz Concerts – Relax on Falkner Winery's lovely lawn area and sip their award-winning wines while listening to free outdoor live Jazz concerts every Sunday afternoon (May-June).

Frangipani Estate Winery
 **39750 De Portola Road, Temecula, CA 92592 ◆ Tel: 951-699-8845 ◆
Hours: Daily 10-5 ◆ Website:** *www.frangipaniwinery.com*

"Wine, Dine and Entertain Series" and *"Shakespeare in the Vines"* – This hilltop winery and tasting room is Wine Country's answer for theater lovers. Frangipani Estate Winery hosts a wide variety of small stage productions throughout the year – ranging from musical reviews and Broadway classics to Shakespeare's comedies. Some of the past productions featured an Elvis tribute artist, the Tony Award-winning drama "Proof," the Las Vegas lounge-style "Sinatra and Friends," and an Andrew Lloyd Webber musical review. In 2008, Shakespeare's *Twelfth Night* and *Taming of the Shrew* will be presented.

✺ *Grape Escapes Discount!* - Present a copy of this book and receive a **30% discount** on all wines purchased on the day of your visit.

Keyways Vineyard & Winery
**37338 De Portola Road, Temecula, CA 92592 ◆ Tel: 1-877-539-9297 ◆
Hours: Daily 10-6, Winter 5 ◆ Website:** *www.keywayswine.com*

"Music and Wine" – Most Sundays, Keyways Winery presents four hours of free musical concerts ranging from Country to Smooth Jazz. Bring a picnic and experience the exciting and up-beat entertainment in a laid-back outdoor setting. In summer, Keyways Winery sometimes creates homemade sangria "smoothies" for you to enjoy while listening to your favorite tunes.

✺ *Grape Escapes Discount!* - Present a copy of this book and receive **Two-for-One tasting** from their "standard" tasting menu. Sorry, but offer is valid on weekdays only.

Longshadow Ranch Vineyard & Winery
**39847 Calle Contento, Temecula, CA 92591 ◆ Tel: 951-587-6221 ◆
Hours: Mon-Fri 12-5, Sat 10-4 (Sat Bonfire 5-9 PM April through October), Sun 10-5 ◆ Website:** *www.longshadowranchwinery.com*

"Bonfire Saturday Nights" – Every Saturday night at 5 PM from mid-April until November, Longshadow Ranch Winery hosts one of the most talked about high-energy, *family* fun night events in the Temecula area! Live music (including Classic Rock) is the highlight, but there is also dancing,

horse drawn carriage rides, and kid's movies in the barn with free popcorn. BBQ and snacks are available for a nominal fee. On some nights, you can even try your luck on a mechanical bull! Although this event is for wine club members only, guest passes and reservations can sometimes be acquired through the tasting room.

☺ *Grape Escapes Discount!* - Present a copy of this book and receive a **10% discount** on all wines purchased on the day of your visit.

Maurice Car'rie Winery & La Cereza Vineyard & Winery
34225 Rancho California Road, Temecula, CA 92591 ♦ Tel: 951-676-1711 ♦ Hours: Daily 10-5 ♦ Website: *www.mauricecarriewinery.com; www.lacerezawinery.com*

Summer Concert Series – Sister wineries Maurice Car'rie and La Cereza host some of the nation's best known musicians, soloists, and groups in their Summer Concert Series. Ranging from Flamenco Spanish guitar artists to 80's rock music groups to star performers, the live concerts are held in the La Cereza courtyard in summer. In 2008, performers scheduled to appear include The Motels with Martha Davis, Benise, and Kris Kristofferson.

☺ *Grape Escapes Discount!* - Present a copy of this book on and receive a **10% discount** on all wines and tasting room merchandise purchased on the day of your visit. Sorry, but offer is not valid on weekends.

Miramonte Winery / Celebration Cellars
33410 Rancho California Road, Temecula, CA 92591 ♦ Tel: 951-506-5500 ♦ Hours: Daily 11-6, Music Fri & Sat 5:30-8:30 PM ♦ Website: *www.miramontewinery.com*

Join Miramonte Winery for some unique after-hours wine tasting and entertainment! Enjoy Miramonte's famous Sangria, delicious food, beautiful sunsets, and panoramic valley views. A $6 - $8 per person cover charge includes your initial wine tasting. *(Wine Club members are admitted free.)* For an additional fee, you can taste delicious appetizers, snacks, or dinners prepared by local chefs, as well as Miramonte's wines. Attire is casual. Reservations are not accepted

Flamenco Fridays – Every Friday night from 5:30 until 8:30 PM, the spotlight is on hot Latin rhythms – Rumba, Flamenco, Latin Jazz – performed by some of Southern California's hottest up-and-coming musicians.

Saturday Night Blues Jam – Soulful jammin' every Saturday from 5:30-8:30 PM by many of the best blues musicians in California!

Mount Palomar Winery
33820 Rancho California Road, Temecula, CA 92591 ◆ Tel: 951-676-5047 ◆ Summer Hours: Mon-Thurs 10-6, Fri-Sun 10-7; Winter Hours: Closed Mon & Tues; Wed-Thur 10-5, Fri-Sun 10-6 ◆ Website: *www.mountpalomar. com*

Music on the Mount – Every Saturday and Sunday in September and October, Mount Palomar Winery hosts a free live music concert from 3:30-6:30 PM. Enjoy music, wines and BBQ on their beautiful Mediterranean-themed outdoor patio areas.

✪ *Grape Escapes Discount!* - Present a copy of this book and receive a **Two-for-One tasting!!!**

South Coast Winery
34843 Rancho California Road, Temecula, CA 92591 ◆ Tel: 951-587-9463 ◆ Hours: Daily 10-6 ◆ Website: *www.wineresort.com*

Wednesday Nights – "After Hours" on the Grand Veranda – Do you dream about stepping back to a slower, more romantic time? Escape to South Coast Winery's Grand Veranda every Wednesday evening in June, July and August from 6 to 9 PM for live musical performances and entertainment under the stars. Enjoy their award-winning wines while you stroll about and get "mellow." But don't forget to sample some of their delicious Tuscany inspired food. (**Note:** This series of events is generally only open to wine club members and their guests.)

Thornton Winery
32575 Rancho California Road, Temecula, CA 92591 ♦ Tel: 951-699-0099 ♦ Hours: Daily 10-5 ♦ Website: *www.thorntonwinery.com*

Champagne Jazz Series – Thornton Winery is known as one of the finest outdoor entertainment venues in Southern California. Each summer, their *Champagne Jazz Series* presents live outdoor concerts featuring nationally renowned contemporary jazz artists.

Artists perform "up close and personal" in the intimate Mediterranean fountain terrace area at the winery's entrance. This area not only overlooks the Valley's scenic rolling hills and vineyards, but the terrace also has remarkable acoustics so you won't miss a note! Visit the winery's website or call 951-699-3021 for information on tickets, schedule of performers, and special supper packages.

Wiens Family Cellars
35055 Via Del Ponte, Temecula, CA   92592 ♦ Tel: 951-694-9892 ♦ Hours: Daily 10-5 ♦ Website: *www.wienscellars.com*

Blending Party – Want to try your hand at creating wine? Join winemaker Doug Wiens at a "Blending Party" and work with him to develop the winery's next "big red" premium blend. In addition to getting to sample unique wines created by you and other guests, you also get to enjoy some of the Wiens Family Cellars delicious appetizers. What more could you ask? This exciting and fun event is held only a few times each year, so don't miss it! Cost is approximately $50 per person.

Summer Concert Series – Wiens Family Cellars presents nationally known rock artists and music groups each summer. In 2008, the line-up includes Berlin (of "Top Gun" fame), Dave Wakeling, and Stan Ridgway / Wall of Voodoo. For the list of performers, concert schedule, price, and reservation information, contact the Wiens Family Cellars or visit Golden Crown Productions' website: *www.goldencrownproductions.com*

Shakespeare in the Vines – Wiens Family Cellars displays its commitment to community theater by serving as one of the venues for the Valley's *Shakespeare in the Vines* productions which are presented each summer and fall at various Temecula wineries. During August 2008, Wiens Family Cellars is hosting Shakespeare's classic, *"Romeo and Juliet."*

✪ *Grape Escapes Discount!* - Present a copy of this book and receive **Two-for-One wine tasting**, plus a **10% discount** on all wines purchased on the day of your visit. Also, present a copy of this book and receive a **free "back-stage" tour** of the winery with the winemaker. *Advance appointment is required*. Phone (951) 694-9892 to schedule.

Wilson Creek Winery & Vineyards
35960 Rancho California Road, Temecula, CA 92591 ◆ Tel: 951-699-9463 ◆ Hours: Daily 10-5 ◆ Website: *www.wilsoncreekwinery.com*

"Sunset Jazz in the Vines" Concert Series – Enjoy spectacular live smooth jazz performed by critically acclaimed artists while enjoying Wilson Creek's famous Almond Champagne and wine along with beautiful sunsets. Tickets for the summer concert series usually go on sale around March each year and sell out quickly. Visit Wilson Creek Winery's website for more information.

✪ *Grape Escapes Discount!* - Present a copy of this book and receive **Two-for-One tasting** for up to four guests (a $20 value). PLUS, present a copy of this book and receive a **10% discount** on all wines purchased on the day of your visit. Offers good Monday – Friday only, except on holidays. And if this is not reason enough to visit one of our favorite wineries, present a copy of *The Grape Escapes 2* and receive a **free glass of Almond Champagne** for up to four guests (one glass per entrée) with your purchase of an Entrée at the **Creekside Grille** located at Wilson Creek Winery. This is a $28 value and is valid Monday – Friday only, except on holidays.

WINE SHOPS

Temecula House of Wine
28522 Old Town – Front Street, Temecula, CA 92590 ◆ Tel: 951-699-6929 ◆ Hours: Mon-Thur, 10 – 6, Fri – Sat, 10 – 8:30 PM, Sun, 11- 5:30 PM ◆ Website: *www.palomarinntemecula.com*

Located in the historic Palomar Inn Hotel, the Temecula House of Wine offers guests a chance to sample the local wines at a "one-stop" convenient location. Beginning in the Summer of 2008, the Temecula House of Wine will host live music on weekends, as well as spotlighting five to six Temecula wines in its tasting bar and garden.

✪ *Grape Escapes Discount!* - Present a copy of this book at the ***Temecula House of Wine*** (28522 Front Street) in Old Town Temecula and receive a **10% discount** on all wines purchased on the day of your visit. If you purchase a case or more of wine during your visit, you will receive an additional **5%** (total 15%) **discount**. Tel: 951-699-0929 ◆ Hours: 10 AM to 8 PM weekdays and 10 AM to 10 PM on weekends ◆ Website: *www.palomarinntemecula.com*

Stellar Cellar
28636 Old Town – Front Street, Temecula, CA 92590 ◆ Tel: 951-6676-2722 ◆ Hours: Hours: Tuesday & Wednesday: 3 -11, Thurs & Friday: 3-10, Saturday: 11-10, Sunday: 11-6 ◆ Website: *www.stellarcellar.com*

Each Thursday at 6:30 PM, Stellar Cellar hosts a special wine tasting event featuring wines from a specific region or winery. On Friday and Saturday evenings from 7 to 10 PM, Stellar Cellar presents live entertainment with no cover charge. Enjoy a wide range of performers and musical styles while you sip their international line-up of wines.

"Simplicity is the ultimate sophistication."
~ Leonardo da Vinci

NO FRILLS, NO THRILLS, JUST GOOD WINES
(A Walk on the Rustic Side)

No bells and whistles. No super fancy gift shops or restaurants. In short – no distractions outside of a friendly winery dog or two. If you simply want to concentrate on the wine, and nothing but the wine, then here are some spots we heartily recommend.

Alex's Red Barn Winery
39820 Calle Contento, Temecula, CA 92951 ◆ Tel: 951-693-3201 ◆ Hours: Sat-Sun and most holidays 11-6, Winter 10-5 ◆ Website: *www.redbarnwine.com*

Foote Print Winery
36650 Glen Oaks Road, Temecula, CA 92592 ◆ Tel: 951-265-9951 ◆ Hours: Fri 12-5, Sat-Sun 10-5, Mon-Thurs By Appointment ◆ Website: *www.footeprintwinery.com*

✪ *Grape Escapes Discount!* - Present a copy of this book and receive a **Two-for-One tasting!!!**

Hart Winery
41300 Avenida Biona, Temecula, CA 92591 ◆ Tel: 951-676-6300 ◆ Hours: Daily 9-4:30 ◆ Website: *www.thehartfamilywinery.com*

Longshadow Ranch Vineyard & Winery
39847 Calle Contento, Temecula, CA 92591 ◆ Tel: 951-587-6221 ◆ Hours: Mon-Fri 12-5, Sat 10-4 (Sat Bonfire 5-9 PM April through October), Sun 10-5 ◆ Website: *www.longshadowranchwinery.com*

✪ *Grape Escapes Discount!* - Present a copy of this book and receive a **10% discount** on all wines purchased on the day of your visit.

Palumbo Family Vineyards & Winery
40150 Barksdale Circle, Temecula, CA 92591 ✦ Tel: 951-676-7900 ✦ Hours: Fri 12-5, Sat-Sun 10-5, Mon-Thurs By Appointment ✦ Website: *www.palumbofamilyvineyards.com*

✪ *Grape Escapes Complimentary Tasting!* - Present a copy of this book and receive a **complimentary tasting for two people** in your party.

"Wine and cheese are ageless companions,
like aspirin and aches, or June and moon…"
~ M.F.K. Fisher

"A JUG OF WINE, A LOAF OF BREAD AND THOU…"
(Favorite Winery Picnic Sites)

OK, it's a little after lunch time. The wine has been tasting really good. You're feeling good. You're convinced you're looking good. In fact, you're certain you look better than ever and have been amazing everyone you meet with your clever and funny conversational skills! If this sounds like you or a member of your group, it is time to get something in your stomach besides wine.

Why not have a picnic? Temecula wineries are the perfect place! So… take a break, stretch your legs, spread out your picnic, and enjoy the beautiful countryside while you munch away.

Failed to bring picnic items with you? No problem. In our *Feed Me* chapter, we have listed tasting rooms that offer deli items so you can create your own picnic on the spot.

☞ **Authors' Tip:** *This may be the best advice we give you in the entire book. Before you even think about going to Temecula Wine Country, you have to stop off at Barons - The Marketplace. Why? Glad you asked. This is a magnificent market. They have meats, some amazing cheeses, dozens of types of olives, more peppers than we can name, fresh-baked bread, crackers, fresh fruit, desserts… everything you need to have the most perfect picnic of your life. This is truly a great store.*

While you are there, check out the wine section as well. They have an excellent selection of local wines. Chances are the prices here will be at least 10% lower than those in the tasting rooms.

Don't have a cooler? Not to worry, Barons will fix you up with an inexpensive "cold bag." Barons is located at 31939 Rancho California Road.

Bella Vista Winery
41220 Calle Contento, Temecula, CA 92592 ◆ Tel: 951-676-5250 ◆ Hours: Daily 10-6, Winter 10-5 ◆ Website: *www.bellavistawinery.com*

If you want to get away from the tasting room crowds, this is the place! Located up the hill from Bella Vista Winery, this quiet and serene area overlooks the valley and vineyards below and seems like it is a world unto itself. Emery (Imre) Cziraki, the winemaker / owner, has created a picnic paradise – complete with numerous picnic tables under three huge, shady palapas that are surrounded by lawns, shrubs and trees. After eating, you can sit back and enjoy the sound of water from the fountain in the nearby duck pond or take a stroll along the brick pathway and enjoy the "Bella Vista" from the hilltop.

Filsinger Vineyards & Winery, Inc.
39050 De Portola Road, Temecula, CA 92592 ◆ Tel: 951-302-6363 ◆ Hours: Fri 11-4, Sat-Sun 10-5 ◆ Website: *www.filsingerwinery.com*

Filsinger Winery has the perfect picnic location if you are looking for some cool shade or an escape from the rain. (Yes, it really does rain in Southern California.) Its picnic area is located under a huge gazebo that is surrounded by trees. There is even a fountain in the middle of the raised platform that houses the gazebo. This winery has the least expensive tasting fees, as well as budget-priced wines and a picnic area. What more could you ask for?

Frangipani Estate Winery
39750 De Portola Road, Temecula, CA 92592 ◆ Tel: 951-699-8845 ◆ Hours: Daily 10-5 ◆ Website: *www.frangipaniwinery.com*

Although limited in number, the picnic tables on the patio outside the hillside tasting room at the Frangipani Estate Winery offer imposing views of the Mount Palomar foothills and the vineyards, olive trees, and horse ranches that run along De Portola Road. Since the picnic area is connected to the tasting bar via a sliding glass service window, you can have wine upon request right at your fingertips.

If you need a little exercise after a morning of tasting, take the stairs down the hillside and you will find two beautiful bocce ball lawns in the middle of the immaculately cultivated vineyard. Nearby there are a couple of tables with umbrellas for those that want a little solitude with their picnic.

☺ *Grape Escapes Discount!* - Present a copy of this book and receive a **30% discount** on all wines purchased on the day of your visit.

Keyways Vineyard & Winery
37338 De Portola Road, Temecula, CA 92592 ◆ Tel: 1-877-539-9297 ◆ Hours: Daily 10-6, Winter 10-5 ◆ Website: *www. ywayswine.com*

Reminiscent of "Old California," the gazebo with its red clay roof tiles shelters multiple wrought iron picnic tables. More tables are on the adjacent patio near the trees and rosebushes that line the area and the pathways to the winery. Another picnic area lies across from the tasting room. Surrounded by immaculate lawns and the Keyways vineyard, this mission-style pavilion offers a few additional picnic tables on its raised patio. Lunch here while you enjoy the soft sounds from the nearby fountain.

☺ *Grape Escapes Discount!* - Present a copy of this book and receive **Two-for-One tasting** from their "standard" tasting menu. Sorry, but offer is valid on weekdays only.

Longshadow Ranch Vineyard & Winery
39847 Calle Contento, Temecula, CA 92591 ◆ Tel: 951-587-6221 ◆ Hours: Mon-Fri 12-5, Sat 10-4 (Sat Bonfire 5-9 PM April through October), Sun 10-5 ◆ Website: *www.longshadowranchwinery.com*

Susan and John Brodersen have created the most unique and family-friendly winery in the Temecula area. Situated in the valley, this picturesque Western-themed winery looks out on white "horse country" fences, vineyards, and rolling hills.

⇨ **By The Way** – **Longshadow Ranch is truly a ranch – big Belgian draft horses that were used to plant the vineyard can be found in nearby corrals.**

Picnic tables are scattered on the wide, green lawns that surround the tasting room. Near many of tables are shade trees that help off-set the summer sun and fire rings for bonfires to keep you warm near sundown when the air becomes chilly. Another picnic area has been created on the large covered patio next to the tasting room so you are just steps away from your favorite wine!

✿ *Grape Escapes Discount!* - Present a copy of this book and receive a **10% discount** on all wines purchased on the day of your visit.

Maurice Car'rie Winery
34225 Rancho California Road, Temecula, CA 92591 ◆ Tel: 951-676-1711 ◆ Hours: Daily 10-5 ◆ Website: *www.mauricecarriewinery.com*

La Cereza Vineyard & Winery
34567 Rancho California Road, Temecula, CA 92591 ◆ Tel: 951-699-6961 ◆ Hours: Daily 10-5 ◆ Website: *www.lacerezawinery.com*

These "sister" wineries have lots of picnic sites where you can enjoy their signature food item on weekends – melted brie cheese encased in a hot loaf of Sourdough bread. *It is so delicious that we almost devoured a whole loaf by ourselves during our last tasting trip!* (See our **Feed Me!** chapter for details.)

Maurice Car'rie has wooden picnic tables scattered throughout its large lawn and concrete tables / benches are available on a patio near the gazebo. There are also seating areas under the Southern style veranda that encircles the tasting room where you can enjoy a glass of wine along with your picnic.

La Cereza provides numerous iron tables and chairs on the grassy area separating the La Cereza tasting room and the Spanish style plaza in front of Hemingway's Cigar Bar. On weekend afternoons, you can also get the warm brie and bread at Hemingway's open air bar.

✿ *Grape Escapes Discount!* - Present a copy of this book on and receive a **10% discount** on all wines and tasting room merchandise purchased on the day of your visit. Sorry, but offer is not valid on weekends.

Robert Renzoni Vineyards
37350 De Portola Road, Temecula, CA 92592 ◆ Tel: 951-302-8466 ◆ Hours: Daily 11-6 ◆ Website: *www. robertrenzonivineyards.com*

The picnic area in this newly opened winery overlooks the Mount Palomar foothills, two thoroughbred horse ranches, and the Renzoni olive trees and vineyards. You can relax and enjoy your lunch at umbrella-shaded picnic tables located next to the winery's cabernet vines.

✿ *Grape Escapes Discount!* - Present a copy of this book and receive a **10% discount** on all wines and tasting room merchandise purchased on the day of your visit. Also, present a copy of this book and receive an additional **10% discount** (total of 20%) on a case or more of wine.

Stuart Cellars
33515 Rancho California Road, Temecula, CA 92591 ◆ Tel: 951-676-6414 ◆ Hours: Daily 10-5 ◆ Website: *www.stuartcellars.com*

On a hilltop at over 1400 feet, Stuart Cellar's picnic area has one of the most impressive hilltop views in Temecula! Across from the tasting room entrance, there are wooden picnic tables scattered throughout a circular grassy area that is ringed with trees, shrubs and flowers. From each table, you can see close to a 360-degree view of the vineyards, farmland, and winding roads of the Temecula Valley below. To one side of the lawn, there is a large flagstone-paved patio and fire pit that also has seating for a picnic or just a glass of wine while you relax and take in the amazing view.

Wilson Creek Winery & Vineyards
35960 Rancho California Road, Temecula, CA 92591 ◆ Tel: 951-699-9463 ◆ Hours: Daily 10-5 ◆ Website: *www.wilsoncreekwinery.com*
Wilson Creek's picnic area is one of the most beautifully landscaped sites in the area. Take the left pathway at the three-tiered fountain that marks the winery's entrance, cross the footbridge that spans Wilson Creek, and you are transported to an enchanted world – complete with a stone alligator lazing in the shallow water and a playful (concrete) baby elephant sitting upright with its trunk in the air!

Multiple grassy picnic areas flank the meandering gravel trails. Split rail fences run along the creek. Follow the paths nestled among rose bushes, shade trees, shrubs, and wine barrel flowerpots and you will come to a beautiful 24 foot wide, white gazebo on a raised platform that overlooks the creek. Wilson Creek Winery also keeps its dedication to creating a "family atmosphere" in mind. All of the large lawns areas are definitely "kid friendly." In addition, near one of the picnic table groupings is a specially designed playground area that features swings and a rustic two-story slide house.

✪ *Grape Escapes Discount!* - Present a copy of this book and receive **Two-for-One tasting** for up to four guests (a $20 value). PLUS, present a copy of this book and receive a **10% discount** on all wines purchased on the day of your visit. Offers good Monday – Friday only, except on holidays. And if this is not reason enough to visit one of our favorite wineries, present a copy of *The Grape Escapes 2* and receive a **free glass of Almond Champagne** for up to four guests (one glass per entrée) with your purchase of an entrée at the **Creekside Grille** located at Wilson Creek Winery. This is a $28 value and is valid Monday – Friday only, except on holidays.

"How long a minute is depends on which
side of the bathroom door you're on." ~ Anonymous

"GOING" IN STYLE
(Cindy's Favorite Winery Bathroom)

OK, we'll be honest. We had to make up this category because Cindy wanted to share her enthusiasm over the décor in the Keyways Vineyard and Winery renovated bathroom with our readers. Keyways produces great wines, but Cindy says it is also worth the visit just to see the Ladies Room with its hammered copper stalls and the inlaid Brazilian onyx sink counter that is lit from below so its golden color seems to glow! *(And every woman knows that a soft golden light from below makes you look years younger!)*

Keyways Vineyard & Winery
37338 De Portola Road, Temecula, CA 92592 ♦ **Tel: 1-877-539-9297** ♦
Hours: Daily 10-6, Winter 10-5 ♦ **Website:** *www.keywayswine.com*

❂ *Grape Escapes Discount!* - Present a copy of this book and receive **Two-for-One tasting** from their "standard" tasting menu. Sorry, but offer is valid on weekdays only.

"I grew up with six brothers. That's how I learned
to dance – waiting for the bathroom." ~ Bob Hope

"In my next life, I'm going to be Italian!" ~ Bob Rhodes

DOING IT ITALIAN STYLE
(We *Love* Italian Varietals!)

We're not talking Gucci here. And don't even let your mind wander where we think it's going – at least not until you're back in the privacy of your own room. Although, we're told that barrel rooms are reportedly an incredible aphrodisiac. The smell of wine, French Oak… No, now stop that! Okay, but if you get caught, don't tell 'em we're the ones who told you.

Where were we? Oh, yeah. You are looking for Italian varietals. Fortunately, you've come to the right place. Temecula Wine Country has loads of Italian varietals, such as Sangiovese, Pinot Grigio, Nebbiolo, Montepulciano, Dolcetto, Malvasia Bianca, Vermentino, Aglianico, and Barbera. Let us guide you where you need to go…

Callaway Vineyard & Winery
32720 Rancho California Road, Temecula, CA 92591 ♦ Tel: 951-676-4001 ♦ Summer Hours: Daily 10-6, Winter Hours: 10-5 ♦ Website: *www.callawaywinery.com*

✪ *Grape Escapes Discount!* - Present a copy of this book and receive a **20% discount** on all wines and tasting room merchandise purchased on the day of your visit. Also, present a copy of this book and receive **Two-for-One tasting!!!**

Cougar Vineyard & Winery
39870 De Portola Road, Temecula, CA 92592 ♦ Tel: 951-491-0825 ♦ Hours: Daily 11-6, Winter 11-5 ♦ Website: *www.cougarvineyards.com*

Ponte Family Estate Winery
35053 Rancho California Road, Temecula, CA 92591 ♦ Tel: 951-694-8855 ♦ Hours: Daily 10-5 ♦ Website: *www.pontewinery.com*

✪ *Grape Escapes Discount!* - Present a copy of this book and receive a **Two-for-One tasting**!!! Offer valid Monday Through Thursday, excluding holidays.

Robert Renzoni Vineyards
37350 De Portola Road, Temecula, CA 92592 ✦ Tel: 951-302-8466 ✦ Hours: Daily 11-6 ✦ Website: *www. robertrenzonivineyards.com*

✪ *Grape Escapes Discount!* - Present a copy of this book and receive a **10% discount** on all wines and tasting room merchandise purchased on the day of your visit. Also, present a copy of this book and receive an additional **10% discount** (total of 20%) on a case or more of wine.

Wiens Family Cellars
35055 Via Del Ponte, Temecula, CA 92592 ✦ Tel: 951-694-9892 ✦ Hours: Daily 10-5 ✦ Website: *www.wienscellars.com*

✪ *Grape Escapes Discount!* - Present a copy of this book and receive **Two-for-One wine tasting**, plus a **10% discount** on all wines purchased on the day of your visit. Also, present a copy of this book and receive a **free "back stage" tour** of the winery with the winemaker. *Advance appointment is required*. Phone (951) 694-9892 to schedule.

Forget love – I'd rather fall in chocolate!
~ Attributed to Sandra J. Dykes

JUST HAND OVER THE CHOCOLATE AND NO ONE GETS HURT!

If there is anything that excites us as much as wine, it has to be *chocolate*. Fortunately, chocolate and wine go together quite nicely. If you are possibly thinking that it is too bad that our wonderful little *Grape Escapes* Wine Country travel guide does not have a chocolate tasting tour, well, take heart. We do. Our favorite tasting rooms that serve chocolate with specially selected wines are listed below:

Leonesse Cellars
38311 De Portola Road, Temecula, CA 92592 ◆ Tel: 951-302-7601 ◆ Hours: Daily 10-5 ◆ Website: *www.leonessecellars.com*

First stop is **Leonesse Cellars** which has the best chocolate truffles. They began carrying these when they first opened in 2003. We guarantee that even your sullen Designated Driver will put on a smile after trying one or two of these wonderful chocolates. It simply does not get any better than these truffles – unless you choose to pair the tasty morsels with Leonesse's wonderful Cinsault dessert wine.

Longshadow Ranch Vineyard & Winery
39847 Calle Contento, Temecula, CA 92591 ◆ Tel: 951-587-6221 ◆ Hours: Mon-Fri 12-5, Sat 10-4 (Sat Bonfire 5-9 PM April through October), Sun 10-5 ◆ Website: *www.longshadowranchwinery.com*

Next stop, **Longshadow Ranch**. They have a chocolate cowboy "boot shooter" that is filled with their Ponderosa Port. And the best part is that, after "bottoms up," you get to eat the boot. Oh, man. This is about as close to that "big ranch house in the sky" as you are likely to get in Temecula.

✪ *Grape Escapes Discount!* - Present a copy of this book and receive a **10% discount** on all wines purchased on the day of your visit.

Wilson Creek Winery & Vineyards
35960 Rancho California Road, Temecula, CA 92591 ◆ Tel: 951-699-9463 ◆ Hours: Daily 10-5 ◆ Website: *www.wilsoncreekwinery.com*

Wilson Creek has a Port wine, called Decadencia, that is infused with just a hint of chocolate essence to make it even more delicious. They serve it to you in a chilled and edible chocolate cup. If you stand outside the tasting room and watch people leaving Wilson Creek, you will notice two things. First, they are all smiling and second, they almost always have a small amount of chocolate at the corners of their mouths. We're convinced that the chocolate is why they are smiling.

✪ *Grape Escapes Discount!* - Present a copy of this book and receive **Two-for-One tasting** for up to four guests (a $20 value). PLUS, present a copy of this book and receive a **10% discount** on all wines purchased on the day of your visit. Offers good Monday – Friday only, except on holidays. And if this is not reason enough to visit one of our favorite wineries, present a copy of *The Grape Escapes 2* and receive a **free glass of Almond Champagne** for up to four guests (one glass per entrée) with your purchase of an entrée at the **Creekside Grille** located at Wilson Creek Winery. This is a $28 value and is valid Monday – Friday only, except on holidays.

☞ **Authors' Tip:** *Being a dedicated, un-reformed chocoholic, Cindy loves Wilson Creek's Dutch Chocolate "shot glass." Not only can you fill it with their award-winning chocolate port, but it can also be used for a very unique dessert when frozen and filled with chocolate mousse or slightly softened ice cream. It never fails to get a "Wow!" from our friends. Wilson Creek sells twelve shot glasses in a gold foiled box for approximately $20. (A word of caution: If you use a liquid, fill the shot glass to just below the rim and "sip first, then nibble." If you bite too aggressively, you will be wearing the contents – so take it slow and savor the flavor.)*

"Seize the moment. Remember all those women on the
Titanic who waved off the dessert cart." ~ Irma Bombeck

YOU SAY YOU HAVE THIS SWEET TOOTH

Well, you've come to the right place. Temecula has always catered to those
who like wines that are a bit on the sweet side. We found some excellent
sweeter-style wines at the wineries and tasting rooms listed below.

We have selected a broad sampling of different wines that have little in
common except the desire to please your sweet tooth. (Ports, Sherries and
Muscat Canelli are addressed in **The Wines** section of this guidebook. See
our chapters on these varietals if they are what you are seeking.)

Callaway Vineyard & Winery
Bronze Medal-winning "Sweet Nancy"
**32720 Rancho California Road, Temecula, CA 92591 ◆ Tel: 951-676-
4001 ◆ Summer Hours: Daily 10-6, Winter Hours: 10-5 ◆ Website:**
www.callawaywinery.com

❂ *Grape Escapes Discount!* - Present a copy of this book and receive a
20% discount on all wines and tasting room merchandise purchased on
the day of your visit. Also, present a copy of this book and receive **Two-
for-One tasting!!!**

⇨ **By The Way – Callaway has an entire section of sweet wines on its
tasting menu and is well worth a visit.**

Lumière Winery
Late Harvest Sauvignon Blanc (4.5% residual sugar)
**39555 Calle Contento, Temecula, CA 92591 ◆ Tel: 951-972-0585 ◆
Hours: To Be Determined; Open Weekends and by Appointment**

Keyways Vineyard & Winery
"Sweet Surrender" Sauvignon Blanc
37338 De Portola Road, Temecula, CA 92592 ◆ Tel: 1-877-539-9297 ◆ Hours: Daily 10-6, Winter 10-5 ◆ Website: *www.keywayswine.com*

✿ *Grape Escapes Discount!* - Present a copy of this book and receive **Two-for-One tasting** from their "standard" tasting menu. Sorry, but offer is valid on weekdays only.

Maurice Car'rie Winery
"Sweet Christa" Late Harvest Chardonnay
34225 Rancho California Road, Temecula, CA 92591 ◆ Tel: 951-676-1711 ◆ Hours: Daily 10-5 ◆ Website: *www.mauricecarriewinery.com*

✿ *Grape Escapes Discount!* - Present a copy of this book and receive a **10% discount** on all wines and tasting room merchandise purchased on the day of your visit. Sorry, but offer is not valid on weekends.

Mount Palomar Winery
Late Harvest Semillon (8.5% residual sugar)
33820 Rancho California Road, Temecula, CA 92591 ◆ Tel: 951-676-5047 ◆ Summer Hours: Mon-Thurs 10-6, Fri-Sun 10-7; Winter Hours: Closed Mon & Tues; Wed-Thur 10-5, Fri-Sun 10-6 ◆ Website: *www.mountpalomar. com*

✿ *Grape Escapes Discount!* - Present a copy of this book and receive a **Two-for-One tasting**!!!

Ponte Family Estate Winery
Beverino and Moscato NV sweet-style wines
35053 Rancho California Road, Temecula, CA 92591 ◆ Tel: 951-694-8855 ◆ Hours: Daily 10-5 ◆ Website: *www.pontewinery.com*

✿ *Grape Escapes Discount!* - Present a copy of this book and receive a **Two-for-One tasting**!!! Offer valid Monday Through Thursday, excluding holidays.

Tesoro Winery
Dolce Innocenza" (Sweet Innocence) – a slightly sweet wine
28475 Old Town Front Street, Temecula, CA 92590 ◆ Tel: 951-308-0000 ◆ Hours: Daily 10-5 ◆ Website: *www. tesorowines.com*

✪ *Grape Escapes Discount!* - Present a copy of this book and receive a **Two-for-One tasting** for up to four people in your party!!! Present a copy of this book and receive a **10% discount** on all wines and tasting room merchandise purchased on the day of your visit.

Wilson Creek Winery & Vineyards
"Duet" Late Harvest blend of Cab & Zin
35960 Rancho California Road, Temecula, CA 92591 ◆ **Tel: 951-699-9463** ◆ **Hours: Daily 10-5** ◆ **Website:** *www.wilsoncreekwinery.com*

✪ *Grape Escapes Discount!* - Present a copy of this book and receive **Two-for-One tasting** for up to four guests (a $20 value). PLUS, present a copy of this book and receive a **10% discount** on all wines purchased on the day of your visit. Offers good Monday – Friday only, except on holidays. And if this is not reason enough to visit one of our favorite wineries, present a copy of *The Grape Escapes 2* and receive a **free glass of Almond Champagne** for up to four guests (one glass per entrée) with your purchase of an entrée at the **Creekside Grille** located at Wilson Creek Winery. This is a $28 value and is valid Monday – Friday only, except on holidays.

"Sometimes I sits and thinks, and sometimes I just sits." ~ Satchel Paige

A SIT-DOWN AFFAIR
(Slow Down – You're Movin' Too Fast)

Have a seat. Literally. At the following tasting rooms, there is no need to jostle for a place at the tasting bar. At these tasting rooms, you are pampered and your wine is delivered to you in a relaxed and very pleasant setting. What could be better than this?

Boorman Vineyards Estate Winery
21630 Ave de Arboles, Murrieta, CA 92562 ◆ Tel: 951-600-9333 ◆ Hours: By Appointment Only ◆ Website: *www.boormanvineyards.com*

✿ *Grape Escapes Special Benefit* - Present a copy of this book and receive a **free "back-stage" tour** of the winery with the winemaker. *Advance appointment is required._*

Briar Rose Winery
41720 Calle Cabrillo, Temecula, CA 92592 ◆ Tel: 951-308-1098 ◆ Hours: By Appointment Only ◆ Website: *www.briarrosewinery.com*

Gershon Bachus Vintners
37750 De Portola Road, Temecula, CA 92592 ◆ Tel: 951-458-8428 ◆ Hours: By Appointment Only ◆ Website: *www.gershonbachus.com*

Thornton Winery
32575 Rancho California Road, Temecula, CA 92591 ◆ Tel: 951-699-0099 ◆ Hours: Daily 10-5 ◆ Website: *www.thorntonwinery.com*

Stellar Cellar (Wine Tasting Bar)
28636 Old Town Front Street, Suite 102, Temecula, CA 92590 ◆ Tel: 951-676-2722 ◆ Hours: Tuesday & Wednesday: 3 -11, Thurs & Friday: 3-10, Saturday: 11-10, Sunday: 11-6 ◆ Website: *www.stellarcellar.com*

☞ **Authors' Tip:** *Stellar Cellar features an outstanding wine list of Northern California and European wines. They also offer entertainment most weekends. See our "Now, That's Entertainment" chapter or their website for details.*

Temecula House of Wine
(Wine Shop, Tasting Bar and Garden)
28522 Old Town Front Street, Temecula, CA 92590 ◆ Tel: 951-699-0929 ◆ Hours: 10 AM to 8 PM weekdays and 10 AM – 10 PM on weekends ◆ Website: *www.palomarinntemecula.com*

✿ *Grape Escapes Discount!* - Present a copy of this book at the *Temecula House of Wine* (28522 Front Street) in Old Town Temecula and receive a **10% discount** on all wines purchased on the day of your visit. If you purchase a case or more of wine during your visit, you will receive an additional **5%** (total 15%) **discount.** Tel: 951-699-0929 ◆ Hours: 10 AM to 8 PM weekdays and 10 AM to 10 PM on weekends ◆ Website: *www.palomarinntemecula.com*

☞ **Authors' Tip:** *At the time we went to press, Carlos Palma, owner of the Palomar Inn Hotel, was putting the finishing touches on the addition of a wine tasting bar and garden to this historic downtown Temecula hotel. Each week the tasting bar will feature five or six different Temecula wines.*

"If food is the body of good living, wine is its soul."
~ Clifton Fadiman

FEED ME!

Let's face it, wine tasting is hard work and you can really develop an appetite from lifting all those *heavy* wine glasses. Don't worry. You do not have to drive back into town to get a delicious meal. More and more high-quality premier restaurants are being constructed at the wineries. Plus, the majority of the tasting rooms have some type of deli items available for purchase.

WINERY RESTAURANTS

Carol's Restaurant
Baily Vineyard & Winery
33440 La Serena Way, Temecula, CA 92591 ✦ Tel: 951-676-9243 ✦ Open for Lunch Wednesday-Friday 11:30 to 2:30; Saturday-Sunday 11:30 to 3:00 ✦ Website: *www.bailywinery. com/carols.html*

Located next to the Tasting Room, Carol's Restaurant continues Baily Winery's medieval theme. Its masonry block walls are festooned with tapestries and ancient weaponry. To ensure your dining experience is safe and pleasant, a knight in armor stands guard on a pedestal in the center of the room! Though the palladium windows, you can see the scenic outside dining area which is on a covered patio overlooking the vineyard. The restaurant features a wide selection of appetizers, salads, sandwiches, pasta, fish and steak.

☞ **Authors' Tip:** *During our visit in January 2008, we sampled a Reuben sandwich and one of the daily pasta specials. Both were very good with artful presentations and attentive service.*

Meritage Restaurant
Callaway Vineyard & Winery
32720 Rancho California Road, Temecula, CA 92591 ◆ Tel: 951-676-4001 ◆ Open for Lunch Mon-Thurs 11 AM to 4 PM; Open for Lunch and Dinner Fri-Sat from 11 AM to 9 PM; Open Sunday from 9 AM to 6 PM ◆ Website: *www.callawaywinery.com*

The Meritage Restaurant with panoramic views of the area's rolling hills and the winery's vineyards is located across from the tasting room. Guests are able to sit back and enjoy the breezes and scenery while enjoying Spanish tapas (appetizer-sized portions of entrees and side dishes) and wine on its arbor-shaded, multi-terraced dining areas.

✪ *Grape Escapes Discount!* - Present a copy of this book and receive a **20% discount** on all wines and tasting room merchandise purchased on the day of your visit. Also, present a copy of this book and receive **Two-for-One tasting!!!**

The Dining Room of the Inn at Churon Winery
33233 Rancho California Road, Temecula, CA 92591 ◆ Tel: 951-694-9070 ◆ Open for Dinner Friday & Saturday 6:00 to 9:00 PM ◆ Website: *www.innatchuronwinery.com*

The dining room of this beautiful French chateau-inspired Inn overlooks the winery's vineyards. Each Friday and Saturday evening, the dining room offers fixed price four-course wine pairing dinners that include a gourmet meal and three glasses of Inn at Churon Winery wines. Reservations are required.

Pinnacle Restaurant
Falkner Winery
40620 Calle Contento, Temecula, CA 92591 ◆ Tel: 951-676-8231 ◆ Open for Lunch Monday – Thursday 11:30 to 4:00 and Friday-Sunday 11:30 to 2:30 ◆ Website: *www.falknerwinery.com*

At an elevation of over 1400 feet, this modern, circular, clay-colored restaurant hugs the hill high above the Temecula Valley and offers one of the best views in the area. Located across from the Falkner Winery, the restaurant's open-air balcony looks out on the distant foothills, lush vineyards, and rolling wine country landscapes which stretch for miles. Inside, huge windows encircle the spacious dining area so that each table has a magnificent outdoor view. Appetizers, soup, salad, sandwiches, and a wide range of entrees (chicken, fish, beef) and scrumptious desserts are served by knowledgeable and friendly staff.

☞ **Authors' Tip:** *We had a quick, light lunch at The Pinnacle while visiting the winery. The soup was delicious, as was the Mediterranean shrimp and pasta dish we shared.*

Gershon Bachus Vintners
37750 De Portola Road, Temecula, CA 92592 ♦ Tel: 951-458-8428 ♦ By Appointment Only ♦ Website: *www.gershonbachus.com*

This elegant villa offers an exclusive, first-class wine tasting experience in its Tuscan-style event center. If you wish, your tasting can include a wine and food pairing gourmet luncheon package for approximately $50 per person. The luncheon package is limited to groups of eight or more wine aficionados who wish to enjoy an unsurpassed wine tasting experience. Each private wine and food pairing luncheon lasts approximately 1-1/2 to 2 hours and is by advance appointment only. (Vegetarian and vegan meals are available upon request.)

Block Five Restaurant
Leonesse Cellars
38311 De Portola Road, Temecula, CA 92592 ♦ Tel: 951-302-7601 ext 100 ♦ Open for Lunch Wednesday – Sunday 11:30 to 3:30 and for Dinner Friday 5:30 to 9:30 PM♦ Website: *www.leonessecellars.com/block-five.html*

The restaurant was named after the Vineyard Irrigation Block that had to be removed in order for the building to be constructed. The covered patio dining area overlooks the winery's beautifully landscaped grounds and lush vineyards. Serving appetizers, soups, salads, sandwiches and a wide range of entrees, Block Five has dishes for everyone's taste.

☞ **Authors' Tip:** *The Block 5 fried calamari appetizer was one of the best we have ever had: large, crisp strips that were fork-tender served with a tasty wasabi mayonnaise – delicious!*

The Smokehouse Restaurant
Ponte Family Estate Winery
35053 Rancho California Road, Temecula, CA 92591 ◆ Tel: 951-694-8855 ◆ Open for Lunch Monday-Saturday 10:00 to 5:00; Call for current Dinner and Sunday Brunch hours ◆ Website: *www.pontewinery.com*

This spacious, open air patio restaurant serves delicious seasonal cuisine with many of its fresh ingredients obtained from local farmers' markets. It has two seating areas depending on your desires: covered seating under a giant pergola or outside seating under umbrellas. In winter, both areas offer portable outdoor heaters to ensure diners are comfy. Begin your meal with one of their imaginative appetizers such as baked figs and gorgonzola wrapped in pancetta or the warm artichoke-spinach-parmesan cheese dip. Meal choices include soups, salads, sandwiches, "comfort" food (meat loaf and pastas), light Mediterranean dishes, and traditional entrees.

☞ **Authors' Tip:** *We ate at The Smokehouse twice during our visit to Temecula. Everything we tried was scrumptious and promptly served by friendly, courteous wait staff.*

✪ *Grape Escapes Discount!* - Present a copy of this book and receive a **Two-for-One tasting** in the Ponte Tasting Room!!! Offer valid Monday Through Thursday, excluding holidays.

Vineyard Rose Restaurant
South Coast Winery
34843 Rancho California Road, Temecula, CA 92591 ◆ Tel: 951-587-9463 ◆ Open Daily for Breakfast, Lunch & Dinner: Sunday – Thursday: 7:00 AM to 9:00 PM; Friday & Saturday: 7:00 AM to 10:00 PM ◆ Website: *www. wineresort.com*

South Coast Winery's casual elegance extends to its premier restaurant. Wooden tables and leather-topped tapestry booths in warm tones lend a welcoming and gracious feel to the enormous great room with open oak-beamed ceilings. The Vineyard Rose Restaurant dining room and outside dining terrace overlook South Coast Resort's beautiful landscape filled with flowers, lawns, statues, and the surrounding vineyard. The Italian-born Executive Chef, Allesandro Serni, showcases Tuscan style and classic American dishes, as well as global cuisine perfected during his previous posts at Four Seasons properties world-wide.

Lunch and dinner items range from fruit and light meals to full gourmet entrees. Desserts are almost too beautiful to eat. Reservations are recommended, especially on Friday and weekends.

Café Champagne
Thornton Winery
32575 Rancho California Road, Temecula, CA 92591 ♦ Tel: 951-699-0088 ♦ Open for Lunch Daily 11:00 to 3:30; Open for Dinner Daily 5:00 to 9:00 PM; Sunday Brunch 11:00 to 4:00 ♦ Website: *www.thorntonwinery.com*

Winner of the Gold Award for Contemporary Cuisine for 11 consecutive years from the Southern California Writers Association, Café Champagne serves delicious, creative "fusion" cuisine and classic American favorites. With vineyard and courtyard views, the open terrace café is located near the herb garden at the entrance of the French chateau-inspired winery. The menus feature a wide variety of dishes for lunch, brunch, and dinner. Café Champagne serves delicious appetizers, soups, salads, and sandwiches, as well as fish / seafood, steak, and poultry dishes. In addition, suggested wine pairings are listed along with each menu item to take the guesswork out of deciding which of its still and sparkling wines you should order to accompany your meal.

☞ **Authors' Tip:** *At Café Champagne, we enjoyed some wonderful appetizers. The pepper and sesame crusted ahi tuna was layered with avocado and accompanied with marinated mushrooms – an unexpected combination that was simply delicious. The "warm brie en croute" is remarkable. Melted brie, encased in toasted puff pastry, is topped with a warm honey and walnut sauce. It is hard to believe this is an appetizer and not dessert!*

Creekside Grill
Wilson Creek Winery & Vineyards
35960 Rancho California Road, Temecula, CA 92591 ♦ Tel: 951-699-9463 ♦ Hours: Daily 10-5 ♦ Website: *www.wilsoncreekwinery.com*

Wilson Creek's new restaurant, the Creekside Grille, opened in Spring / Summer of 2008. Located in the new event center building and overlooking Wilson Creek, the restaurant focuses on providing fresh luncheons, light fare and homemade specialties. Sit back and relax in your chair under the Tuscan balcony while you enjoy a glass of Wilson Creek wines.

✪ *Grape Escapes Discount!* - Present a copy of this book and receive **Two-for-One tasting** for up to four guests (a $20 value). PLUS, present a copy of this book and receive a **10% discount** on all wines purchased on the day of your visit. Offers good Monday – Friday only, except on holidays. And if this is not reason enough to visit one of our favorite wineries, present a copy of *The Grape Escapes 2* and receive a **free glass of Almond Champagne** for up to four guests (one glass per entrée) with your purchase of an entrée at the **Creekside Grille** located at Wilson Creek Winery. This is a $28 value and is valid Monday – Friday only, except on holidays.

"It's more fun to talk with someone who doesn't use
long, difficult words, but rather short, easy words
like, *What about lunch?*" ~ Pooh's Little Instruction Book

TASTING ROOMS OFFERING LIGHT FOOD or DELI ITEMS

If you get the munchies while on your Grape Escapes excursion, we recommend stopping at any of the tasting rooms listed below. Some offer light food freshly prepared on-site while you wait, such as sandwiches, salads, pizza, etc.

All the wineries listed have deli items and packaged food perfect for snacking or picnicking.

LIGHT FARE (Salads, sandwiches, etc.)

The Bistro
Keyways Vineyard & Winery
37338 De Portola Road, Temecula, CA 92592 ◆ Tel: 1-877-539-9297 ◆
Hours: Daily 10-6, Winter 10-5 ◆ Website: *www.keywayswine.com*

✪ *Grape Escapes Discount!* - Present a copy of this book and receive **Two-for-One tasting** from their "standard" tasting menu. Sorry, but offer is valid on weekdays only.

Mount Palomar Taverna
Mount Palomar Winery
33820 Rancho California Road, Temecula, CA 92591 ◆ **Tel: 951-676-5047** ◆ **Summer Hours: Mon-Thurs 10-6, Fri-Sun 10-7; Winter Hours: Closed Mon & Tues; Wed-Thur 10-5, Fri-Sun 10-6** ◆ **Website:** *www.mountpalomar. com*

✪ *Grape Escapes Discount!* - Present a copy of this book and receive a **Two-for-One tasting!!!**

DELI SELECTIONS
(Cheese, salami, lunch meats, salsa, crackers, soft drinks, bottled water)

Baily Vineyard & Winery
33440 La Serena Way, Temecula, CA 92591 ◆ **Tel: 951-676-9463** ◆ **Hours: Sun-Fri 11-5, Sat 10-5** ◆ **Website:** *www.bailywinery.com*

Bella Vista Winery
41220 Calle Contento, Temecula, CA 92592 ◆ **Tel: 951-676-5250** ◆ **Hours: Daily 10-6, Winter 10-5** ◆ **Website:** *www.bellavistawinery.com*

Callaway Vineyard & Winery
32720 Rancho California Road, Temecula, CA 92591 ◆ **Tel: 951-676-4001** ◆ **Summer Hours: Daily 10-6, Winter Hours: 10-5** ◆ **Website:** *www.callawaywinery.com*

✪ *Grape Escapes Discount!* - Present a copy of this book and receive a **20% discount** on all wines and tasting room merchandise purchased on the day of your visit. Also, present a copy of this book and receive **Two-for-One tasting!!!**

Inn at Churon Winery
33233 Rancho California Road, Temecula, CA 92591 ◆ **Tel: 951-694-9070** ◆ **Hours: Daily 10-4:30** ◆ **Website:** *www.innatchuronwinery.com*

Cougar Vineyard & Winery
39870 De Portola Road, Temecula, CA 92592 ◆ **Tel: 951-491-0825** ◆ **Hours: Daily 11-6, Winter 11-5** ◆ **Website:** *www.cougarvineyards.com*

☞ **Authors' Tip:** *Try Cougar's salmon-stuffed marinated olives which are harvested from the trees near their vineyard.*

Falkner Winery
40620 Calle Contento, Temecula, CA 92591 ♦ Tel: 951-676-8231 ♦ Hours: Daily 10-5 ♦ Website: *www.falknerwinery.com*

Keyways Vineyard & Winery
37338 De Portola Road, Temecula, CA 92592 ♦ Tel: 1-877-539-9297 ♦ Hours: Daily 10-6, Winter 10-5 ♦ Website: *www.keywayswine.com*

✪ *Grape Escapes Discount!* - Present a copy of this book and receive **Two-for-One tasting** from their "standard" tasting menu. Sorry, but offer is valid on weekdays only.

La Cereza Vineyard & Winery
34567 Rancho California Road, Temecula, CA 92591 ♦ Tel: 951-699-6961 ♦ Hours: Daily 10-5 ♦ Website: *www.lacerezawinery.com*

✪ *Grape Escapes Discount!* - Present a copy of this book on Monday through Friday and receive a **10% discount** on all wines and tasting room merchandise purchased on the day of your visit. Sorry, but offer is not valid on weekends.

Leonesse Cellars
38311 De Portola Road, Temecula, CA 92592 ♦ Tel: 951-302-7601 ♦ Hours: Daily 10-5 ♦ Website: *www.leonessecellars.com*

Maurice Car'rie Winery
34225 Rancho California Road, Temecula, CA 92591 ♦ Tel: 951-676-1711 ♦ Hours: Daily 10-5 ♦ Website: *www.mauricecarriewinery.com*

☞ **Authors' Tip:** *On weekends, order Maurice Car'rie's "baked brie" (hot brie encased in a toasted loaf of sourdough bread) for a yummy and filling snack. Call ahead so it will be piping hot and ready upon your arrival at the winery. It takes approximately 30 minutes to prepare. If you cannot call ahead, place your order at the "Brie Table" on the porch as soon as you arrive. An unbaked version is also available for purchase for you to take home and prepare for your guests.*

✪ *Grape Escapes Discount!* - Present a copy of this book and receive a **10% discount** on all wines and tasting room merchandise purchased on the day of your visit. Sorry, but offer is not valid on weekends.

Miramonte Winery / Celebration Cellars
33410 Rancho California Road, Temecula, CA 92591 ♦ Tel: 951-506-5500 ♦ Hours: Daily 11-6, Music Fri & Sat 5:30-8:30 ♦ Website: *www.miramontewinery.com*

Mount Palomar Winery
33820 Rancho California Road, Temecula, CA 92591 ♦ Tel: 951-676-5047 ♦ Summer Hours: Mon-Thurs 10-6, Fri-Sun 10-7; Winter Hours: Closed Mon & Tues; Wed-Thur 10-5, Fri-Sun 10-6 ♦ Website: *www.mountpalomar.com*

✪ *Grape Escapes Discount!* -   Present a copy of this book and receive a **Two-for-One tasting!!!**

Oak Mountain Winery / Temecula Hills Winery
36522 Via Verde, Temecula, CA 92592 ♦ Tel: 951-699-9102 ♦ Hours: Daily 11-5 ♦ Website: *www.oakmountainwinery.com*

✪ *Grape Escapes Discount!* - Present a copy of this book and receive a **10% discount** on all wines purchased on the day of your visit. Also, present a copy of this book and receive **Two-for-One tasting** for up to four guests. Offer does not include the souvenir logo glass.

Ponte Family Estate Winery
35053 Rancho California Road, Temecula, CA 92591 ♦ Tel: 951-694-8855 ♦ Hours: Daily 10-5 ♦ Website: *www. pontewinery.com*

✪ *Grape Escapes Discount!* - Present a copy of this book and receive a **Two-for-One tasting!!!** Offer valid Monday Through Thursday, excluding holidays.

Robert Renzoni Vineyards
37350 De Portola Road, Temecula, CA 92592 ♦ Tel: 951-302-8466 ♦ Hours: Daily 11-6 ♦ Website: *www. robertrenzonivineyards.com*

✪ *Grape Escapes Discount!* - Present a copy of this book and receive a **10% discount** on all wines and tasting room merchandise purchased on the day of your visit. Also, present a copy of this book and receive an additional **10% discount** (total of 20%) on a case or more of wine.

South Coast Winery
34843 Rancho California Road, Temecula, CA 92591 ♦ Tel: 951-587-9463 ♦ Hours: Daily 10-6 ♦ Website: *www.wineresort.com*

Stuart Cellars
33515 Rancho California Road, Temecula, CA 92591 ♦ Tel: 951-676-6414 ♦ Hours: Daily 10-5 ♦ Website: *www.stuartcellars.com*

Thornton Winery
32575 Rancho California Road, Temecula, CA 92591 ♦ Tel: 951-699-0099 ♦ Hours: Daily 10-5 ♦ Website: *www.thorntonwinery.com*

Wiens Family Cellars
35055 Via Del Ponte, Temecula, CA 92592 ♦ Tel: 951-694-9892 ♦ Hours: Daily 10-5 ♦ Website: *www.wienscellars.com*

✪ *Grape Escapes Discount!* - Present a copy of this book and receive **Two-for-One** wine tasting, plus a **10% discount** on all wines purchased on the day of your visit. Also, present a copy of this book and receive a **free "back-stage" tour** of the winery with the winemaker. *Advance appointment is required.* Phone (951) 694-9892 to schedule.

Wilson Creek Winery & Vineyards
35960 Rancho California Road, Temecula, CA 92591 w Tel: 951-699-9463 w Hours: Daily 10-5 w Website: *www.wilsoncreekwinery.com*

✪ *Grape Escapes Discount!* - Present a copy of this book and receive **Two-for-One tasting** for up to four guests (a $20 value). PLUS, present a copy of this book and receive a **10% discount** on all wines purchased on the day of your visit. Offers good Monday – Friday only, except on holidays. And if this is not reason enough to visit one of our favorite wineries, present a copy of *The Grape Escapes 2* and receive a **free glass of Almond Champagne** for up to four guests (one glass per entrée) with your purchase of an entrée at the **Creekside Grille** located at Wilson Creek Winery. This is a $28 value and is valid Monday – Friday only, except on holidays.

"Drink wine, and you will sleep well.
Sleep well, and you will not sin.
Avoid Sin, and you will be saved. Ergo,
drink wine and be saved." ~ Medieval German Saying

WINE TASTING AFTER HOURS

Let's say it is 6 PM and you've had such a wonderful day of wine tasting that you are not quite ready for it to end. Or maybe you've just arrived in Temecula and can't wait to get an early start on your wine tasting adventure. What's a guy (or gal) to do?

Well, we're glad you asked, 'cause this is why we're here – to provide answers to all your Temecula wine-related questions.

There are three places in Temecula that are just waiting for you "After Hours."

<u>Temecula House of Wine</u>
Suite A, 28522 Old Town Front Street
Temecula, CA 92590
Tel: (951) 699-0929
Website: *www.palomarinntemecula.com.*

The **Temecula House of Wine,** owned and operated by Carlos Palma, is located in the historic Palomar Inn Hotel in Old Town. Carlos only carries Temecula wines. In fact, you can find Temecula wines that you probably have not even heard of. Carlos is proud to carry small lot, private label wines made by some of Temecula's top winemakers.

Carlos plans to expand his wine tasting operation to include a tasting bar and a tasting garden. He will feature five or six Temecula wines each week. Both should be open by the Summer of 2008.

We asked Carlos if he would be willing to disclose the name of his most popular selling wine. He told us that **Boorman Vineyards Estate Winery** produces some of his top sellers. But, don't tell anyone because we told Carlos we would keep it a secret – just between us and our friends. Way-to-go, Todd and Rosie. ☺

☺ *Grape Escapes Discount!* - Present a copy of this book at the *Temecula House of Wine* (28522 Front Street) in Old Town Temecula and receive a **10% discount** on all wines purchased on the day of your visit. If you purchase a case or more of wine during your visit, you will receive an additional **5%** (total 15%) **discount**. Tel: 951-699-0929 ◆ Hours: 10 AM to 8 PM weekdays and 10 AM to 10 PM on weekends ◆ Website: *www.palomarinntemecula.com*

⇨ **By The Way – If you are interested in staying in a genuine historic hotel, consider the Palomar Inn. They have great rates. For more information, contact the Inn at (951) 676-6503.**

Stellar Cellar

28636 Old Town Front Street
Temecula, CA 52590
Tel: (951) 676-2722
Website: *www.stellarcellar.com*

Stellar Cellar, owned by Anna Bienvenue and her husband, David, is a very comfortable and relaxing tasting bar in the heart of Old Town. Whereas the *Temecula House of Wine* only offers Temecula wines, *Stellar Cellar* has taken the opposite approach. They have an excellent menu of well-regarded California and European wines. They also carry a few local wines.

Why the different approach? They cater mostly to locals who are already familiar with Temecula wines and wish to try something different. Most Thursday evenings, Stellar Cellar hosts a wine tasting event that features wines from a specific region or winery.

Frankie's Steak and Seafood

41789 Nicole Lane in Temecula
Tel: (951) 676-8040
Website: www.Frankies-restaurant.com

Frankie's Steak and Seafood is owned by Franco Vessia and is located in the Creekside Center, at the corner of Overland and Nicole Lane, across the street from the Temecula Costco. If you are looking for a great wine list, or perhaps a great place to dine in Temecula, this is our top recommendation. Frankie's has a modern walk-in wine cellar with a fine list of California and Italian wines, but our favorite was his own **Villa Vessia Vineyard Cabernet Sauvignon** which is made by none other than Todd Boorman.

"Fill every glass, for wine inspires us, and fires us with courage, love and joy." ~ John Gay, "The Beggars Opera"

I JUST WANT TO CELEBRATE

You know who you are. You have this little voice in your head. It keeps saying CELEBRATE … CELEBRATE … I JUST WANT TO CELEBRATE! If you are looking for wine tasting in a fun and energy-filled atmosphere, the following wineries are your ticket to a good time and good wines.

Leonesse Cellars
38311 De Portola Road, Temecula, CA 92592 ◆ Tel: 951-302-7601 ◆ Hours: Daily 10-5 ◆ Website: *www.leonessecellars.com*

Ponte Family Estate Winery
35053 Rancho California Road, Temecula, CA 92591 ◆ Tel: 951-694-8855 ◆ Hours: Daily 10-5 ◆ Website: *www.pontewinery.com*

✪ *Grape Escapes Discount!* - Present a copy of this book and receive a **Two-for-One tasting**!!! Offer valid Monday Through Thursday, excluding holidays.

Wiens Family Cellars
35055 Via Del Ponte, Temecula, CA 92592 ◆ Tel: 951-694-9892 ◆ Hours: Daily 10-5 ◆ Website: *www.wienscellars.com*

✪ *Grape Escapes Discount!* - Present a copy of this book and receive **Two-for-One** wine tasting, plus a **10% discount** on all wines purchased on the day of your visit. Also, present a copy of this book and receive a **free "back-stage" tour** of the winery with the winemaker. *Advance appointment is required*. Phone (951) 694-9892 to schedule.

Wilson Creek Winery & Vineyards
35960 Rancho California Road, Temecula, CA 92591 ♦ Tel: 951-699-9463 ♦ Hours: Daily 10-5 ♦ Website: *www.wilsoncreekwinery.com*

✿ *Grape Escapes Discount!* - Present a copy of this book and receive **Two-for-One tasting** for up to four guests (a $20 value). PLUS, present a copy of this book and receive a **10% discount** on all wines purchased on the day of your visit. Offers good Monday – Friday only, except on holidays. And if this is not reason enough to visit one of our favorite wineries, present a copy of *The Grape Escapes 2* and receive a **free glass of Almond Champagne** for up to four guests (one glass per entrée) with your purchase of an entrée at the **Creekside Grille** located at Wilson Creek Winery. This is a $28 value and is valid Monday – Friday only, except on holidays.

This is MY wine. I discovered it. I bought it.
I even put my name on it. It's mine! All mine.

LET'S GET PERSONAL
(Customized Wine Bottles and Labels)

Have you ever tasted a wine and simply thought *"This is my wine. This is me. I want to put my name it. I want to share this wine with my friends. No, wait. What am I thinking? I'm not gonna share this. It is too good. Okay, maybe I'll share it with some of them. If they are nice...or bring steaks...or something."*

Well, if you had even just a few of these thoughts, these wineries have a deal for you. The following wineries will help you design your own custom wine labels and ship their delicious wines suitably personalized. Your labels might read, "Congratulations," "Happy Anniversary," "Cindy's Private Reserve," "Wendy's Wonderful Wine," or "Touch This Wine and I'll Break Your Arm!" No doubt you can come up with something much more creative. If not, the following wineries will help you create a unique and personal label.

Callaway Vineyard & Winery
32720 Rancho California Road, Temecula, CA 92591 ◆ Tel: 951-676-4001 ◆ Summer Hours: Daily 10-6, Winter Hours: 10-5 ◆ Website: *www.callawaywinery.com*

✪ *Grape Escapes Discount!* - Present a copy of this book and receive a **20% discount** on all wines and tasting room merchandise purchased on the day of your visit. Also, present a copy of this book and receive **Two-for-One tasting!!!**

⇨ **By The Way** – Callaway Vineyard and Winery won two Silver Medals at the 2008 New World International Wine Competition. Winners were the 2004 Cab-Franc and their Non-Vintage Dessert wine.

La Cereza Vineyard & Winery
34567 Rancho California Road, Temecula, CA 92591 ◆ Tel: 951-699-6961 ◆ Hours: Daily 10-5 ◆ Website: *www.lacerezawinery.com*

✿ *Grape Escapes Discount!* - Present a copy of this book and receive a **10% discount** on all wines and tasting room merchandise purchased on the day of your visit. Sorry, but offer is not valid on weekends.

Maurice Car'rie Winery
34225 Rancho California Road, Temecula, CA 92591 ◆ Tel: 951-676-1711 ◆ Hours: Daily 10-5 ◆ Website: *www.mauricecarriewinery.com*

✿ *Grape Escapes Discount!* - Present a copy of this book and receive a **10% discount** on all wines and tasting room merchandise purchased on the day of your visit. Sorry, but offer is not valid on weekends.

Miramonte Winery / Celebration Cellars
33410 Rancho California Road, Temecula, CA 92591 ◆ Tel: 951-506-5500 ◆ Hours: Daily 11-6, Music Fri & Sat 5:30-8:30 ◆ Website: *www.miramontewinery.com*

⇨ **By The Way** – Miramonte Winery is associated with Celebration Cellars whose custom painted, etched and engraved wine bottles are literally both works of art and collector's items. If you are looking for a truly unique and special gift, visit their website: www.celebrationcellars. com

---

Orfila Vineyards & Winery
3455 San Pasqual Road, Escondido, CA 92025 ◆ Tel: 760-738-6500 ◆ Hours: Daily 10-6
Website: *www.orfila.com*

Want to know more about this award-winning winery? Check out our ***Road Trip*** chapter.

❂ *Grape Escapes Discount!* - Present a copy of this book and receive **free tasting** for up to four people in your party. In addition, you will also receive a **15% discount** on all wines purchased (except the Ambassador Reserve Merlot), plus a **10% discount** on all tasting room merchandise purchased on the day of your visit. Present a copy of this book and receive an additional **5% discount** (total of 20%) on a case or more of wine. Also, present a copy of this book and receive a **free "back-stage" tour** of the winery. Appointment required.

Wilson Creek Winery & Vineyards
35960 Rancho California Road, Temecula, CA 92591 ◆ Tel: 951-699-9463 ◆ Hours: Daily 10-5 ◆ Website: *www.wilsoncreekwinery.com*

❂ *Grape Escapes Discount!* - Present a copy of this book and receive **Two-for-One tasting** for up to four guests (a $20 value). PLUS, present a copy of this book and receive a **10% discount** on all wines purchased on the day of your visit. Offers good Monday – Friday only, except on holidays. And if this is not reason enough to visit one of our favorite wineries, present a copy of *The Grape Escapes 2* and receive a **free glass of Almond Champagne** for up to four guests (one glass per entrée) with your purchase of an entrée at the **Creekside Grille** located at Wilson Creek Winery. This is a $28 value and is valid Monday – Friday only, except on holidays.

"Searching and learning is where the miracle
process all begins." ~ Jim Rohn

A CLASS ACT
(Favorite Wineries for Learning about Wine)

In our book's Introduction, we mentioned that we have two Rules for Wine
Tasting:
You gotta have fun.
You should learn something.
In our opinion, Rule Number two is really a subset of Rule Number one.

Learning and wine tasting go hand-in-hand. After finding a "WOW!" wine,
your next thought (right after "Can I have more?") is to wonder how the
winemaker created this particular magical elixir.

If you are hooked on wine and want to learn more about wine tasting, viticulture, or the process from the vine to your glass, we suggest you contact one
of the following wineries that offer recurring educational programs about
wine and wine tasting.

Note: The information contained in this guidebook was current at the time of publication,
but is subject to change. Telephone numbers and website addresses are provided to assist
the reader in obtaining up-to-date information.

Falkner Winery
**40620 Calle Contento, Temecula, CA 92591 ◆ Tel: 951-676-8231 ◆ Hours:
Daily 10-5 ◆ Website:** *www.falknerwinery.com*

Wine Appreciation Class – Learn the basic "ins and outs" of wine tasting.
Falkner Winery offers a three-hour class for $35 per person that provides
an introduction to wine tasting, wine identification and food / wine pairing.
The class includes samples of their wines that regularly appear on the tasting room menu and a few premium wines.

Cooking Class Dinners – Chef Dennis from the Pinnacle Restaurant gives a private and fun "hands-on" cooking class for you and your friends or associates while preparing a delicious gourmet dinner. He also entertains you with information on how to pair wine with foods.

Ponte Family Estate Winery
35053 Rancho California Road, Temecula, CA 92591 ◆ Tel: 951-694-8855 ◆ Hours: Daily 10-5 ◆ Website: *www.pontewinery.com*

Wine 101 – Ponte's Master Sommelier Eddie Osterland has teamed with Executive Chef Steve Stawinski to develop a unique and fun wine education class. Eddie discusses the concept of "food-wines" and demonstrates why some wines enhance specific food flavors better than others. He also shares ideas and stories about new, easy and interesting ways to entertain at home with wine and food. Chef Steve has created a delicious menu of unique hors d'oeuvres that are served with Ponte's wines during the class. Check the Ponte website for more information.

✪ *Grape Escapes Discount!* - Present a copy of this book and receive a **Two-for-One tasting**!!! Offer valid Monday Through Thursday, excluding holidays. Discount does not apply to wine education classes.

South Coast Winery
34843 Rancho California Road, Temecula, CA 92591 ◆ Tel: 951-587-9463 ◆ Hours: Daily 10-6 ◆ Website: *www.wineresort.com*

Wine & Food Pairing Class – South Coast Winery takes you on a fun and delicious adventure into the relationship between food and wine. Executive Chef Allesandro Serni and Master Winemaker Jon McPherson have created a special menu (including appetizers, salad, pasta, fish / seafood and dessert) and selected some of South Coast's award-winning wines (including port) for you to sample. This unique wine and food tasting excursion will help you understand how and why various wines are paired with different types of food to enhance the dining experience. Cost for the class is $65 per person. Check the South Coast Winery's website for additional information and to view the specially designed menu of food and wine pairings.

Stuart Cellars
33515 Rancho California Road, Temecula, CA 92591 ◆ Tel: 951-676-6414 ◆ Hours: Daily 10-5 ◆ Website: *www.stuartcellars.com*

Dynamic Wine & Food Pairing Class (SDSU) – Stuart Cellars hosts a special full-day class presented by the San Diego State University (SDSU) Business and Wine Program. The class is presented by a Master Chef who helps you understand how specific food and wine complement each other by sampling a variety of cuisine and varietals. In addition, the class explores each wine's origin and the traditional foods found in that region. Cost for the class is approximately $200 per person. For additional information, schedules, and registration instructions, view the SDSU College of Extended Studies – The Business of Wine website at *http://ces.sdsu.edu/wine. html* or phone 619-594-6924.

Wiens Family Cellars
35055 Via Del Ponte, Temecula, CA 92592 ◆ Tel: 951-694-9892 ◆ Hours: Daily 10-5 ◆ Website: *www.wienscellars.com*

California Wine School – Doug Wiens, winemaker, viticulturist, and one of the owners of Wiens Family Cellars, is also founder and one of the primary instructors for the California Wine School. This organization presents fun, relaxed, informative classes that cover "everything about wine from the soil to the glass." The courses are designed to appeal to a wide variety of students from casual tasters who are just beginning to explore wine to food service professionals.

Classes range from the two-hour "Shootout" sessions where a variety of red wines are tasted and discussed to the in-depth "Introduction to Wine" series which meets one evening a week for four weeks. All the classes are interactive and end with a 30-minute informal mixer where instructors and students talk, taste wine and share wine experiences.

Costs for the classes range from approximately $60 to $230 per person, depending upon the class. (Members of the Wiens Family Cellars Wine Club receive significant discounts off the cost of the classes.) Classes are held in Temecula at the Wiens Family Cellars, as well as in San Diego. In the near future, the California Wine School will begin offering courses for wine lovers in Orange County and Palm Springs. For more information, class descriptions and schedules, visit *www.californiawineschool.com* or call Doug Wiens at (951) 623-9708.

✿ *Grape Escapes Discount!* - Present a copy of this book and receive **Two-for-One wine tasting**, plus a **10% discount** on all wines purchased on the day of your visit. Also, present a copy of this book and receive a **free "back-stage" tour** of the winery with the winemaker. *Advance appointment is required*. Phone (951) 694-9892 to schedule. Discounts do not apply to California Wine School classes.

"Strategy is buying a bottle of fine wine when you take a
lady out for dinner.
Tactics is getting her to drink." ~ Frank Muir

SALUTING OUR ACTIVE DUTY MILITARY
(Tasting Rooms that Offer Military Discounts)

One of the things we like about Temecula is that the people there just seem to have their priorities straight. The wineries and tasting rooms listed below offer discounts to Active Duty Military on tasting fees and / or purchases. It is their way of saying thank you in a small way to our Service Members who, along with their families, have given so much for this country.

Deane Foote of **Foote Print Winery**, in particular, is always on the look out for a short hair cut or a crisp posture that so often signals the presence of a military man and woman. Deane always asks, "You military?" As a former military person himself, Deane can pick a service member out of the crowd. He goes on to tell the person that their tasting will be free. Bravo, Deane! Well done! *OOHRAH!*

In order to obtain the discounts, you must be at least 21 and show a valid Active Duty ID card

Note: The information contained in this guidebook was current at the time of publication, but is subject to change. Telephone numbers and website addresses are provided to assist the reader in obtaining up-to-date information.

Authors' Note: Address, phone number and contact information for the following wineries may be found in the Winery Section of this Guidebook. Happy Tastings!

Baily Vineyard & Winery -
10% discount on wine purchases
Boorman Vineyards Estate Winery -
Free Tasting
Briar Rose Winery -
20% discount on wine purchases
Callaway Vineyard & Winery -
10% discount on wine tasting and wine purchases
10% discount on gift shop merchandise
Cougar Vineyard & Winery -
10% discount on wine purchases;
Falkner Winery
- Active Duty: *50% off Tasting fee and 15% discount on wine purchases*
- Navy League: *50 % off Tasting fee and 15% discount on wine purchases*
Note: Falkner Winery also offers discounts on wedding / event packages to active duty military families.
Filsinger Vineyards & Winery -
10% discount on wine purchases
Foote Print Winery -
Free Tasting and 10% discount on wine purchases
Frangipani Estate Winery -
50% off Tasting fee and 10% discount on wine purchases
Keyways Vineyard & Winery -
10% discount on wine purchases (Monday-Friday only)
La Cereza Vineyards & Winery -
20% off Tasting fee; 20% discount on wine purchases;10% discount on gift shop merchandise
Longshadow Ranch Winery -
15% discount on wine purchases (also applies to spouses)
Maurice Car'rie Winery -
20% off Tasting fee; 20% discount on wine and 20 % discount on gift shop purchases
Mount Palomar Winery -
10% discount on wine purchases
Oak Mountain Winery / Temecula Hills Winery -
50% off Tasting fee; 10% discount on wine purchases
Ponte Family Estate Winery -
Free Tasting

South Coast Winery -
50% off Tasting fee and 15% discount on wine purchases
Stuart Cellars -
50% off Tasting fee
Wiens Family Cellars -
Free Tasting and 20% discount on wine purchases
Wilson Creek Winery & Vineyards -
20% off Tasting fee;
20% discount on wine purchases

"The best kind of wine is that which is most
pleasant to him who drinks it." ~ Pliny the Elder

FOR BEGINNERS ONLY - 102
(A Difference Between the Sexes?)

"Honey, taste this. Isn't this wonderful?" her husband
asks. He has the grin of a hunter that has just brought down a
14-point buck.

Honey smiles at him. Her head is nodding yes, but her
eyes say no.

"What? You don't like it?" he asks, both surprised and disappointed.

"It's OK," Honey says, not wanting to hurt his feelings,
but the "earthy" Syrah he has just given to her smells like a
barnyard – a big, powerful barnyard.

"What do you mean, OK?" he demands.

"Well," Honey says, choosing her words carefully, so as
not to offend her proud hunter. "It is just so overpowering. It
feels like the 4th of July in my mouth."

"Exactly!" her husband exclaims, thinking briefly that she
finally gets it. But no, she really doesn't care for his wonderful
new discovery. Sadly, he turns back to the tasting bar, convinced
that something is definitely wrong with Honey.

What's going on? Well, for one thing, there is nothing "wrong" with
Honey. Men and women are different. Okay, you knew that. But did you
know that tongues are different, too? Some people have fewer taste buds.
These folks may tend to like the big, bold, concentrated wines. Perhaps
Honey's hubby falls into this category.

People with more taste buds might be more sensitive and be "put off"
by wines with strong tannins. They may prefer more delicate or lighter

style wines. (Okay, ladies, this is where you smack your husband on the shoulder and say, "See! I told you there was nothing wrong with my taste buds.")

Simply put, sex does matter. According to Jane Black, wine writer for the *Washington Post*, the female judges' first place choice at a 2006 Pinot Noir judging in San Francisco came in 35th when scored by the men. The first place choice for the men was ranked 35th by the women.

Starting to see a pattern here? In our experience, women tend to be more sensitive tasters. (Now, don't go cranking up the computer to send us a flaming Email over this comment.) We don't say they are better tasters, just different. Terri Pebley of **Keyways Vineyard and Winery** recognizes this and that is why she has created "wine for women, by women." It is not just a clever marketing strategy, but it is also recognition that not all wine tasters are created equal.

So where does that leave us? Glad you asked. Knowing the type of taster you are is important. If you are a beginning wine taster, our recommendation is to focus less on the mumbo-jumbo of wine tasting notes and to concentrate on the basics. Do you like big, bold, lush wines, or softer, lighter style and more delicate wines? Do you like sweeter style wines or wines that are dry (less sweet)?

Next time you are in a large tasting room such as **Callaway**, **Leonesse**, **Wiens**, or **South Coast**, do not follow the normal tasting pattern. Ask your server to pour you two wines in two different glasses. Ask the server to pick something "light and delicate" and perhaps a bit fruity and something "big, bold and lush." We know, we're breaking some traditional how-to-taste-wine rules, but trust us. Go back and forth between the two styles of wines. Start with white wines and repeat the process with reds and pay attention to the alcohol content. You might find you like wines with less alcohol.

Knowing which types of wines "fit" you is a great help in selecting wines to try. Your goal is to be able to answer the question, **"Which wines would you like to taste?"** Your answer might be, "I usually prefer dry (less sweet), lighter style wines." Or you might respond by telling your server that you prefer big, bold wines with lots of tannins.

Contrary to the introduction section of the book in which we state that we only have two Rules of Wine Tasting, there is actually a third. "Trust Your Palate" – not point scores, not awards, not those around you. Just trust yourself. Remember, a great wine for you is one *you* like. But, do not be surprised as you become a more experienced wine taster to find that your palate has changed from when you first began. That's part of the fun of wine tasting. The appreciation of wine is a wonderful and always evolving experience.

Happy Tastings!

THE WINES...

"When it comes to wine, I tell people to
throw away the vintage charts and invest in a
corkscrew. The best way to learn about wine is
the drinking."
~ Alexis Lichine

"Wine is the most healthful and most hygienic
of beverages." ~ Louis Pasteur

- WHITE WINES -

FAVORITE TASTING ROOMS FOR CHARDONNAY

CHARDONNAY (Shar-dun-NAY) *is the best known of the white wine grapes and makes a rich buttery or creamy, medium to full-bodied wine. Chardonnay wines may have pear, apple, and oak flavor and aroma.*

The following wineries / tasting rooms are the ones we recommend for Chardonnay.

Callaway Vineyard & Winery
32720 Rancho California Road, Temecula, CA 92591 ◆ Tel: 951-676-4001 ◆ Hours: Daily 10- 5 ◆ Website: *www.callawaywinery.com*

✪ *Grape Escapes Discount!* - Present a copy of this book and receive a **20% discount** on all wines and tasting room merchandise purchased on the day of your visit. Also, present a copy of this book and receive **Two-for-One tasting!!!**

Filsinger Vineyards & Winery, Inc.
39050 De Portola Road, Temecula, CA 92592 ◆ Tel: 951-302-6363 ◆ Hours: Fri 11-4, Sat-Sun 10-5 ◆ Website: *www.filsingerwinery.com*

Keyways Vineyard & Winery
37338 De Portola Road, Temecula, CA 92592 ◆ Tel: 1-877-539-9297 ◆ Hours: Daily 10-6, Winter 10-5 ◆ Website: *www.keywayswine.com*

✪ *Grape Escapes Discount!* - Present a copy of this book and receive **Two-for-One tasting** from their "standard" tasting menu. Sorry, but offer is valid on weekdays only.

Longshadow Ranch Vineyard & Winery
39847 Calle Contento, Temecula, CA 92591 ◆ Tel: 951-587-6221 ◆ Hours: Mon-Fri 12-5, Sat 10-4 (Sat Bonfire 5-9 PM April through October), Sun 10-5 ◆ Website: *www.longshadowranchwinery.com*

✪ *Grape Escapes Discount!* - Present a copy of this book and receive a **10% discount** on all wines purchased on the day of your visit.

Orfila Vineyards & Winery
13455 San Pasqual Road, Escondido, CA 925025 ◆ Tel: (760) 738-6500 ◆ Hours: Daily 10-6 ◆ Website: *www.Orfila.com*

✪ *Grape Escapes Discount!* - Present a copy of this book and receive **free tasting** for up to four people in your party. In addition, you will also receive a **15% discount** on all wines purchased (except the Ambassador Reserve Merlot), plus a **10% discount** on all tasting room merchandise purchased on the day of your visit. Present a copy of this book and receive an additional **5% discount** (total of 20%) on a case or more of wine. Also, present a copy of this book and receive a **free "back-stage" tour** of the winery. Appointment required.

"Reality is an illusion that occurs due to a lack of wine." ~ Anonymous

FAVORITE TASTING ROOMS FOR CORTESE

CORTESE (Cor-TAY-zee) – *a white grape grown primarily in the Piedmont area of Italy that is known for producing a dry, pale yellow wine with light body and long finish. It may have a crispy, lemony or flinty flavor and aroma.*

<u>Cougar Vineyard & Winery</u>
39870 De Portola Road, Temecula, CA 92592 ◆ **Tel: 951-491-0825** ◆ **Hours: Daily 11-6, Winter 11-5** ◆ **Website:** *www.cougarvineyards.com*

<u>Mount Palomar Winery</u>
33820 Rancho California Road, Temecula, CA 92591 ◆ **Tel: 951-676-5047** ◆ **Summer Hours: Mon-Thurs 10-6, Fri-Sun 10-7; Winter Hours: Closed Mon & Tues; Wed-Thur 10-5, Fri-Sun 10-6** ◆ **Website:** *www.mountpalomar. com*

✪ *Grape Escapes Discount!* - Present a copy of this book and receive a **Two-for-One tasting!!!**

"Wine gives men courage and makes
men more apt for passion." ~ Ovid

FAVORITE TASTING ROOMS FOR GEWÜRZTRAMINER

GEWÜRZTRAMINER (Geh-VERTZ-tram-in-er) – *a white grape (with a tough to pronounce German name) used to produce a golden yellow to copper colored, feisty, strong wine with a perfumey, exotic scent. It is also used to produce an excellent dessert wine. These wines may have spicy gardenia, honeysuckle, peach, mango, lychee nut, and wood flavors and aromas. The late harvest wine has a honey and sweet cabbage taste.*

La Cereza Vineyard & Winery
Silver Medal Winner - 2008 SF Chronicle Wine Competition!
34567 Rancho California Road, Temecula, CA 92591 ✦ Tel: 951-699-6961 ✦ Hours: Daily 10-5 ✦ Website: *www.lacerezawinery.com*

✪ *Grape Escapes Discount!* - Present a copy of this book and receive a **10% discount** on all wines and tasting room merchandise purchased on the day of your visit. Sorry, but offer is not valid on weekends.

Orfila Vineyards & Winery
Silver Medal Winner - 2008 SF Chronicle Wine Competition!
3455 San Pasqual Road, Escondido, CA 92025 ✦ Tel: 760-738-6500 ✦ Hours: Daily 10-6
Website: *www.orfila.com*

✪ *Grape Escapes Discount!* - Present a copy of this book and receive **free tasting** for up to four people in your party. In addition, you will also receive a **15% discount** on all wines purchased (except the Ambassador Reserve Merlot), plus a **10% discount** on all tasting room merchandise purchased on the day of your visit. Present a copy of this book and receive an additional **5% discount** (total of 20%) on a case or more of wine. Also, present a copy of this book and receive a **free "back-stage" tour** of the winery. Appointment required.

South Coast Winery
34843 Rancho California Road, Temecula, CA 92591 ◆ Tel: 951-587-9463 ◆ Hours: Daily 10-6 ◆ Website: *www.wineresort.com*

"Eat thy bread with joy, and drink thy wine with a merry heart."
~ Ecclesiastes

FAVORITE TASTING ROOMS FOR PINOT GRIGIO

PINOT GRIGIO (Pee-noh GREE-zOH") or **PINOT GRIS** (pee-noh GREE) – *a white grape that is used to make a simple, clean, crisp, dry wine with an acid bite. Apple, lemon, pear, peach, vanilla, almond, and smoke may be flavors and aromas in this wine.*

La Cereza Vineyard & Winery
34567 Rancho California Road, Temecula, CA 92591 ◆ Tel: 951-699-6961 ◆ Hours: Daily 10-5 ◆ Website: *www.lacerezawinery.com*

✪ *Grape Escapes Discount!* - Present a copy of this book and receive a **10% discount** on all wines and tasting room merchandise purchased on the day of your visit. Sorry, but offer is not valid on weekends.

Leonesse Cellars
38311 De Portola Road, Temecula, CA 92592 ◆ Tel: 951-302-7601 ◆ Hours: Daily 10-5 ◆ Website: *www.leonessecellars.com*

Robert Renzoni Vineyards
37350 De Portola Road, Temecula, CA 92592 ◆ Tel: 951-302-8466 ◆ Hours: Daily 11-6 ◆ Website: *www. robertrenzonivineyards.com*

✪ *Grape Escapes Discount!* - Present a copy of this book and receive a **10% discount** on all wines and tasting room merchandise purchased on the day of your visit. Also, present a copy of this book and receive an additional **10% discount** (total of 20%) on a case or more of wine.

Stuart Cellars
33515 Rancho California Road, Temecula, CA 92591 ◆ Tel: 951-676-6414 ◆ Hours: Daily 10-5 ◆ Website: *www.stuartcellars.com*

"Give me wine to wash me clean of the
weather-stains of care." ~ Ralph Waldo Emerson

FAVORITE TASTING ROOMS FOR RIESLING

RIESLING (REES-ling) – *a white grape originating in 14th century Germany and used to make a dry, sweet, complex wine. It may have apple, peach, apricot, pear, melon, citrus, honey, rose petal, or musky flavors or aromas.*

Alex's Red Barn Winery
39820 Calle Contento, Temecula, CA 92951 ◆ Tel: 951-693-3201 ◆ Hours: Sat-Sun and most holidays 11-6, Winter 10-5 ◆ Website: *www.redbarnwine.com*

Briar Rose Winery
41720 Calle Cabrillo, Temecula, CA 92592 ◆ Tel: 951-308-1098 ◆ Hours: By Appointment Only ◆ Website: *www.briarrosewinery.com*

Falkner Winery
40620 Calle Contento, Temecula, CA 92591 ◆ Tel: 951-676-8231 ◆ Hours: Daily 10-5 ◆ Website: *www.falknerwinery.com*

Keyways Vineyard & Winery
37338 De Portola Road, Temecula, CA 92592 ◆ Tel: 1-877-539-9297 ◆ Hours: Daily 10-6, Winter 10-5 ◆ Website: *www.keywayswine.com*

✪ *Grape Escapes Discount!* - Present a copy of this book and receive **Two-for-One tasting** from their "standard" tasting menu. Sorry, but offer is valid on weekdays only.

Orfila Vineyards & Winery
Bronze Medal Winner - 2008 NWIWC!
3455 San Pasqual Road, Escondido, CA 92025 ♦ Tel: 760-738-6500 ♦
Hours: Daily 10-6
Website:*www.orfila.com*

☼ *Grape Escapes Discount!* - Present a copy of this book and receive **free tasting** for up to four people in your party. In addition, you will also receive a **15% discount** on all wines purchased (except the Ambassador Reserve Merlot), plus a **10% discount** on all tasting room merchandise purchased on the day of your visit. Present a copy of this book and receive an additional **5% discount** (total of 20%) on a case or more of wine. Also, present a copy of this book and receive a **free "back-stage" tour** of the winery. Appointment required.

Ponte Family Estate Winery
35053 Rancho California Road, Temecula, CA 92591 ♦ Tel: 951-694-8855 ♦ Hours: Daily 10-5 ♦ Website: *www.pontewinery.com*

☼ *Grape Escapes Discount!* - Present a copy of this book and receive a **Two-for-One tasting**!!! Offer valid Monday Through Thursday, excluding holidays.

South Coast Winery
Silver Medal Winner - 2008 NWIWC!
34843 Rancho California Road, Temecula, CA 92591 ♦ Tel: 951-587-9463 ♦ Hours: Daily 10-6 ♦ Website: *www.wineresort.com*

"The juice of the grape is the liquid quintessence
of concentrated sunbeams." ~ Thomas Love Peacock

FAVORITE TASTING ROOMS FOR SAUVIGNON BLANC

SAUVIGNON BLANC (SOH-veen-yawn • Blahnk) – *a white grape that makes dry, sweet, aggressive wines. It may have vanilla, gooseberry, asparagus, green olive, bell pepper, grapefruit, lime, melon, grass, oak or smoke flavors and aromas.*

Alex's Red Barn Winery
39820 Calle Contento, Temecula, CA 92951 ◆ Tel: 951-693-3201 ◆ Hours: Sat-Sun and most holidays 11-6, Winter 10-5 ◆ Website: *www.redbarnwine.com*

Briar Rose Winery
41720 Calle Cabrillo, Temecula, CA 92592 ◆ Tel: 951-308-1098 ◆ Hours: By Appointment Only ◆ Website: *www.briarrosewinery.com*

Falkner Winery
Best of Class Gold Medal Winner - 2008 SF Chronicle Wine Competition!
40620 Calle Contento, Temecula, CA 92591 ◆ Tel: 951-676-8231 ◆ Hours: Daily 10-5 ◆ Website: *www.falknerwinery.com*

⇨ **By The Way** – Only the United States uses the "Fumé Blanc" name. All other countries still call the grape and wine "Sauvignon Blanc." Robert Mondavi was the first winemaker to use "Fumé Blanc" as a varietal name. In 1968, Mondavi was offered a crop of particularly good Sauvignon Blanc grapes, but he knew the varietal needed a different name in order for it to be marketed successfully. At that time, Sauvignon Blanc had a poor reputation and poor sales in California. His newly named wine was aged in oak barrels and it became an immediate success.

Hart Winery
41300 Avenida Biona, Temecula, CA   92591 ✦ Tel: 951-676-6300 ✦ Hours: Daily 9-4:30 ✦ Website: *www.thehartfamilywinery.com*

Keyways Vineyard & Winery
Best of Class Double Gold - 2008 NWIWC!
37338 De Portola Road, Temecula, CA 92592 ✦ Tel: 1-877-539-9297 ✦ Hours: Daily 10-6, Winter 10-5 ✦ Website: *www.keywayswine.com*

✪ *Grape Escapes Discount!* - Present a copy of this book and receive **Two-for-One tasting** from their "standard" tasting menu. Sorry, but offer is valid on weekdays only.

Maurice Car'rie Winery
34225 Rancho California Road, Temecula, CA 92591 ✦ Tel: 951-676-1711 ✦ Hours: Daily 10-5 ✦ Website: *www.mauricecarriewinery.com*

✪ *Grape Escapes Discount!* - Present a copy of this book and receive a **10% discount** on all wines and tasting room merchandise purchased on the day of your visit. Sorry, but offer is not valid on weekends.

Ponte Family Estate Winery
35053 Rancho California Road, Temecula, CA 92591 ✦ Tel: 951-694-8855 ✦ Hours: Daily 10-5 ✦ Website: *www.pontewinery.com*

✪ *Grape Escapes Discount!* - Present a copy of this book and receive a **Two-for-One tasting**!!! Offer valid Monday Through Thursday, excluding holidays.

Wilson Creek Winery & Vineyards
Bronze Medal Winner - 2008 NWIWC!
35960 Rancho California Road, Temecula, CA 92591 ◆ Tel: 951-699-9463 ◆ Hours: Daily 10-5 ◆ Website: *www.wilsoncreekwinery.com*

✪ *Grape Escapes Discount!* - Present a copy of this book and receive **Two-for-One tasting** for up to four guests (a $20 value). PLUS, present a copy of this book and receive a **10% discount** on all wines purchased on the day of your visit. Offers good Monday – Friday only, except on holidays. And if this is not reason enough to visit one of our favorite wineries, present a copy of **The Grape Escapes 2** and receive a **free glass of Almond champagne** for up to four guests (one glass per entrée) with your purchase of an entrée at the **Creekside Grille** located at Wilson Creek Winery. This is a $28 value and is valid Monday – Friday only, except on holidays.

"...all I want out of wines is to enjoy them."
~ Ernest Hemingway

FAVORITE TASTING ROOMS FOR VIOGNIER

VIOGNIER (Vee-own-YAY) *is a classic white grape grown in France's Rhone Valley and in California that produces a complex, full-bodied, heavily perfumed, spicy, and deep yellow wine. In addition, it is one of the few white grapes that can be successfully blended with red grapes. Lime, melons, apricots, pears, tropical fruits, honeysuckle, jasmine, ginger, and white pepper are the flavors and aromas that are often found in Viognier wine.*

Viognier is another of our favorite white wines. Its rich fruit flavors make it an excellent alternative to Chardonnay. We think the following tasting rooms offer superb Viognier:

Alex's Red Barn Winery
39820 Calle Contento, Temecula, CA 92951 ♦ Tel: 951-693-3201 ♦ Hours: Sat-Sun and most holidays 11-6, Winter 10-5 ♦ Website: *www.redbarnwine.com*

Briar Rose Winery
41720 Calle Cabrillo, Temecula, CA 92592 ♦ Tel: 951-308-1098 ♦ Hours: By Appointment Only ♦ Website: *www.briarrosewinery.com*

Falkner Winery
Bronze Medal Winner - 2008 SF Chronicle Wine Competition!
40620 Calle Contento, Temecula, CA 92591 ♦ Tel: 951-676-8231 ♦ Hours: Daily 10-5 ♦ Website: *www.falknerwinery.com*

Hart Winery
41300 Avenida Biona, Temecula, CA   92591 ◆ Tel: 951-676-6300 ◆
Hours: Daily 9-4:30 ◆ Website: *www.thehartfamilywinery.com*

La Cereza Vineyard & Winery
Bronze Medal Winner - 2008 NWIWC!
34567 Rancho California Road, Temecula, CA 92591 ◆ Tel: 951-699-
6961 ◆ Hours: Daily 10-5 ◆ Website: *www.lacerezawinery.com*

✿ *Grape Escapes Discount!* - Present a copy of this book and receive a
10% discount on all wines and tasting room merchandise purchased on
the day of your visit. Sorry, but offer is not valid on weekends.

Oak Mountain Winery / Temecula Hills Winery
36522 Via Verde, Temecula, CA 92592 ◆ Tel: 951-699-9102 ◆ Hours:
Daily 11-5 ◆ Website: *www.oakmountainwinery. com*

✿ *Grape Escapes Discount!* - Present a copy of this book and receive a
10% discount on all wines purchased on the day of your visit. Also, present a copy of this book and receive **two-for-one tasting** for up to four
guests. Offer does not include the souvenir logo glass.

"Compromises are for relationships, not wine."
~ Sir Robert Scott Caywood

FAVORITE TASTING ROOMS FOR WHITE BLENDS

Baily Vineyard & Winery
33440 La Serena Way, Temecula, CA 92591 ♦ Tel: 951-676-9463 ♦ Hours: Sun-Fri 11-5, Sat 10-5 ♦ Website: *www.bailywinery.com*

Gershon Bachus Vintners
37750 De Portola Road, Temecula, CA 92592 ♦ Tel: 951-458-8428 ♦ Hours: By Appointment Only ♦ Website: *www.gershonbachus.com*

Maurice Car'rie Winery
34225 Rancho California Road, Temecula, CA 92591 ♦ Tel: 951-676-1711 ♦ Hours: Daily 10-5 ♦ Website: *www.mauricecarriewinery.com*

✿ *Grape Escapes Discount!* - Present a copy of this book and receive a **10% discount** on all wines and tasting room merchandise purchased on the day of your visit. Sorry, but offer is not valid on weekends.

Tesoro Winery (Tasting Room)
28475 Old Town Front Street, Temecula, CA 92590 ♦ Tel: 951-308-0000 ♦ Hours: Daily 10-5 ♦ Website: *www. tesorowines.com*

✿ *Grape Escapes Discount!* - Present a copy of this book and receive a **Two-for-One tasting** for up to four people in your party!!! Present a copy of this book and receive a **10% discount** on all wines and tasting room merchandise purchased on the day of your visit.

Wilson Creek Winery & Vineyards
Bronze Medal Winner - 2008 NWIWC!
35960 Rancho California Road, Temecula, CA 92591 ◆ Tel: 951-699-9463 ◆ Hours: Daily 10-5 ◆ Website: *www.wilsoncreekwinery.com*

✪ *Grape Escapes Discount!* - Present a copy of this book and receive **Two-for-One tasting** for up to four guests (a $20 value). PLUS, present a copy of this book and receive a **10% discount** on all wines purchased on the day of your visit. Offers good Monday – Friday only, except on holidays. And if this is not reason enough to visit one of our favorite wineries, present a copy of *The Grape Escapes 2* and receive a **free glass of Almond champagne** for up to four guests (one glass per entrée) with your purchase of an entrée at the **Creekside Grille** located at Wilson Creek Winery. This is a $28 value and is valid Monday – Friday only, except on holidays.

"Whiskey!? Never tasted such beastly stuff in my life!
In a civilized country they drink wine." ~ Charlie Chaplin

FAVORITE TASTING ROOMS FOR WHITE CAB

Alex's Red Barn Winery
**39820 Calle Contento, Temecula, CA 92951 ◆ Tel: 951-693-3201 ◆
Hours: Sat-Sun and most holidays 11-6, Winter 10-5 ◆ Website:**
www.redbarnwine.com

Cougar Vineyard & Winery
**39870 De Portola Road, Temecula, CA 92592 ◆ Tel: 951-491-0825 ◆
Hours: Daily 11-6, Winter 11-5 ◆ Website:** *www.cougarvineyards.com*

Wilson Creek Winery & Vineyards
**35960 Rancho California Road, Temecula, CA 92591 ◆ Tel: 951-699-
9463 ◆ Hours: Daily 10-5 ◆ Website:** *www.wilsoncreekwinery.com*

✪ *Grape Escapes Discount!* - Present a copy of this book and receive
Two-for-One tasting for up to four guests (a $20 value). PLUS, present a
copy of this book and receive a **10% discount** on all wines purchased on
the day of your visit. Offers good Monday – Friday only, except on holidays. And if this is not reason enough to visit one of our favorite wineries,
present a copy of *The Grape Escapes 2* and receive a **free glass of Almond
Champagne** for up to four guests (one glass per entrée) with your purchase of an entrée at the **Creekside Grille** located at Wilson Creek Winery.
This is a $28 value and is valid Monday – Friday only, except on holidays.

"Artists and poets still find life's meaning
in a glass of wine." ~ Joy Sterling, A Cultivated Life

FAVORITE TASTING ROOMS FOR WHITE MERLOT

Inn at Churon Winery
33233 Rancho California Road, Temecula, CA 92591 ♦ Tel: 951-694-9070 ♦ Hours: Daily 10-4:30 ♦ Website: *www.innatchuronwinery.com*

Leonesse Cellars
38311 De Portola Road, Temecula, CA 92592 ♦ Tel: 951-302-7601 ♦ Hours: Daily 10-5 ♦ Website: *www.leonessecellars.com*

Longshadow Ranch Vineyard & Winery
39847 Calle Contento, Temecula, CA 92591 ♦ Tel: 951-587-6221 ♦ Hours: Mon-Fri 12-5, Sat 10-4 (Sat Bonfire 5-9 PM April through October), Sun 10-5 ♦ Website: *www.longshadowranchwinery.com*

✪ *Grape Escapes Discount!* - Present a copy of this book and receive a **10% discount** on all wines purchased on the day of your visit.

Oak Mountain Winery / Temecula Hills Winery
36522 Via Verde, Temecula, CA 92592 ♦ Tel: 951-699-9102 ♦ Hours: Daily 11-5 ♦ Website: *www.oakmountainwinery. com*

✪ *Grape Escapes Discount!* - Present a copy of this book and receive a **10% discount** on all wines purchased on the day of your visit. Also, present a copy of this book and receive **two-for-one tasting** for up to four guests. Offer does not include the souvenir logo glass.

Stuart Cellars
33515 Rancho California Road, Temecula, CA 92591 ♦ Tel: 951-676-6414 ♦ Hours: Daily 10-5 ♦ Website: *www.stuartcellars.com*

"If God forbade drinking, would He have
made wine so good?" ~ Attributed to Cardinal Richelieu

FAVORITE TASTING ROOMS FOR ROSÉ

ROSÉ (Roe-ZAY) - *a pink or light red wine made from red grapes. The grapes are crushed and, as the juice separates from the skin and seeds, it picks up pigmentation (color) from the skins. Unlike red wine, the skins are removed early on during fermentation. This decreases the tannins and causes rosé to taste similar to white wine. It is a soft, easy-to-drink wine best served chilled.*

So, is Rosé a red wine or a white wine? A hint – It is neither, but also a little bit of both. Confused? It was once popular for winemakers to simply add a little red wine to a white wine to give it a bit of color and a heartier character. This is rarely done now.

Juice from red wine grapes is actually clear. In order to impart the "blush" or color to Rosé, after crushing the grapes, winemakers leave the red skins in the juice for two or three days. It is the pigmentation from the skins that imparts a slight color or "blush," to the wine.

Sadly, Rosé has fallen out of fashion over the past few decades. Our attitude is: Don't worry about fashion – if Rosé is what you enjoy, by all means, enjoy. We like chilled Rosé – especially on a hot summer day.

We found some excellent Rosé wines in our travels around Temecula. Here are the wineries we recommend if Rosé is what you relish.

Keyways Vineyard & Winery
Rosé of Syrah won a Silver Medal at the 2008 NWIWC!
37338 De Portola Road, Temecula, CA 92592 ◆ Tel: 1-877-539-9297 ◆
Hours: Daily 10-6, Winter 10-5 ◆ Website: *www.keywayswine.com*

✪ *Grape Escapes Discount!* - Present a copy of this book and receive
Two-for-One tasting from their "standard" tasting menu. Sorry, but offer
is valid on weekdays only.

Miramonte Winery / Celebration Cellars
33410 Rancho California Road, Temecula, CA 92591 ◆ Tel: 951-506-
5500 ◆ Hours: Daily 11-6, Music Fri & Sat 5:30-8:30 ◆ Website:
www.miramontewinery.com

Robert Renzoni Vineyards
37350 De Portola Road, Temecula, CA 92592 ◆ Tel: 951-302-8466 ◆
Hours: Daily 11-6 ◆ Website: *www. robertrenzonivineyards.com*

✪ *Grape Escapes Discount!* - Present a copy of this book and receive a
10% discount on all wines and tasting room merchandise purchased on
the day of your visit. Also, present a copy of this book and receive an additional **10% discount** (total of 20%) on a case or more of wine.

Stuart Cellars
33515 Rancho California Road, Temecula, CA 92591 ◆ Tel: 951-676-
6414 ◆ Hours: Daily 10-5 ◆ Website: *www.stuartcellars.com*

"I like a wine you can drink a bottle of and
find pleasure all the way to the end of the bottle."
~ James Dunstan

- RED WINES -

FAVORITE TASTING ROOMS FOR BARBERA

BARBERA (Bar-BEAR-ah) *is a red grape that has low tannins and high acidity. The wine has medium body and may have a fruity or berry flavor. These grapes give wine an intense, deep red color.*

We like Barbera and are surprised that it is not in more demand. Since it is a medium-bodied wine, it is great for pairing with food. The wineries listed below produce some excellent wine from this varietal.

Boorman Vineyards Estate Winery
21630 Ave de Arboles, Murrieta, CA 92562 ◆ Tel: 951-600-9333 ◆ Hours: By Appointment Only ◆ Website: *www.boormanvineyards.com*

✪ *Grape Escapes Special Benefit* - Present a copy of this book and receive a **free "back-stage" tour** of the winery with the winemaker. *Advance appointment is required._*

Cowper Family Vineyards (Rey Sol Wines) (Not open to the Public.)
Etienne Cowper's excellent Barbera is available from *Temecula House of Wine* on Front Street in Temecula ◆ Tel: (951) 699-0929, or online at: *www.shoptemeculawines.com*

✪ *Grape Escapes Discount!* - Present a copy of this book at the ***Temecula House of Wine*** (28522 Front Street) in Old Town Temecula and receive a **10% discount** on all wines purchased on the day of your visit. If you purchase a case or more of wine during your visit, you will receive an additional **5%** (total 15%) **discount**. Tel: 951-699-0929 ◆ Hours: 10 AM to 8 PM weekdays and 10 AM to 10 PM on weekends ◆ Website: *www.palomarinntemecula.com*

Keyways Vineyard & Winery
37338 De Portola Road, Temecula, CA 92592 ◆ Tel: 1-877-539-9297 ◆ Hours: Daily 10-6, Winter 10-5 ◆ Website: *www.keywayswine.com*

✪ *Grape Escapes Discount!* - Present a copy of this book and receive **Two-for-One tasting** from their "standard" tasting menu. Sorry, but offer is valid on weekdays only.

"A date with a great bottle of Cabernet Sauvignon
is like a bedroom rendezvous with royalty..."
~ Campbell Mattinson, Wine Writer

FAVORITE TASTING ROOMS FOR CABERNET SAUVIGNON

CABERNET SAUVIGNON (Cah-burr-NAY • So-veen-YAWN) *is one of the most well known varieties of red grapes. It produces a full-bodied wine with a high sugar content that may have blueberry, black current, raspberry and an oak flavor and aroma.*

Boorman Vineyards Estate Winery
21630 Ave de Arboles, Murrieta, CA 92562 ♦ Tel: 951-600-9333 ♦ Hours: By Appointment Only ♦ Website: *www.boormanvineyards.com*

✪ *Grape Escapes Special Benefit* - Present a copy of this book and receive a free **"back-stage" tour** of the winery with the winemaker. *Advance appointment is required.*

Briar Rose Winery
41720 Calle Cabrillo, Temecula, CA 92592 ♦ Tel: 951-308-1098 ♦ Hours: By Appointment Only ♦ Website: *www.briarrosewinery.com*

⇨ **By The Way** – Cabernet Sauvignon, a grape varietal originally transplanted from Bordeaux, France, is California's most recognized varietal.

Gershon Bachus Vintners
37750 De Portola Road, Temecula, CA 92592 ◆ **Tel: 951-458-8428** ◆ **Hours: By Appointment Only** ◆ **Website:** *www.gershonbachus.com*

Mount Palomar Winery
33820 Rancho California Road, Temecula, CA 92591 ◆ **Tel: 951-676-5047** ◆ **Summer Hours: Mon-Thurs 10-6, Fri-Sun 10-7; Winter Hours: Closed Mon & Tues; Wed-Thur 10-5, Fri-Sun 10-6** ◆ **Website:** *www.mountpalomar.com*

✿ *Grape Escapes Discount!* - Present a copy of this book and receive a **Two-for-One tasting!!!**

South Coast Winery
Silver Medal Winner - 2008 NWIWC!
34843 Rancho California Road, Temecula, CA 92591 ◆ **Tel: 951-587-9463** ◆ **Hours: Daily 10-6** ◆ **Website:** *www.wineresort.com*

Tesoro Winery
28475 Old Town Front Street, Temecula, CA 92590 ◆ **Tel: 951-308-0000** ◆ **Hours: Daily 10-5** ◆ **Website:** *www. tesorowines.com*

✿ *Grape Escapes Discount!* - Present a copy of this book and receive a **Two-for-One tasting** for up to four people in your party!!! Present a copy of this book and receive a **10% discount** on all wines and tasting room merchandise purchased on the day of your visit.

Villa Vessia Vineyard Cabernet Sauvignon
Frankie's Steak and Seafood, 41789 Nicole Lane #1, Temecula, CA 92591 ◆ **Tel:** ◆ (951) 676.8040 ◆ **Website:** *www.Frankies-restaurant.com.* Villa Vessia Cabernet can also be purchased at *Temecula House of Wine* or online at *www.ShopTemeculaWines.com*

✿ *Grape Escapes Discount!* - Present a copy of this book at the *Temecula House of Wine* (28522 Front Street) in Old Town Temecula and receive a **10% discount** on all wines purchased on the day of your visit. If you purchase a case or more of wine during your visit, you will receive an additional **5%** (total 15%) **discount**. Tel: 951-699-0929 ◆ Hours: 10 AM to 8 PM weekdays and 10 AM to 10 PM on weekends ◆ Website: *www.palomarinntemecula.com*

If a life of wine, women and song becomes too much,
give up the singing. ~ Anonymous

FAVORITE TASTING ROOMS FOR CAB-FRANC

CABERNET FRANC (Cah-burr-NAY • Frahnk) – *a red grape used for deep purple, full-bodied wines. It has black current or earth fruit aromas and flavors.*

Baily Vineyard & Winery
Bronze Medal Winner - 2008 NWIWC!
33440 La Serena Way, Temecula, CA 92591 ◆ Tel: 951-676-9463 ◆ Hours: Sun-Fri 11-5, Sat 10-5 ◆ Website: *www. bailywinery.com*

Boorman Vineyards Estate Winery
21630 Ave de Arboles, Murrieta, CA 92562 ◆ Tel: 951-600-9333 ◆ Hours: By Appointment Only ◆ Website: *www.boormanvineyards.com*

✪ *Grape Escapes Special Benefit* - Present a copy of this book and receive a **free "back-stage" tour** of the winery with the winemaker. *Advance appointment is required._*

Callaway Vineyard & Winery
Silver Medal Winner - 2008 NWIWC!
32720 Rancho California Road, Temecula, CA 92591 ◆ Tel: 951-676-4001 ◆ Summer Hours: Daily 10- 6, Winter Hours: 10-5 ◆ Website: *www.callawaywinery.com*

✪ *Grape Escapes Discount!* - Present a copy of this book and receive a **20% discount** on all wines and tasting room merchandise purchased on the day of your visit. Also, present a copy of this book and receive **Two-for-One tasting!!!**

Hart Winery
Silver Medal Winner - 2008 NWIWC!
41300 Avenida Biona, Temecula, CA 92591 ◆ Tel: 951-676-6300 ◆ Hours: Daily 9-4:30 ◆ Website: *www.thehartfamilywinery.com*

Mount Palomar Winery
33820 Rancho California Road, Temecula, CA 92591 ◆ Tel: 951-676-5047 ◆ Summer Hours: Mon-Thurs 10-6, Fri-Sun 10-7; Winter Hours: Closed Mon & Tues; Wed-Thur 10-5, Fri-Sun 10-6 ◆ Website: *www.mountpalomar. com*

✪ *Grape Escapes Discount!* - Present a copy of this book and receive a **Two-for-One tasting!!!**

Stuart Cellars
Bronze medal Winner - 2008 NWIWC!
33515 Rancho California Road, Temecula, CA 92591 ◆ Tel: 951-676-6414 ◆ Hours: Daily 10-5 ◆ Website: *www. stuartcellars.com*

"Making good wine is a skill.
Fine wine is an art." ~ Robert Mondavi

FAVORITE TASTING ROOMS FOR GRENACHE

GRENACHE (Gren-AHSH) – *a red grape that is one of the most widely planted in the world. It is used to make pale red, peppery and sweet, fruity wines. Grenache wines may have the flavors and aromas of black currant, blackberry, apricot, and vanilla, sweet wood, oak, or smoke.*

Frangipani Estate Winery
39750 De Portola Road, Temecula, CA 92592 ◆ Tel: 951-699-8845 ◆ Hours: Daily 10-5 ◆ Website: *www.frangipaniwinery.com*

✿ *Grape Escapes Discount!* - Present a copy of this book and receive a **30% discount** on all wines purchased on the day of your visit.

Hart Winery
41300 Avenida Biona, Temecula, CA 92591 ◆ Tel: 951-676-6300 ◆ Hours: Daily 9-4:30 ◆ Website: *www.thehartfamilywinery.com*

Oak Mountain Winery / Temecula Hills Winery
36522 Via Verde, Temecula, CA 92592 ◆ Tel: 951-699-9102 ◆ Hours: Daily 11-5 ◆ Website: *www.oakmountainwinery. com*

✿ *Grape Escapes Discount!* - Present a copy of this book and receive a **10% discount** on all wines purchased on the day of your visit. Also, present a copy of this book and receive **two-for-one tasting** for up to four guests. Offer does not include the souvenir logo glass.

South Coast Winery
Silver Medal Winner - 2008 NWIWC!
34843 Rancho California Road, Temecula, CA 92591 ◆ Tel: 951-587-9463 ◆ Hours: Daily 10-6 ◆ Website: *www. wineresort.com*

"Wine gives strength to weary men." ~ Homer

FAVORITE TASTING ROOMS FOR MERLOT

MERLOT (Mehr-LOW) *is a classic grape that is used to produce an extremely popular, easy-to-drink wine with soft, smooth tannins. It may have flavors and aromas of currant, black cherry, plum, caramel, clove, vanilla, bay leaf, bell pepper, green olive, coconut, or oak.*

Bella Vista Winery
41220 Calle Contento, Temecula, CA 92592 ♦ Tel: 951-676-5250 ♦ Hours: Daily 10-6, Winter 10-5 ♦ Website: *www.bellavistawinery.com*

Foote Print Winery
36650 Glen Oaks Road, Temecula, CA 92592 ♦ Tel: 951-265-9951 ♦ Hours: Fri 12-5, Sat-Sun 10-5, Mon-Thurs By Appointment ♦ Website: *www.footeprintwinery.com*

❂ *Grape Escapes Discount!* - Present a copy of this book and receive a **Two-for-One tasting**!!!

Hart Winery
41300 Avenida Biona, Temecula, CA 92591 ♦ Tel: 951-676-6300 ♦ Hours: Daily 9-4:30 ♦ Website: *www.thehartfamilywinery.com*

Keyways Vineyard & Winery
37338 De Portola Road, Temecula, CA 92592 ♦ Tel: 1-877-539-9297 ♦ Hours: Daily 10-6, Winter 10-5 ♦ Website: *www.keywayswine.com*

❂ *Grape Escapes Discount!* - Present a copy of this book and receive **Two-for-One tasting** from their "standard" tasting menu. Sorry, but offer is valid on weekdays only.

Leonesse Cellars
(★ Signature Selection Merlot – This is a big, wonderful Merlot!)
**38311 De Portola Road, Temecula, CA 92592 ♦ Tel: 951-302-7601 ♦
Hours: Daily 10-5 ♦ Website:** *www.leonessecellars.com*

Orfila Vineyards & Winery
Gold Medal Winner - 2008 SF Chronicle Wine Competition!
**3455 San Pasqual Road, Escondido, CA 92025 ♦ Tel: 760-738-6500 ♦
Hours: Daily 10-6
Website:***www.orfila.com*

✪ *Grape Escapes Discount!* - Present a copy of this book and receive **free
tasting** for up to four people in your party. In addition, you will also
receive a **15% discount** on all wines purchased (except the Ambassador
Reserve Merlot), plus a **10% discount** on all tasting room merchandise
purchased on the day of your visit. Present a copy of this book and receive
an additional **5% discount** (total of 20%) on a case or more of wine. Also,
present a copy of this book and receive a **free "back-stage" tour** of the
winery. Appointment required.

Palumbo Family Vineyards & Winery
**40150 Barksdale Circle, Temecula, CA 92591 ♦ Tel: 951-676-7900 ♦
Hours: Fri 12-5, Sat-Sun 10-5, Mon-Thurs By Appointment ♦ Website:** *www.palumbofamilyvineyards.com*
✪ *Grape Escapes Complimentary Tasting!* - Present a copy of this book
and receive a **complimentary tasting for two people** in your party.

Wiens Family Cellars
**35055 Via Del Ponte, Temecula, CA   92592 ♦ Tel: 951-694-9892 ♦
Hours: Daily 10-5 ♦ Website:** *www.wienscellars.com*

✪ *Grape Escapes Discount!* - Present a copy of this book and receive
Two-for-One wine tasting, plus a **10% discount** on all wines purchased
on the day of your visit. Also, present a copy of this book and receive a **free
"back-stage" tour** of the winery with the winemaker. *Advance appointment is required.* Phone (951) 694-9892 to schedule.

"Up to the age of forty, eating is beneficial.
After forty, drinking." ~ The Talmud, 200BC

FAVORITE TASTING ROOMS FOR PETITE SYRAH

PETITE SIRAH (Peh-TEET • sih-RAH) – *a cross between two grapes (Syrah and Peloursin) that was developed in France in 1880. The grape makes a dark, blue-red (inky), full-bodied, peppery wine with high tannins. Raspberry, blackberry, plum, violets, black pepper, tobacco and chocolate aromas and flavors may be present in this wine.*

(Inn at) Churon Winery
33233 Rancho California Road, Temecula, CA 92591 ♦ Tel: 951-694-9070 ♦ Hours: Daily 10-4:30 ♦ Website: *www.innatchuronwinery.com*

Frangipani Estate Winery
39750 De Portola Road, Temecula, CA 92592 ♦ Tel: 951-699-8845 ♦ Hours: Daily 10-5 ♦ Website: *www.frangipaniwinery.com*

✪ *Grape Escapes Discount!* - Present a copy of this book and receive a **30% discount** on all wines purchased on the day of your visit.

Keyways Vineyard & Winery
37338 De Portola Road, Temecula, CA 92592 ♦ Tel: 1-877-539-9297 ♦ Hours: Daily 10-6, Winter 10-5 ♦ Website: *www.keywayswine.com*

✪ *Grape Escapes Discount!* - Present a copy of this book and receive **Two-for-One tasting** from their "standard" tasting menu. Sorry, but offer is valid on weekdays only.

Wilson Creek Winery & Vineyards
Gold Medal Winner - 2008 NWIWC Competition!
35960 Rancho California Road, Temecula, CA 92591 ◆ Tel: 951-699-9463 ◆ Hours: Daily 10-5 ◆ Website: *www.wilsoncreekwinery.com*

✿ *Grape Escapes Discount!* - Present a copy of this book and receive **Two-for-One tasting** for up to four guests (a $20 value). PLUS, present a copy of this book and receive a **10% discount** on all wines purchased on the day of your visit. Offers good Monday – Friday only, except on holidays. And if this is not reason enough to visit one of our favorite wineries, present a copy of *The Grape Escapes 2* and receive a **free glass of Almond Champagne** for up to four guests (one glass per entrée) with your purchase of an entrée at the **Creekside Grille** located at Wilson Creek Winery. This is a $28 value and is valid Monday – Friday only, except on holidays.

> "I have lived temperately…
> I double the doctor's recommendation
> of a glass and a half of wine a day…"
> ~ Thomas Jefferson

FAVORITE TASTING ROOMS FOR PINOT NOIR

PINOT NOIR (Pee-noh NWAHR) – *a hard-to-grow red grape that is used to produce a light-red, rich (but not heavy) wine. It may have aromas and flavors of cherry, strawberry, raspberry, mint, cinnamon, sassafras, mushroom, violet, vanilla, coconut, black olive, rosemary, caraway and toast.*

<u>Maurice Car'rie Winery</u>
34225 Rancho California Road, Temecula, CA 92591 ◆ Tel: 951-676-1711 ◆ Hours: Daily 10-5 ◆ Website: *www.mauricecarriewinery.com*

✪ *Grape Escapes Discount!* - Present a copy of this book and receive a **10% discount** on all wines and tasting room merchandise purchased on the day of your visit. Sorry, but offer is not valid on weekends.

<u>Wiens Family Cellars</u>
35055 Via Del Ponte, Temecula, CA   92592 ◆ Tel: 951-694-9892 ◆ Hours: Daily 10-5 ◆ Website: *www.wienscellars.com*

✪ *Grape Escapes Discount!* - Present a copy of this book and receive **Two-for-One wine tasting**, plus a **10% discount** on all wines purchased on the day of your visit. Also, present a copy of this book and receive a **free "back-stage" tour** of the winery with the winemaker. *Advance appointment is required.* Phone (951) 694-9892 to schedule.

"Wine, madam, is God's next best gift to man."
~ Ambrose Bierce

FAVORITE TASTING ROOMS FOR PRIMITIVO

PRIMITIVO (Pree-mi-TEE-voh) – *a dark red grape that was transported to Italy from Greece and was named by the Benedictine monks in the 17th century. It is considered to be the "father" of the Zinfandel grape. Recent studies at UC Davis show that both the Italian grown Primitivo and California Zinfandel have the same DNA characteristics. This deeply colored, rich and zesty wine can have flavors of wild cherry, clove, blackberry, raspberry, and spice.*

Cougar Vineyard & Winery
39870 De Portola Road, Temecula, CA 92592 ◆ Tel: 951-491-0825 ◆ Hours: Daily 11-6, Winter 11-5 ◆ Website: *www.cougarvineyards.com*

Palumbo Family Vineyards & Winery
40150 Barksdale Circle, Temecula, CA 92591 ◆ Tel: 951-676-7900 ◆ Hours: Fri 12-5, Sat-Sun 10-5, Mon-Thurs By Appointment ◆ Website: *www.palumbofamilyvineyards.com*

✪ *Grape Escapes Complimentary Tasting!* - Present a copy of this book and receive a **complimentary tasting for two people** in your party.

"The First Duty of wine is to be Red..." ~ Harry Waugh

FAVORITE TASTING ROOMS FOR RED BLENDS AND MERITAGE

MERITAGE (Mehr-ri-TAHJ) *is another word for Bordeaux-style blended wine – but not just any blend will do. Technically, to be called a red Meritage, the wine must be made from a combination of three or more of the following varietals: Cabernet Sauvignon, Cab Franc, Malbec, and Petit Verdot.*

Temecula is "Blend Country." Blending allows the winemaker to take the best from specific grape varietals and create wines that are quite literally greater than the sum of their component parts. The following wineries served us outstanding blends during our recent visits to Temecula.

⇨ **By The Way** – The word "Meritage" was chosen as a name for blended red wine in a national contest with over 6000 entries.

Bella Vista Winery
41220 Calle Contento, Temecula, CA 92592 ♦ Tel: 951-676-5250 ♦ Hours: Daily 10-6, Winter 10-5 ♦ Website: *www.bellavistawinery.com*

Gershon Bachus Vintners
37750 De Portola Road, Temecula, CA 92592 ♦ Tel: 951-458-8428 ♦ Hours: By Appointment Only ♦ Website: *www.gershonbachus.com*

Hart Winery
41300 Avenida Biona, Temecula, CA 92591 ♦ Tel: 951-676-6300 ♦ Hours: Daily 9-4:30 ♦ Website: *www.thehartfamilywinery.com*

Leonesse Cellars
38311 De Portola Road, Temecula, CA 92592 ♦ Tel: 951-302-7601 ♦ Hours: Daily 10-5 ♦ Website: *www.leonessecellars.com*

Mount Palomar Winery
33820 Rancho California Road, Temecula, CA 92591 ◆ Tel: 951-676-5047 ◆ Summer Hours: Mon-Thurs 10-6, Fri-Sun 10-7; Winter Hours: Closed Mon & Tues; Wed-Thur 10-5, Fri-Sun 10-6 ◆ Website: *www.mountpalomar. com*

✪ *Grape Escapes Discount!* - Present a copy of this book and receive a **Two-for-One tasting!!!**

Oak Mountain Winery / Temecula Hills Winery
36522 Via Verde, Temecula, CA 92592 ◆ Tel: 951-699-9102 ◆ Hours: Daily 11-5 ◆ Website: *www.oakmountainwinery. com*

✪ *Grape Escapes Discount!* - Present a copy of this book and receive a **10% discount** on all wines purchased on the day of your visit. Also, present a copy of this book and receive **Two-for-One tasting** for up to four guests. Offer does not include the souvenir logo glass.

Palumbo Family Vineyards & Winery
40150 Barksdale Circle, Temecula, CA 92591 ◆ Tel: 951-676-7900 ◆ Hours: Fri 12-5, Sat-Sun 10-5, Mon-Thurs By Appointment ◆ Website: *www.palumbofamilyvineyards.com*

✪ *Grape Escapes Complimentary Tasting!* - Present a copy of this book and receive a **complimentary tasting for two people** in your party.

Santa Maria Winery
Benny Rodriguez's wonderful blended wines are available at *Temecula House of Wine* located on Front Street in Old Town Temecula or online at: *www.shoptemeculawines.com*

✪ *Grape Escapes Discount!* - Present a copy of this book at the ***Temecula House of Wine*** (28522 Front Street) in Old Town Temecula and receive a **10% discount** on all wines purchased on the day of your visit. If you purchase a case or more of wine during your visit, you will receive an additional **5%** (total 15%) **discount**. Tel: 951-699-0929 ◆ Hours: 10 AM to 8 PM weekdays and 10 AM to 10 PM on weekends ◆ Website: *www.palomarinntemecula.com*

Thornton Winery
32575 Rancho California Road, Temecula, CA 92591 ◆ Tel: 951-699-0099 ◆ Hours: Daily 10-5 ◆ Website: *www.thorntonwinery.com*

"Wine is the drink of the gods, milk the drink of babes…
and water the drink of beasts." ~ John Stuart Blackie

FAVORITE TASTING ROOMS FOR SANGIOVESE

SANGIOVESE (San-jo-VAY-zay) – a red grape that makes a medium bodied, dry red wine that sometimes has an orange tint. The wine may have black cherry, plum, strawberry, blueberry, orange peel, violet, cinnamon, clove, thyme, vanilla and smoke flavors and aromas.

Baily Vineyard & Winery
Silver Medal Winner - 2008 NWIWC!
33440 La Serena Way, Temecula, CA 92591 ✦ Tel: 951-676-9463 ✦ Hours: Sun-Fri 11-5, Sat 10-5 ✦ Website: *www.bailywinery.com*

Cougar Vineyard & Winery
39870 De Portola Road, Temecula, CA 92592 ✦ Tel: 951-491-0825 ✦ Hours: Daily 11-6, Winter 11-5 ✦ Website: *www.cougarvineyards.com*

Las Piedras Vineyards (Not Open to the Public.)
Steve Hagata's 2002 Sangiovese is available at *Temecula House of Wine* located on Front Street ✦ Tel: (951) 699-0929 ✦ or online at: *www.shoptemeculawines.com*

✪ *Grape Escapes Discount!* - Present a copy of this book at the ***Temecula House of Wine*** (28522 Front Street) in Old Town Temecula and receive a **10% discount** on all wines purchased on the day of your visit. If you purchase a case or more of wine during your visit, you will receive an additional **5%** (total 15%) **discount**. Tel: 951-699-0929 ✦ Hours: 10 AM to 8 PM weekdays and 10 AM to 10 PM on weekends ✦ Website: *www.palomarinntemecula.com*

Maurice Car'rie Winery
Silver Medal Winner - 2008 SF Chronicle Wine Competition!
34225 Rancho California Road, Temecula, CA 92591 ◆ Tel: 951-676-1711 ◆ Hours: Daily 10-5 ◆ Website: *www. mauricecarriewinery.com*

✪ *Grape Escapes Discount!* - Present a copy of this book and receive a **10% discount** on all wines and tasting room merchandise purchased on the day of your visit. Sorry, but offer is not valid on weekends.

Mount Palomar Winery
33820 Rancho California Road, Temecula, CA 92591 ◆ Tel: 951-676-5047 ◆ Summer Hours: Mon-Thurs 10-6, Fri-Sun 10-7; Winter Hours: Closed Mon & Tues; Wed-Thur 10-5, Fri-Sun 10-6 ◆ Website: *www.mountpalomar. com*

✪ *Grape Escapes Discount!* - Present a copy of this book and receive a **Two-for-One tasting!!!**

Orfila Vineyards & Winery
Bronze Medal Winner - 2008 NWIWC!
3455 San Pasqual Road, Escondido, CA 92025 ◆ Tel: 760-738-6500 ◆ Hours: Daily 10-6
Website:*www.orfila.com*

✪ *Grape Escapes Discount!* - Present a copy of this book and receive **free tasting** for up to four people in your party. In addition, you will also receive a **15% discount** on all wines purchased (except the Ambassador Reserve Merlot), plus a **10% discount** on all tasting room merchandise purchased on the day of your visit. Present a copy of this book and receive an additional **5% discount** (total of 20%) on a case or more of wine. Also, present a copy of this book and receive a **free "back-stage" tour** of the winery. Appointment required.

Palumbo Family Vineyards & Winery
40150 Barksdale Circle, Temecula, CA 92591 ◆ Tel: 951-676-7900 ◆ Hours: Fri 12-5, Sat-Sun 10-5, Mon-Thurs By Appointment ◆ Web-site: *www.palumbofamilyvineyards.com*

✪ *Grape Escapes Complimentary Tasting!* - Present a copy of this book and receive a **complimentary tasting for two people** in your party.

Stuart Cellars
33515 Rancho California Road, Temecula, CA 92591 ◆ Tel: 951-676-6414 ◆ Hours: Daily 10-5 ◆ Website: *www. stuartcellars.com*

Tesoro Winery
28475 Old Town Front Street, Temecula, CA 92590 ◆ Tel: 951-308-0000 ◆ Hours: Daily 10-5 ◆ Website: *www. tesorowines.com*

✪ *Grape Escapes Discount!* - Present a copy of this book and receive a **Two-for-One tasting** for up to four people in your party!!! Present a copy of this book and receive a **10% discount** on all wines and tasting room merchandise purchased on the day of your visit.

☞ **Authors' Tip:** *If you are a Sangio lover, you have to stop by and try Tesoro's 2005 Sangiovese. It is exceptional and one of the best in the Valley.*

"The soft extractive note of an aged cork being withdrawn
has the true sound of a man opening his heart."
~ William S. Benwell

FAVORITE TASTING ROOMS FOR SUPER TUSCAN-STYLE BLEND

SUPER TUSCAN – *a red wine made from a blend of grapes with San-giovese being the main varietal. Super Tuscans include other grapes, such as Cabernet Sauvignon or Merlot, which are intended to make a richer and somewhat more full-bodied wine.*

Falkner Winery
40620 Calle Contento, Temecula, CA 92591 ◆ Tel: 951-676-8231 ◆ Hours: Daily 10-5 ◆ Website: *www.falknerwinery.com*

Ponte Family Estate Winery
35053 Rancho California Road, Temecula, CA 92591 ◆ Tel: 951-694-8855 ◆ Hours: Daily 10-5 ◆ Website: *www. pontewinery.com*

❂ *Grape Escapes Discount!* - Present a copy of this book and receive a **Two-for-One tasting**!!! Offer valid Monday Through Thursday, excluding holidays.

Tesoro Winery Tasting Room
28475 Old Town Front Street, Temecula, CA 92590 ◆ Tel: 951-308-0000 ◆ Hours: Daily 10-5 ◆ Website: *www. tesorowines.com*

❂ *Grape Escapes Discount!* - Present a copy of this book and receive a **Two-for-One tasting** for up to four people in your party!!! Present a copy of this book and receive a **10% discount** on all wines and tasting room merchandise purchased on the day of your visit.

☞ **Authors' Tip:** *The Tesoro Trinità is a Super Tuscan-Style blend that will knock your socks off. It is simply a marvelous wine and was easily our favorite of the "Super Tuscan" wines that we tasted.*

"Wine is inspiring and adds greatly to the joy of living."
~ Napoleon

FAVORITE TASTING ROOMS FOR SYRAH / SHIRAZ

SYRAH or **SIRAH** (See-RAH), also known as **SHIRAZ** (SHEAR-oz), *is a thick-skinned red grape that is used to produce a spicy, deep violet (almost black), rich full-bodied wine. The wine tends to be more spicy than fruity, but can have the flavors and aromas of black currant, black-berry, grass, black pepper, licorice, clove, thyme, bay leaf, sweet wood, oak and smoke.*

True or False? **Syrah** (or Sirah) is just a larger version of **Petite Sirah**. *False.* Although both Syrah and Petite Sirah are Rhone varietals with similar names, the two grapes are completely different. To make things more confusing, the Australians went and renamed their Syrah wines "Shiraz." But do not let confusion stop you from exploring this wine – especially ones produced in the Temecula area.

What will you receive if you order a glass of Syrah? This wine is most frequently described as "inky." It has medium to large tannins when it is young, but the tannins decrease as the wine ages. Often, the wine is suggested as an alternative to Cabernet Sauvignon or Zinfandel. The following wineries produce outstanding Syrah:

Atwood Estate Vineyard (Not Open to the Public.)
Tim Kramer's exceptional Atwood Syrah is one of our favorite Temecula wines. This wine is available at *Temecula House of Wine* ◆ **Tel: (951) 699-0929** ◆ or online at: *www. shoptemeculawines.com*

Curry Vineyards (Not Open to the Public.)
Charlie Curry's excellent Syrah can be purchased by contacting Charlie direct at (909) 821-1282 or (951) 302-5647. His wines are also available at *Temecula House of Wine* ◆ **Tel: (951) 699-0929** ◆ or online at: *www.shoptemeculawines.com*

✪ *Grape Escapes Discount!* - Present a copy of this book at the ***Temecula House of Wine*** (28522 Front Street) in Old Town Temecula and receive a **10% discount** on all wines purchased on the day of your visit. If you purchase a case or more of wine during your visit, you will receive an additional **5%** (total 15%) **discount**. Tel: 951-699-0929 ◆ Hours: 10 AM to 8 PM weekdays and 10 AM to 10 PM on weekends ◆ Website: *www.palomarinntemecula.com*

Foote Print Winery
36650 Glen Oaks Road, Temecula, CA 92592 ◆ Tel: 951-265-9951 ◆ Hours: Fri 12-5, Sat-Sun 10-5, Mon-Thurs By Appointment ◆ Website: *www.footeprintwinery.com*

✪ *Grape Escapes Discount!* - Present a copy of this book and receive **Two-for-One tasting.**

Keyways Vineyard & Winery
37338 De Portola Road, Temecula, CA 92592 ◆ Tel: 1-877-539-9297 ◆ Hours: Daily 10-6, Winter 10-5 ◆ Website: *www.keywayswine.com*

✪ *Grape Escapes Discount!* - Present a copy of this book and receive **Two-for-One tasting** from their "standard" tasting menu. Sorry, but offer is valid on weekdays only.

La Cereza Vineyard & Winery
34567 Rancho California Road, Temecula, CA 92591 ◆ Tel: 951-699-6961 ◆ Hours: Daily 10-5 ◆ Website: *www. lacerezawinery.com*

✪ *Grape Escapes Discount!* - Present a copy of this book and receive a **10% discount** on all wines and tasting room merchandise purchased on the day of your visit. Sorry, but offer is not valid on weekends.

Las Piedras Vineyards (Not Open to the Public.)
Steve Hagata's 2004 Syrah is available at *Temecula House of Wine* located on Front Street ♦ **Tel: (951) 699-0929** ♦ or online at: *www.shoptemeculawines.com*

✿ *Grape Escapes Discount!* - Present a copy of this book at the **Temecula House of Wine** (28522 Front Street) in Old Town Temecula and receive a **10% discount** on all wines purchased on the day of your visit. If you purchase a case or more of wine during your visit, you will receive an additional **5%** (total 15%) **discount**. Tel: 951-699-0929 ♦ Hours: 10 AM to 8 PM weekdays and 10 AM to 10 PM on weekends ♦ Website: *www.palomarinntemecula.com*

Leonesse
38311 De Portola Road, Temecula, CA 92592 ♦ Tel: 951-302-7601 ♦ Hours: Daily 10-5 ♦ Website: *www.leonessecellars.com*

Orfila Vineyards & Winery
Bronze Medal Winner - 2008 SF Chronicle Wine Competition!
3455 San Pasqual Road, Escondido, CA 92025 ♦ Tel: 760-738-6500 ♦ Hours: Daily 10-6
Website:*www.orfila.com*

✿ *Grape Escapes Discount!* - Present a copy of this book and receive **free tasting** for up to four people in your party. In addition, you will also receive a **15% discount** on all wines purchased (except the Ambassador Reserve Merlot), plus a **10% discount** on all tasting room merchandise purchased on the day of your visit. Present a copy of this book and receive an additional **5% discount** (total of 20%) on a case or more of wine. Also, present a copy of this book and receive a **free "back-stage" tour** of the winery. Appointment required.

South Coast Winery
34843 Rancho California Road, Temecula, CA 92591 ♦ Tel: 951-587-9463 ♦ Hours: Daily 10-6 ♦ Website: *www. wineresort.com*

Wiens Family Cellars
35055 Via Del Ponte, Temecula, CA 92592 ♦ Tel: 951-694-9892 ♦ Hours: Daily 10-5 ♦ Website: *www.wienscellars.com*

✪ *Grape Escapes Discount!* - Present a copy of this book and receive **Two-for-One wine tasting,** plus a **10% discount** on all wines purchased on the day of your visit. Also, present a copy of this book and receive a **free "back-stage" tour** of the winery with the winemaker. *Advance appointment is required.* Phone (951) 694-9892 to schedule.

⇨ **By The Way** – **Although not on the tasting menu when we visited, the Falkner 2004 Syrah won the Silver Medal at the 2008 NWIWC and at the 2008 SF Chronicle Wine Competition. At the time we went to press, this wine was still available for purchase at the winery.**

"Wine is light, held together by water." ~ Galileo

FAVORITE TASTING ROOMS FOR TEMPRANILLO

TEMPRANILLO (Temp-rah-NEE-yoh) – *a red grape originating in Spain used primarily in low-acid, low-tannin wine for blends. Blackberry, plum, leather, cedar, vanilla, and spices are the predominant flavors and aromas.*

Hart Winery
41300 Avenida Biona, Temecula, CA   92591 ♦ Tel: 951-676-6300 ♦ Hours: Daily 9-4:30 ♦ Website: *www.thehartfamilywinery.com*

Keyways Vineyard & Winery
37338 De Portola Road, Temecula, CA 92592 ♦ Tel: 1-877-539-9297 ♦ Hours: Daily 10-6, Winter 10-5 ♦ Website: *www.keywayswine.com*

✪ *Grape Escapes Discount!* - Present a copy of this book and receive **Two-for-One tasting** from their "standard" tasting menu. Sorry, but offer is valid on weekdays only.

La Cereza Vineyard & Winery
Silver Medal Winner - 2008 NWIWC!
34567 Rancho California Road, Temecula, CA 92591 ♦ Tel: 951-699-6961 ♦ Hours: Daily 10-5 ♦ Website: *www. lacerezawinery.com*

✪ *Grape Escapes Discount!* - Present a copy of this book and receive a **10% discount** on all wines and tasting room merchandise purchased on the day of your visit. Sorry, but offer is not valid on weekends.

Oak Mountain Winery / Temecula Hills Winery
36522 Via Verde, Temecula, CA 92592 ◆ Tel: 951-699-9102 ◆ Hours: Daily 11-5 ◆ Website: *www.oakmountainwinery. com*

✪ *Grape Escapes Discount!* - Present a copy of this book and receive a **10% discount** on all wines purchased on the day of your visit. Also, present a copy of this book and receive **Two-for-One tasting** for up to four guests. Offer does not include the souvenir logo glass.

"Zinfandel is a captivating grape –
Zinfandel draws you in, if you let it.
Or maybe it just gets its hooks into you,
and gets ahold of you."
~ Frank Nerelli, Zin Alley

FAVORITE TASTING ROOMS FOR ZINFANDEL

ZINFANDEL (Zin-fan-DELL) *is a tough, hearty, versatile red grape that is used to produce remarkably different wines. The popular blush wine called White Zinfandel is light and fruity, but the Red Zinfandel is a robust, mouth-filling, deeply fruity, high alcohol wine with a lasting finish. The Red Zinfandel traditionally has jammy fruit (raspberry, blackberry, boysenberry, and black cherry), licorice, briar, cinnamon, black pepper, bubblegum, oak, and smoke flavors and aromas.*

We recommend you stop by one or all of the following wineries in your quest for the perfect Zin. *Our attitude is, go ahead and Zin. To do otherwise would be … well, unforgivable.*

Bella Vista Winery
41220 Calle Contento, Temecula, CA 92592 ♦ Tel: 951-676-5250 ♦ Hours: Daily 10-6, Winter 10-5 ♦ Website: *www.bellavistawinery.com*

Gershon Bachus Vintners
37750 De Portola Road, Temecula, CA 92592 ♦ Tel: 951-458-8428 ♦ Hours: By Appointment Only ♦ Website: *www.gershonbachus.com*

Hart Winery
Silver Medal Winner - 2008 NWIWC!
41300 Avenida Biona, Temecula, CA 92591 ♦ Tel: 951-676-6300 ♦ Hours: Daily 9-4:30 ♦ Website: *www.thehartfamilywinery.com*

Orfila Vineyards & Winery
Gold Medal Winner - 2008 SF Chronicle Wine Competition!
3455 San Pasqual Road, Escondido, CA 92025 ◆ Tel: 760-738-6500 ◆
Hours: Daily 10-6
Website:*www.orfila.com*

✪ *Grape Escapes Discount!* - Present a copy of this book and receive **free tasting** for up to four people in your party. In addition, you will also receive a **15% discount** on all wines purchased (except the Ambassador Reserve Merlot), plus a **10% discount** on all tasting room merchandise purchased on the day of your visit. Present a copy of this book and receive an additional **5% discount** (total of 20%) on a case or more of wine. Also, present a copy of this book and receive a **free "back-stage" tour** of the winery. Appointment required.

Stuart Cellars
Bronze Medal Winner - 2008 NWIWC!
33515 Rancho California Road, Temecula, CA 92591 ◆ Tel: 951-676-6414 ◆ Hours: Daily 10-5 ◆ Website: *www.stuartcellars.com*

Thornton Winery
32575 Rancho California Road, Temecula, CA 92591 ◆ Tel: 951-699-0099 ◆ Hours: Daily 10-5 ◆ Website: *www.thorntonwinery.com*

Wilson Creek Winery & Vineyards
Double Gold Medal Winner - 2008 NWIWC!
35960 Rancho California Road, Temecula, CA 92591 ◆ Tel: 951-699-9463 ◆ Hours: Daily 10-5 ◆ Website: *www.wilsoncreekwinery.com*

✪ *Grape Escapes Discount!* - Present a copy of this book and receive **Two-for-One tasting** for up to four guests (a $20 value). PLUS, present a copy of this book and receive a **10% discount** on all wines purchased on the day of your visit. Offers good Monday – Friday only, except on holidays. And if this is not reason enough to visit one of our favorite wineries, present a copy of **The Grape Escapes 2** and receive a **free glass of Almond Champagne** for up to four guests (one glass per entrée) with your purchase of an entrée at the **Creekside Grille** located at Wilson Creek Winery. This is a $28 value and is valid Monday – Friday only, except on holidays.

⇨ **By The Way** – Zinfandel first appeared on California wine labels in the late 1800s. Today, it is known as "California's grape" since most of the world's Zinfandel vineyard acreage is planted in California.

"A Mind the caliber of mine cannot
derive its nutrient from cows." ~ George Bernard Shaw

- DESSERT WINES -

FAVORITE TASTING ROOMS FOR MUSCAT CANELLI

MUSCAT CANELLI (Mus-CAT • Ka-NELL- ee) – *a white grape that makes a creamy, sweet, highly perfumed, light bodied, low alcohol wine with a honey-like texture and a long finish. It is a delicious aperitif, cocktail or dessert wine. It may have peach, honeydew melon, rose petals, lichee fruit, fig, orange blossom, candied ginger, and almond flavors and aromas.*

If you are a Muscat Canelli fan, we have some special treats in store for you.

Bella Vista Winery
41220 Calle Contento, Temecula, CA 92592 ◆ Tel: 951-676-5250 ◆ Hours: Daily 10-6, Winter 10-5 ◆ Website: *www.bellavistawinery.com*

Callaway Vineyard & Winery
32720 Rancho California Road, Temecula, CA 92591 ◆ Tel: 951-676-4001 ◆ Summer Hours: Daily 10-6, Winter Hours: 10-5 ◆ Website: *www.callawaywinery.com*

✪ *Grape Escapes Discount!* - Present a copy of this book and receive a **20% discount** on all wines and tasting room merchandise purchased on the day of your visit. Also, present a copy of this book and receive **Two-for-One tasting**!!!

Cougar Vineyard & Winery
39870 De Portola Road, Temecula, CA 92592 ◆ Tel: 951-491-0825 ◆
Hours: Daily 11-6, Winter 11-5 ◆ Website: *www.cougarvineyards.com*

Keyways Vineyard & Winery
Silver Medal Winner - 2008 NWIWC!
37338 De Portola Road, Temecula, CA 92592 ◆ Tel: 1-877-539-9297 ◆
Hours: Daily 10-6, Winter 10-5 ◆ Website: *www.keywayswine.com*

✪ *Grape Escapes Discount!* - Present a copy of this book and receive
Two-for-One tasting from their "standard" tasting menu. Sorry, but offer
is valid on weekdays only.

Orfila Vineyards & Winery
Gold Medal Winner 2007 VinoChallenge IWC!
3455 San Pasqual Road, Escondido, CA 92025 ◆ Tel: 760-738-6500 ◆
Hours: Daily 10-6
Website: *www.orfila.com*

☞ **Authors' Tip:** *We had a group of eight friends over to help us taste
wine one evening. All but one of these guests are "hard-core" red wine
drinkers. Even so, and against some very tough competition, the Orfila
Muscat Canelli was selected as our "Best of Show" from a selection of
twelve Temecula area wines.*

✪ *Grape Escapes Discount!* - Present a copy of this book and receive **free
tasting** for up to four people in your party. In addition, you will also
receive a **15% discount** on all wines purchased (except the Ambassador
Reserve Merlot), plus a **10% discount** on all tasting room merchandise
purchased on the day of your visit. Present a copy of this book and receive
an additional **5% discount** (total of 20%) on a case or more of wine. Also,
present a copy of this book and receive a **free "back-stage" tour** of the
winery. Appointment required.

South Coast Winery
Bronze Medal Winner - 2008 NWIWC!
4843 Rancho California Road, Temecula, CA 92591 ◆ Tel: 951-587-
9463 ◆ Hours: Daily 10-6 ◆ Website: *www.wineresort.com*

"I only drink fortified wines during bad weather.
Snowstorm, hurricane, tornado –
I'm not particular as long as it's bad.
After all, any storm for a Port." ~ Paul S. Winalski

FAVORITE TASTING ROOMS FOR PORT

PORT *wine is a thick, sweet, smooth wine that has usually been fortified (normally by adding brandy or other alcohol) to raise the alcohol content to18% – 20%. Port has the flavor and aroma of dried fruit, spices and wood. It is generally served after meals like a dessert wine or with cheese or chocolate.*

Temecula area winemakers produce great Ports. Here are our favorites:

Briar Rose Winery
41720 Calle Cabrillo, Temecula, CA 92592 ◆ Tel: 951-308-1098 ◆ Hours: By Appointment Only ◆ Website: *www.briarrosewinery.com*

Hart Winery
41300 Avenida Biona, Temecula, CA 92591 ◆ Tel: 951-676-6300 ◆ Hours: Daily 9-4:30 ◆ Website: *www.thehartfamilywinery.com*

Leonesse Cellars
38311 De Portola Road, Temecula, CA 92592 ◆ Tel: 951-302-7601 ◆ Hours: Daily 10-5 ◆ Website: *www.leonessecellars.com*

⇨ **By The Way – True Port wine comes from Portugal and is grown and produced in the Douro region. Under Portuguese law, only wine from this area can legally be called "Port."**

Oak Mountain Winery / Temecula Hills Winery
36522 Via Verde, Temecula, CA 92592 ◆ Tel: 951-699-9102 ◆ Hours: Daily 11-5 ◆ Website: *www.oakmountainwinery. com*

✿ *Grape Escapes Discount!* - Present a copy of this book and receive a **10% discount** on all wines purchased on the day of your visit. Also, present a copy of this book and receive **Two-for-One tasting** for up to four guests. Offer does not include the souvenir logo glass.

Stuart Cellars
33515 Rancho California Road, Temecula, CA 92591 ◆ Tel: 951-676-6414 ◆ Hours: Daily 10-5 ◆ Website: *www. stuartcellars.com*

Wilson Creek Winery & Vineyards
35960 Rancho California Road, Temecula, CA 92591 ◆ Tel: 951-699-9463 ◆ Website: *www.wilsoncreekwinery.com*

✿ *Grape Escapes Discount!* - Present a copy of this book and receive **Two-for-One tasting** for up to four guests (a $20 value). PLUS, present a copy of this book and receive a **10% discount** on all wines purchased on the day of your visit. Offers good Monday – Friday only, except on holidays. And if this is not reason enough to visit one of our favorite wineries, present a copy of **The Grape Escapes 2** and receive a **free glass of Almond Champagne** for up to four guests (one glass per entrée) with your purchase of an entrée at the **Creekside Grille** located at Wilson Creek Winery. This is a $28 value and is valid Monday – Friday only, except on holidays.

"If penicillin can cure those that are ill, Spanish sherry
can bring the dead back to life." ~ Sir Alexander Fleming

FAVORITE TASTING ROOMS FOR SHERRY

If you were paying attention in your high school literature class, you might
recall a short story published in 1846 by Edgar Allan Poe entitled, "The Cask
of Amontillado." Remember? Poor Fortunado is chained inside a wall niche
while Montressor mercilessly seals him in, brick-by-brick. Creepy! Anyway,
Amontillado is (you guessed it) a type of Sherry. Once you taste the Sherries
that Temecula Wine Country has to offer, you will understand why a man
could be led to his death in pursuit of this wonderful wine.

☞ **Authors' Tip:** *One of the special things about Sherry is that it can
last weeks or months after opening without spoiling. Perhaps this is why
it was a popular provision on long ocean voyages. Christopher Columbus
reportedly took it with him on his voyage to the New World. In Britain,
Sherry became very popular in the early 1600s after Sir Francis Drake
brought back 2900 barrels that he "liberated" from the Spanish city of
Cadiz.*

Sherry has been around so long that its origin is in dispute. Some think the
wine draws its name from a town in Spain called Sherish. Some think that
the Sherry's birthplace is Shiraz, Iran. In either event, everyone agrees that
Sherry is a *fortified* wine. By fortification, we mean that another spirit,
most commonly brandy, is added <u>after</u> the wine has fermented. As a result,
Sherry is not typically as sweet as traditional dessert wines.

You will often see Sherries referred to as "NV" or "non-vintage." This is
because solera-style Sherry is created in a "cascading" series of barrels.
Wine ready for bottling is drawn off from the "oldest" end of the barrel
series. Barrels are "topped of" with wine from the barrel preceding it. Care

is taken to make sure that the amounts of wine transferred from barrel to barrel are equal in volume in order to maintain consistency. New wine is added at the opposite end. Since the aging process also blends the wines from year to year, a vintage cannot be assigned. To be called Sherry, a wine must be aged in this fashion for at least three years.

Temecula wineries make wonderful Sherry and no trip to Temecula Wine Country is complete without trying it. We recommend visiting at least one of the wineries listed below to sample this ancient style of wine. Happy Tastings!

Alex's Red Barn Winery
39820 Calle Contento, Temecula, CA 92951 ♦ Tel: 951-693-3201 ♦ Hours: Sat-Sun and most holidays 11-6, Winter 10-5 ♦ Website: *www.redbarnwine.com*

Inn at Churon Winery
33233 Rancho California Road, Temecula, CA 92591 ♦ Tel: 951-694-9070 ♦ Hours: Daily 10-4:30 ♦ Website: *www.innatchuronwinery.com*

Mount Palomar Winery
33820 Rancho California Road, Temecula, CA 92591 ♦ Tel: 951-676-5047 ♦ Summer Hours: Mon-Thurs 10-6, Fri-Sun 10-7; Winter Hours: Closed Mon & Tues; Wed-Thur 10-5, Fri-Sun 10-6 ♦ Website: *www.mountpalomar. com*

☺ *Grape Escapes Discount!* - Present a copy of this book and receive a **Two-for-One tasting!!!**

Wilson Creek Winery & Vineyards
Silver Medal Winner - 2008 NWIWC!
35960 Rancho California Road, Temecula, CA 92591 ♦ Tel: 951-699-9463 ♦ Hours: Daily 10-5 ♦ Website: *www.wilsoncreekwinery.com*

☺ *Grape Escapes Discount!* - Present a copy of this book and receive **Two-for-One tasting** for up to four guests (a $20 value). PLUS, present a copy of this book and receive a **10% discount** on all wines purchased on the day of your visit. Offers good Monday – Friday only, except on holidays. And if this is not reason enough to visit one of our favorite wineries, present a copy of *The Grape Escapes 2* and receive a **free glass of Almond Champagne** for up to four guests (one glass per entrée) with your purchase of an entrée at the **Creekside Grille** located at Wilson Creek Winery. This is a $28 value and is valid Monday – Friday only, except on holidays.

"I drink Champagne when I win, to celebrate…
and I drink Champagne when I lose, to console myself."
~ Napoleon Bonaparte

- SPARKLING WINE -

FAVORITE TASTING ROOMS FOR SPARKLING WINES
(Do We Detect a Sparkling [Wine] in Your Eye?)

If sparkling wines are what bring a smile to your face or a twinkling to your eye, then Temecula Wine Country is a great place for you to be. The following are our favorite stops for the bubbly:

South Coast Winery
34843 Rancho California Road, Temecula, CA 92591 ◆ Tel: 951-587-9463 ◆ Hours: Daily 10-6 ◆ Website: *www.wineresort.com*

☞ **Authors' Tip:** *Be sure to try to the Sparkling Cuvée at South Coast. This wine is actually a Sparkling Syrah and was one of our highest scoring Sparkling Wines. Also of note, South Coast's Non-vintage Extra Dry Méthode Champenoise received a Silver Medal at the 2007 Riverside International Wine Competition.*

Thornton Winery
32575 Rancho California Road, Temecula, CA 92591 ◆ Tel: 951-699-0099 ◆ Hours: Daily 10-5 ◆ Website: *www.thorntonwinery.com*

⇨ **By The Way** – Thornton received a Bronze Medal for their Brut and Non-vintage Blanc de Noirs at the 2007 San Diego International Wine Competition.

Wilson Creek Winery & Vineyards
35960 Rancho California Road, Temecula, CA 92591 ◆ Tel: 951-699-9463 ◆ Hours: Daily 10-5 ◆ Website: *www.wilsoncreekwinery.com*

☺ *Grape Escapes Discount!* - Present a copy of this book and receive **Two-for-One tasting** for up to four guests (a $20 value). PLUS, present a copy of this book and receive a **10% discount** on all wines purchased on the day of your visit. Offers good Monday – Friday only, except on holidays. And if this is not reason enough to visit one of our favorite wineries, present a copy of **The Grape Escapes 2** and receive a **free glass of Almond Champagne** for up to four guests (one glass per entrée) with your purchase of an entrée at the **Creekside Grille** located at Wilson Creek Winery. This is a $28 value and is valid Monday – Friday only, except on holidays.

⇨ **By The Way** – Wilson Creek's Grand Cuvée was awarded a Bronze Medal at the 2007 San Diego International Wine Competition. According to Angel Castaneda, Wine and Liquor Manager at the Longs Drug Store just outside Wine Country along Rancho California Road, the Wilson Creek Almond Champagne is one of their most popular sellers. His exact words were, "We can't keep it on the shelf."

☞ **Authors' Tip:** *If you like sparkling wines with fruit flavors, we also suggest you try La Cereza's "Peach Girls" flavored champagnes and Maurice Car'rie's Pineapple-flavored bubbly.*

"Making wines is like having children; you love them all, but boy, are they different." ~ Bunny Finkelstein

FAVORITE TASTING ROOMS FOR LESS COMMON WINES AND VARIETALS

The following wineries had less common varietals on their tasting menus during our visit. We have organized our list by varietal headings to make it easier for you to find what you are looking for.

☞ **Authors' Tip:** *Most of these wineries are small lot producers, so they may sell out of the less common varietals. If you are specifically searching for one of these varietals, call ahead to ensure that the wine is still available and that it will be on the tasting room menu on the day you plan to visit.*

Aglianico

Cougar Vineyard & Winery
39870 De Portola Road, Temecula, CA 92592 ◆ Tel: 951-491-0825 ◆ Hours: Daily 11-6, Winter 11-5 ◆ Website: *www.cougarvineyards.com*

Aleatico

Briar Rose Winery
41720 Calle Cabrillo, Temecula, CA 92592 ♦ Tel: 951-308-1098 ♦
Hours: By Appointment Only ♦ Website: *www.briarrosewinery.com*

Hart Winery
41300 Avenida Biona, Temecula, CA 92591 ♦ Tel: 951-676-6300 ♦
Hours: Daily 9-4:30 ♦ Website: *www.thehartfamilywinery.com*

Chenin Blanc

Keyways Vineyard & Winery
Best of Class Gold Medal Winner - 2008 NWIWC!
37338 De Portola Road, Temecula, CA 92592 ♦ Tel: 1-877-539-9297 ♦
Hours: Daily 10-6, Winter 10-5 ♦ Website: *www.keywayswine.com*
✪ GE Discount

Cinsault

Leonesse Cellars
38311 De Portola Road, Temecula, CA 92592 ♦ Tel: 951-302-7601 ♦
Hours: Daily 10-5 ♦ Website: *www.leonessecellars.com*

Claret

Frangipani Estate Winery
39750 De Portola Road, Temecula, CA 92592 ♦ Tel: 951-699-8845 ♦
Hours: Daily 10-5 ♦ Website: *www.frangipaniwinery.com*
✪ GE Discount

Cortese

Cougar Vineyard & Winery
39870 De Portola Road, Temecula, CA 92592 ♦ Tel: 951-491-0825 ♦
Hours: Daily 11-6, Winter 11-5 ♦ Website: *www.cougarvineyards.com*

Mount Palomar Winery
33820 Rancho California Road, Temecula, CA 92591 ♦ Tel: 951-676-5047 ♦ Summer Hours: Mon-Thurs 10-6, Fri-Sun 10-7; Winter Hours: Closed Mon & Tues; Wed-Thur 10-5, Fri-Sun 10-6 ♦ Website: *www.mountpalomar. com* ✪ GE Discount

Dolcetto

Callaway Vineyard & Winery
32720 Rancho California Road, Temecula, CA 92591 ◆ Tel: 951-676-4001 ◆ Summer Hours: Daily 10-6, Winter Hours: 10-5 ◆ Website: *www.callawaywinery.com*
✪ GE Discount

Grenache

Frangipani Estate Winery
39750 De Portola Road, Temecula, CA 92592 ◆ Tel: 951-699-8845 ◆ Hours: Daily 10-5 ◆ Website: *www.frangipaniwinery.com*
✪ GE Discount

Hart Winery
Bronze Medal Winner - 2008 NWIWC!
41300 Avenida Biona, Temecula, CA 92591 ◆ Tel: 951-676-6300 ◆ Hours: Daily 9-4:30 ◆ Website: *www.thehartfamilywinery.com*

Oak Mountain Winery / Temecula Hills Winery
36522 Via Verde, Temecula, CA 92592 ◆ Tel: 951-699-9102 ◆ Hours: Daily 11-5 ◆ Website: *www.oakmountainwinery. com* ✪ GE Discount

Ice Wine

Keyways Vineyard & Winery
37338 De Portola Road, Temecula, CA 92592 ◆ Tel: 1-877-539-9297 ◆ Hours: Daily 10-6, Winter 10-5 ◆ Website: *www.keywayswine.com*
✪ GE Discount

Late Harvest Petite Syrah

Bella Vista Winery
41220 Calle Contento, Temecula, CA 92592 ◆ Tel: 951-676-5250 ◆ Hours: Daily 10-6, Winter 10-5 ◆ Website: *www.bellavistawinery.com*

Late Harvest Sèmillon

Wiens Family Cellars
35055 Via Del Ponte, Temecula, CA 92592 ◆ Tel: 951-694-9892 ◆ Hours: Daily 10-5 ◆ Website: *www.wienscellars.com* ✪ GE Discount

Lemberger

Keyways Vineyard & Winery
37338 De Portola Road, Temecula, CA 92592 ✦ Tel: 1-877-539-9297 ✦
Hours: Daily 10-6, Winter 10-5 ✦ Website: *www.keywayswine.com*
✪ GE Discount

Malbec

Doffo Winery
(Not Open to the Public at the time of publication.)
36083 Summitville, Temecula, CA 92592 ✦ Tel: 951-676-6989 ✦
Hours: By Appointment only ✦ Website: *www.doffowines.com* Wines
are also available at the *Temecula House of Wine* in Old Town and via
ShopTemeculaWines.com

Stuart Cellars
33515 Rancho California Road, Temecula, CA 92591 ✦ Tel: 951-676-
6414 ✦ Hours: Daily 10-5 ✦ Website: *www.stuartcellars.com*

Malvasia Bianca

Cougar Vineyard & Winery
39870 De Portola Road, Temecula, CA 92592 ✦ Tel: 951-491-0825 ✦
Hours: Daily 11-6, Winter 11-5 ✦ Website: *www.cougarvineyards.com*

Robert Renzoni Vineyards
37350 De Portola Road, Temecula, CA 92592 ✦ Tel: 951-302-8466 ✦
Hours: Daily 11-6 ✦ Website: *www. robertrenzonivineyards.com*
✪ GE Discount

Montepulciano

Cougar Vineyard & Winery
39870 De Portola Road, Temecula, CA 92592 ✦ Tel: 951-491-0825 ✦
Hours: Daily 11-6, Winter 11-5 ✦ Website: *www.cougarvineyards.com*

Mourvédre

Oak Mountain Winery / Temecula Hills Winery
36522 Via Verde, Temecula, CA 92592 ✦ Tel: 951-699-9102 ✦ Hours:
Daily 11-5 ✦ Website: *www.oakmountainwinery. com* ✪ GE Discount

Cougar Vineyard & Winery
39870 De Portola Road, Temecula, CA 92592 ◆ Tel: 951-491-0825 ◆ Hours: Daily 11-6, Winter 11-5 ◆ Website: *www.cougarvineyards.com*

Nebbiolo

Ponte Family Estate Winery
35053 Rancho California Road, Temecula, CA 92591 ◆ Tel: 951-694-8855 ◆ Hours: Daily 10-5 ◆ Website: *www.pontewinery.com*
✪ GE Discount

Thornton Winery
32575 Rancho California Road, Temecula, CA 92591 ◆ Tel: 951-699-0099 ◆ Hours: Daily 10-5 ◆ Website: *www. thorntonwinery.com*

Primitivo

Cougar Vineyard & Winery
39870 De Portola Road, Temecula, CA 92592 ◆ Tel: 951-491-0825 ◆ Hours: Daily 11-6, Winter 11-5 ◆ Website: *www.cougarvineyards.com*

Wiens Family Cellars
35055 Via Del Ponte, Temecula, CA 92592 ◆ Tel: 951-694-9892 ◆ Hours: Daily 10-5 ◆ Website: *www.wienscellars.com* ✪ GE Discount

Roussanne

Callaway Vineyard & Winery
32720 Rancho California Road, Temecula, CA 92591 ◆ Tel: 951-676-4001 ◆ Summer Hours: Daily 10-6, Winter Hours: 10-5 ◆ Website: *www.callawaywinery.com*
✪ GE Discount

TEMECULA WINE COUNTRY INTERNET LINKS AND RESOURCES

Note: *The websites listed below were active at the time of publication. None of the website sponsors or supporters paid or offered any type of compensation to be included in this guidebook.*

www.TheGrapeEscapes.com -
Official website for *"The Grape Escapes"* Guidebooks

<u>Temecula Wine, Wineries, Maps, Tours, Festivals, and Tourist Information</u>

cityoftemecula.org – The City of Temecula
swcv.org – Southwest California Vintners Association
temecula.org – Temecula Chamber of Commerce
temeculacalifornia.com – Old Town Temecula
temeculacvb.org – Temecula Convention and Visitors Bureau
temeculawines.org – Temecula Valley Winegrowers Association
beachcalifornia.com/temecula-wineries.html – Guide to California
    Beaches
calwineries.com – Guide to California's Wine Country
cheers2wine.com – Guide to California's Wine Country
citytowninfo.com/places/california/temecula - Information on U.S. Cities
en.wikipedia.org/wiki/Temecula – Wikipedia on Temecula's history,
    statistics, tourism, etc.
ShopTemeculaWines.com – Winery Information & Wine Shop
temecula.winecountry.com – Wine Country Information
temeculamapguide.com – Tour of Temecula Map Guide
temecula-tourism.com – Temecula Valley Events
temeculawinery.info – Temecula Winery Information
travelenvoy.com/wine/temecula_wineries.htm – Travel Envoy: The Wine
    Guide
tv.winelibrary.com – Gary Vaynerchuk's daily wine video blog
winecountry.com/regions/temecula – Wine Country Information

Temecula Wine Shops

ShopTemeculaWines.com – Online Wine Shopping and Winery Information

palomarinntemecula.com – *Temecula House of Wine* in Old Town Temecula ✪ GE Discount

stellarcellar.com – Stellar Cellar in Old Town Temecula

Temecula Tours & Transportation

gogrape.com – The Grapeline® Wine Country Shuttle

sterlingroselimo.com – Sterling Rose Limousine

wctrans.com – West Coast Chauffeur & Transportation
    ✪ GE Discount

hotairtours.com – A Grape Escape Balloon Adventure
    ✪ GE Discount

Temecula Valley Area Newspapers and Journals

myvalleynews.com – The Valley News

nctimes.com – The North County Times (includes wine / winery articles)

nctimes.com/news/californian/temecula – Temecula Edition of North County Times

neighborsnewspaper.com – Neighbors Newspaper (Temecula Valley Community News)

sandiegan.com – The San Diegan - Guide to San Diego Area Dining & Attractions

thevillagenews.com – Fallbrook Village News (includes wine / winery news)

topix.net/city/fallbrook-ca – Fallbrook Press-Enterprise (includes wine / winery news)

valleybusinessjournal.com – The Valley Business Journal (includes wine / winery news)

vine-times.com – The Vine Times Magazine

Wine Information, Tasting Notes, Chat Rooms & Forums and Blogs

abwine.com – Wine: The Online Connoisseur

affairsofthevine.com – Affairs of the Vine

bellaonline.com/site/wine – Bella Online Wine Site

california-wineonline.com – Online Information & Shopping for California Wine

cellarnotes.net – Wine-Related Information & References

chiff.com/wine – Wine-Related Information & References

decanter.com – Wine-Related Information & References

drvino.com – Winner 2007 Best Wine Blog Award

erobertparker.com – Robert Parker's Guide to Fine Wines

fortheloveofport.com – Roy Hersh's Port Related Information & References

grape-nutz.com – Wine Review and Journal

ilikewine.com – Wine-Related Information & References

intowine.com – Wine-Related Information & References

stratsplace.com – Wine-Related Information & References

vivisjournal.com – Wine Life Today

wine.appellationamerica.com – Information about Wine & American Wine Regions

wineanswers.com – Wine Answers

winebusiness.com – Wine Industry Information and Resources

winecountry.com – Wine Country Information

winecountrygetaways.com – Wine Country Travel Tips & Winery Visit Journal

winefiles.org – Wine, Wine Making & Grape Growing Info &References

winegeeks.com – Winery Information & Wine Reviews

wineloverspage.com – Wine-Related Information & References

winepros.org – Wine-Related Information & References

wines.com – Wine-Related Information & References

winespectator.com – Wine Spectator Magazine: Wine-Related Info & References

winetalk.com – Wine-Related Information

zinfandel.org – Zinfandel Info & References by Zinfandel Advocates & Producers (ZAP)

- INDEX -

TEMECULA WINERIES, TASTING ROOMS, and WINE MERCHANTS

Note: Index of *Wines and Varietals* follows the last Winery / Tasting Room entry

The "✪ **GE Discount**" notation indicates the wineries or merchants that offer money-saving *Grape Escapes* Discounts or Special Promotions when you show your copy of this book.

WINES and VARIETALS

ABOUT THE AUTHORS

Bob and Cindy Rhodes lived in California's Orange and San Diego counties for fifteen years and spent their free time discovering and enjoying California's beautiful wine regions and their remarkable wines. The authors recently relocated from Southern California to the quiet, rural life in Sequim (pronounced "Skwim") in Washington's Olympic Peninsula. When they are not at their residence in the beautiful state of Washington, they can usually be found in Wine Country. You may write to them via their website at *www.TheGrapeEscapes.com*.

> **"And Noah said to his wife when they sat down
> to dine, 'I don't care where the water goes,
> if it doesn't get into the wine!' "**
> ~ G. K. Chesterton

Printed in the United States
121123LV00002B/1-18/P